The Text of the Bible

ALSO BY DAVID S. NEW

*Christian Fundamentalism in America:
A Cultural History* (McFarland, 2012)

*Holy War: The Rise of Militant Christian, Jewish and
Islamic Fundamentalism* (McFarland, 2002)

# The Text of the Bible

*Its Path Through History and to the People*

DAVID S. NEW

McFarland & Company, Inc., Publishers
*Jefferson, North Carolina, and London*

LIBRARY OF CONGRESS CATALOGUING-IN-PUBLICATION DATA

New, David S.
 The text of the Bible : its path through history and to the people / David S. New.
   p.    cm.
 Includes bibliographical references and index.

 **ISBN 978-0-7864-7353-3**
 softcover : acid free paper ∞

1. Bible—History.   I. Title.
BS445.N48 2013
220.09—dc23                                    2013011596

BRITISH LIBRARY CATALOGUING DATA ARE AVAILABLE

© 2013 David S. New. All rights reserved

*No part of this book may be reproduced or transmitted in any form or by any means, electronic or mechanical, including photocopying or recording, or by any information storage and retrieval system, without permission in writing from the publisher.*

On the cover: scribe at desk © 2012 Clipart.com

Manufactured in the United States of America

*McFarland & Company, Inc., Publishers*
  *Box 611, Jefferson, North Carolina 28640*
    *www.mcfarlandpub.com*

# Table of Contents

| | |
|---|---:|
| *Preface* | 1 |
| 1. In the Beginning Was the Word | 5 |
| 2. Of Making Many Books | 10 |
| 3. Gothic | 17 |
| 4. Doctor Maximus | 25 |
| 5. Cloistered | 33 |
| 6. Magic Talisman | 39 |
| 7. The Emerald Isle | 44 |
| 8. A Light in the Dark | 56 |
| 9. Life in the Big City | 64 |
| 10. Birds of the Air, Lilies of the Field | 72 |
| 11. Clandestine Operation | 81 |
| 12. Archheretic | 93 |
| 13. Prison of Doubt | 97 |
| 14. A Scholar and a Gentleman | 104 |
| 15. Hijacked | 112 |
| 16. Room with a View | 122 |
| 17. The Gutenberg Bible | 128 |
| 18. Cloak and Dagger | 135 |
| 19. The King James Bible | 144 |
| 20. Man on a Mission | 150 |
| 21. A Young Photographer | 158 |

| | |
|---|---|
| 22. Discovery | 162 |
| 23. Ancient Treasure | 165 |
| 24. Scandal | 174 |
| 25. The Original Text | 182 |
| 26. A Babel of Bibles | 188 |
| *Bibliography* | 193 |
| *Index* | 215 |

# Preface

Outside the windows of the air-conditioned tourist bus scorching heat shimmers off rock cliffs in a natural oven which reaches brutal temperatures. In this seemingly God-forsaken wasteland the brassy sun shows no mercy for any living thing. I strain to peer through the haze and catch a glimpse of the sea, languid under humid mist.

"This is the land of the damned. The story is from the biblical book of Genesis," our guide Angie informs us. "Abraham pleaded with his god Yahweh to not destroy Sodom and Gomorrah. Yahweh agreed, provided there were ten righteous people among the wicked in these cities. There were not. Yahweh's anger raged; down rained a sulphurous fire. All plant life was destroyed; the valley became a furnace. Just before this destruction, angels from Yahweh had warned a man named Lot that he and his family should flee for their lives into the hills. They must not look back or stop anywhere in the valley. But," Angie smiles, "we all know that women can be curious." There is conspiratorial but cautious laughter from the men on the tour. Angie continues. "So it was with Lot's wife. She could not resist a look back. She had to see what she was forbidden to see. So she looked back, and was turned into a pillar of salt. If you look out the windows you will see pillars of salt, although we don't know which one is Lot's wife. Yahweh's curse upon the land was for eternity. Nothing changes here. Everything speaks of death. The Dead Sea."

The forbidding scene outside the windows of the bus causes a bead of sweat to trickle down my brow. Thank God for air conditioning! "When do we stop for refreshments?" someone in the rear of the bus asks. No sooner are these words spoken than the bus turns onto a gentle incline, away from the sea. We pull into a parking lot and lurch to a halt. Another group of tourists is getting back onto their bus; they look relaxed and refreshed. The door of the bus opens and the breath is sucked from my lungs. Not even a hint of breeze. It's absolutely stifling. The sunlight is blinding. And that sulphurous smell! My legs can't get me into the snack bar fast enough.

Soon our thirsts are quenched, our lungs filled with cooler air. Our bodies have resumed some degree of normal equilibrium. "Is everyone finished?" Angie asks. There are reluctant sighs; no one is in a hurry to leave this oasis of comfort. "Okay ... okay," Angie beams her understanding smile, "seeing as no other tour bus has arrived, I'll give you a break and start my spiel inside." This garners a hearty round of affirming applause.

Just a few feet from the snack bar — fortunately it isn't going to be a long walk in the heat — is what appears to be a labyrinth fashioned from stones of every size and shape. Angie tells us that back in Jesus's time the walls that stood on these foundations formed the habitation for a group of monks. Signs in Hebrew and English point to the location of what had once been a dining hall, what had once been a kitchen. She points out the scriptorium, where scribes copied manuscripts onto leather scrolls. The finished scrolls were deposited in nearby caves. "For this is where the famous Dead Sea Scrolls originated," Angie informs us.

One of our group says she had read that this is just a theory, that scholars disagree: some say it was inhabited by monks, but others think it may have been a fortress. Angie nods acknowledgment. "That's scholars for you! Never can agree on anything." People laugh and look in my direction. I raise my hands in supplication as if to say, What can you do?, and smile.

Angie resumes. "For now, we'll stick with the conventional opinion, that this establishment was inhabited by a group of Jews who had separated from other Jews, and who had their own beliefs and religious practices. They weren't here for long before the Romans came and put an end to their desert existence."

Reluctantly we follow Angie's lead outside, into the sweltering heat. We haven't examined the remains of the ancient foundations for more than a few minutes when an older woman expresses her disappointed wishes for the tour: "When are we going to visit some place where it's not so hot and barren? You know, like those illustrations you see in the Bible — the cool green places where Jesus spoke gentle words of wisdom and love." Angie offers an indulgent smile. "Soon. You'll have to be patient for just a little while longer."

Back on the bus several tourists question Angie about the connection between the Dead Sea Scrolls and the Bible.

The Dead Sea Scrolls. Just part of the long and fascinating saga of the Bible. The story of the Bible is a layperson's Baedeker to events and persons from the Roman Empire to the present, a roistering romp through popular history: the myths surrounding Saint Columba, the beauty and magic of illuminated Irish manuscripts, the barbarian invasions, the Black Death, the Waldensian heresy, the color and pageantry of medieval romance, the gluttonous sumptuous life of medieval monk and clergy, the scandalous debauchery of the medieval Vatican, the spirit of the Renaissance, the tradition of monk and scholar.

Shining against these backdrops are the dramatis personae, for the story of the Bible is primarily a story about people, the drama of their lives woven into the tapestry of their times: The translator who is forced to flee town because of his love for women. The Gothic bishop of an heretical sect in Transylvania. Burning at the stake, kidnapping, smuggling, secret rendezvous, danger, raw ambition, scandal, chicanery. It's all there.

Recently a hand-lettered copy of the Bible in seven large volumes was commissioned. Inscribed on parchment, replete with colored illumination, it would take six years to complete. In today's information-technology world, why lavish such loving and expensive attention on a single piece of literature?

It is because the Bible is the most widely disseminated literature and the best-selling book of all time, even today. In 2300 languages and dialects, it reaches remote regions and peoples of the globe. The first book to be printed, it is the oldest and most quoted written work; its million words have yielded everyday expressions: "pearls before swine," "root of all evil." For two thousand years it has inspired and guided and influenced human lives. Generations have turned to this literature for wisdom and strength. Its words have helped millions walk beside still waters, lie down in green pastures. The Bible is a public symbol. It is used to swear in witnesses at courts of law. The Bible has shaped our civilization; inspired art, literature, and music. Considered by many the holy word of God, it provides documentary evidence and witness for the beliefs of three major world religions. Some consider the Bible dangerous, others have died for it; response to the Bible seems always to be passionate. This is the story of such passions.

But it is also the story of the words of the Bible, its text. Today there are available a confusing number of versions of the Bible—from the traditional King James Version to the multiplying new translations and paraphrases. Why so many? And which one is the *real* Bible? For the forty percent of Americans who regard the Bible as the actual Word of God, to be taken literally word for word, it may prove dismaying to learn that the text of the Bible has been corrupted and distorted through its two-thousand-year history—witness the 1631 edition of the King James Bible, where the seventh commandment reads, "Thou *shalt* commit adultery." What light have the Dead Sea Scrolls and other recent manuscript discoveries shed on this contentious issue?

Renewed interest in the Bible and Christian history is an acknowledged phenomenon of recent years. There is a hunger to get back to the source of our Christian heritage. How did the text of the Bible come to be what it is today?

The story of the Bible provides a deep feeling and appreciation for the richness of its text. Those words and phrases bound to our hearts when we first began to search for meaning in our lives, those passages of Scripture first heard in the quiet security of our parents' love, made sacred by repetition in times of joy and celebration ... these we can savor once more with deeper understanding of all that brought them to us down through the ages.

# 1

# In the Beginning Was the Word

Nearly two thousand years ago in the Middle East north of the Dead Sea a man named John proclaimed the coming of the Kingdom of Heaven. The present order would be soon be swept away and a new age inaugurated.

John wore animal skins, and ate what he could scrounge in the rocky wilderness—wild honey and insects. He looked much like the prophets of old who had preached to the Jewish people of wondrous things. But it was said that the age of the prophets had past. If not a prophet, then what? ... could he possibly be the awaited Anointed One of God, the Messiah, the Christ?

The local ruler, the tetrarch Herod, looked on with an anxious heart: John was becoming far too popular, stirring up far too much excitement among the populace. An ambitious man, Herod had won office by cunning and bold acts. Neither a Jew nor a Roman citizen, he could not expect loyalty or love from the people over whom he was sovereign, but he knew that those who mattered in Rome respected a man who could keep the peace, who ruled with law and order. Rome needed men like Herod. It was at the peak of its power and dominion, proud to claim that its empire had made of the Mediterranean Sea "a Roman lake." Less than a century had passed since the great Julius Caesar led Roman legions into the far western isles of Britannia. Gaul and Spain were Roman provinces.

Palestine, settled by Jews, Samaritans, Greeks, Syrians, and many other ethnic groups, was rife with political and religious unrest. Even among the Jews there existed bad feelings: The wealthy classes had forsaken their religious heritage for the life of material luxury. Even the high priests had proven vulnerable to the lure of mammon. This caused many Jews, tired of successive waves of foreign rule and customs, to ache for a return to traditional religious mores. The more fanatically religious among them, driven to despair, went about armed with daggers, plunging their weapons deep into the entrails of whomever they suspected of religious infidelity. Many Jews, particularly the Pharisees, despised these Zealots as ruffians and gangsters.

The area over which Herod was sovereign was a sea of dissension about to boil over, and John's incendiary preaching was turning up the heat. Herod was not about to risk what he had worked so hard to attain. He had John arrested and imprisoned. Then, on the entreaty of his wife Herodias and her daughter, Herod had John put to death.

But Herod's problems were not over. A new figure arose in John's footsteps, one reputed to perform miracles. Herod gasped in horror. Miracles? Could this be John, risen from the dead?

It wasn't John. Instead, it was the one John had said would follow him —"he that cometh." He was a man of thirty years, unknown to the public until this time, having lived a private life as an ordinary citizen. Yet here he was, this man from Nazareth, this Jesus, proclaiming, "The time is fulfilled, and the kingdom of God is at hand." In an era of religious charlatans, sorcerers, and wandering philosophers, Jesus drew a crowd. Had he not healed the sick and cast out demons from those possessed?

But Jesus was no ordinary miracle-worker. He spoke as no other, with seeming authority. He called God "my Father." His manner of speech indicated that he *knew* whereof he spoke. He castigated the institutional religious authorities, contradicted and challenged the religious leaders, the scribes and the Pharisees: "You have heard it said ... but I say unto you...." To the man and woman along the rural byway his words were beguiling, persuasive. Jesus said there was no need to worry about food and clothing, no need to fret about tomorrow. "Ask, and it shall be given."

Jesus soon gathered around him a following. Here was a man who knew the human heart, who responded to human needs. He spoke of human love, and of a loving God. He talked not in esoteric priestly jargon, but in everyday words: sowing and reaping, fish and bread. He told stories: "A certain man...." His fame spread, the crowds grew. They came from all over — Galilee in the north, Jerusalem and Judaea in the south, even east beyond the Jordan, from Decapolis.

While the poor and underprivileged clung to every word from Jesus's lips, others began to despise and detest this arrogant figure. Blasphemer! screamed the scribes and the Pharisees, outraged at this upstart's cavalier abrogation of Sabbath law. Hypocrites! Vipers! Blind guides! Jesus responded to those who considered legality and human institutions more important than justice toward one's fellows and love for God.

Disrespect for wealth and position, for ritual and tradition, was sure to get Jesus in trouble. Political and religious leaders conspired to put an end to this rabble-rouser, this pretender. Some among the people were beginning to see Jesus as the Messiah of the house of David, that expected political savior who would liberate the Jews from foreign rule and custom. They wished to make him king. This would not do. Soon Roman legions would arrive in Palestine to quell possible revolt. And then what would become of Jewish society and its religious institutions? Jesus must be stopped.

The religious authorities got their way. Jesus was tried before the high priest, and found guilty of blasphemy. He was nailed to a giant cross and left to die a slow painful death. Normally anyone put to death in this way remained fastened to the cross, but because of the Sabbath and Passover the Jews asked that Jesus be taken down. The Roman authorities allowed this but thrust a spear through Jesus's side to make sure he was dead. A wealthy man claimed the body and laid it in a tomb.

Had that been the end of the story, Jesus would likely have been forgotten. But it was not the end. Soon Jesus's disciples and others close to him were proclaiming the amazing news that Jesus had risen from the dead. All of this—the story of Jesus's life and death and resurrection—would eventually be recorded in the four gospels, the first four books of the Bible's New Testament. No other literature surviving from ancient times contains this story in such detail.

But these books were not found in the Bible of the earliest Christians, for their Bible consisted only of those books we now refer to as "the Old Testament," the Bible of the Jews. Jesus himself was a Jew, as likely were all of his disciples and most of those who first followed him. Although the Jews who came to be called "Christians" soon broke away from the Jews who continued to worship in the synagogue tradition, they retained the Jewish Scripture.

Why? Because it was through the books of this Scripture that these early Jewish followers of Jesus were able to understand the marvelous news spread by Jesus's disciples and others close to him. It was through passages found in Jewish Scripture that these first Christians understood Jesus to be the Christ, the Messiah long awaited by those of the Jewish faith. Jesus was the fulfillment of what had been prophesied in Jewish Scripture. Even the fact that Jesus suffered such a painful death on the cross was explained with reference to the "suffering servant" of the book of Isaiah. Jesus's life, death, and resurrection were understood as part of God's plan. The new Christian faith was seen as continuous with Jewish religious tradition. This was important, even for the early Gentile church. Several generations after Jesus's death Saint Ignatius claimed that Jewish Scripture remained the certain proof that Jesus was the Christ. To this day passages from the Old Testament, which are considered to foretell Jesus's birth, are read from the pulpit during the Christmas season.

This belief of the earliest Christians, that God had resurrected Jesus from the dead in fulfillment of his promises in Jewish Scripture, formed the essential core of the new faith. This was the "good news" that the earliest Christians were excited to make known: that God had acted in the marvelous event of Jesus's resurrection, revealing his love and giving new hope for the meaning of human life.

So eager were the earliest Christians to spread the good news, they did not take the time to put it down in writing. Besides, what would be the point? Most people could not read in those times, and the written word was prohibitively expensive. The material used for writing was far more costly than the paper used today. Papyrus was made from strips cut from the pith of the papyrus plant glued together in alternate layers placed at right angles, then polished smooth. Large quantities of papyrus were shipped from the Syrian port of Byblos, which is probably the source for the ancient Greek word for "book"—"biblion." The plural of this Greek word—"biblia"—came to be used for the collection of books which we call the Bible.

There was another reason why the good news was spread with an urgency that precluded its written form in the earliest days. There was prevalent a belief that Jesus would soon return, probably within a single generation, to bring on the eschaton—the end of the world. This belief did not encourage the writing of books for future generations.

As time passed, however, this expectancy of an imminent eschaton began to wane. As well, the original disciples, the first-hand witnesses, were nearing the end of their days. It seemed a good idea to get a record of their recollections in writing before they were gone.

There was another reason to put the good news in writing. As missionaries spread the faith to the Gentiles it came into competition with other religious movements. The Gentile world was filled with magicians, sorcerers, and miracle-workers, individuals believed to have access to the realm of supernatural forces and powers; Jesus was one among many. The gospels tell us that persons sought to touch the hem of Jesus's clothing, believing thus to be healed of disease. The biblical book of Acts tells how handkerchiefs and pieces of clothing belonging to the apostle Paul retained healing powers (19:12).

The boundary between miracle-worker and divinity was not clearly defined. In the Greek world many believed that the human soul held within it the spark of divinity. Leading figures of the time were believed to be gods who descended from above to live and die as human beings. On the island of Crete one could visit the grave of Zeus, the greatest of the gods. In such an environment many pretenders arose, claiming to be a god or a son of some god. As Jesus says in Luke's gospel, many will come saying, "'I am he' and 'the time is at hand'" (21:8). The apostle Paul in his second letter to the Corinthians writes concerning "another Jesus" and "another gospel" (11:4).

Clearly, early Christianity needed some advantage over other faiths in the religious marketplace. If it could convince prospective converts that Jesus was the Messiah long awaited by the Jews, this would help its cause. The Greek world was one of ideas and books. Literate people in the major cities knew that the Jewish faith was one of ancient tradition — that alone gave it status among so many upstart religions and philosophies. So the gospels were written in Greek, addressed to the literate society of the major cities. (Greek was the language of international commerce and literature; Jesus likely spoke Aramaic, the indigenous language of the local people.) Only in centers of commerce were the wealth and human resources for implementing the gospels in writing available.

The gospels of the New Testament attempted to convince people in the wider Greek-speaking world that Jesus was indeed the Messiah long awaited by the Jews. John's gospel states this clearly: it is "written that you might believe that Jesus is the Christ" (20:31). Matthew's gospel is full of quotations from Jewish Scripture meant to demonstrate that Jesus is that Christ.

As the years passed, debate arose among Christians as to what exactly Jesus said and did. What had he said about divorce, about the Sabbath, about various food laws? Varying accounts were springing up. Which were true? Which were false? Only a few years after Jesus's death the apostle Paul had to contend with "false prophets" within the Christian community. Setting down in writing what Jesus had said and done was necessary to prevent the Christian community from exploding into a number of diverse sects.

The Jesus who walked this earth, the Jesus modern scholars call "the historical Jesus," will never be known. He died two thousand years ago, and might well have been forgotten were it not for his disciples and followers who spread their astounding story. The Jesus loved by Christians today, the Christ acknowledged in churches around the world, is the savior revealed in the canon of the New Testament. As John writes, in the first words of his revered gospel, "In the beginning was the Word...."

# 2

# Of Making Many Books

At the beginning of his gospel Luke remarks that "many have taken in hand to set forth in order a declaration of those things which are most surely believed among us." Luke is writing his gospel so that "the certainty of those things" would become known. He proceeds to give an account of Jesus's life, death, and resurrection which in many parts mirrors the accounts given in the biblical gospels of Matthew and Mark, but includes material not found in any of the other three biblical gospels. What was Luke's purpose? While acknowledging other accounts, was he implying that his account was written to correct misinformation provided in the former? This is not clear.

John's gospel refers to acts of Jesus "not written in this book" (20:30), and repeats this point in the final verse: "there are also many other things which Jesus did," concerning which are not written. The penultimate verse emphasizes that the preceding gospel is the work of one of Jesus's disciples who "wrote these things: and we know that his testimony is true." What does this imply? That there were other, differing accounts which were *not* true? Again, this is not clear.

In 1945 at Nag Hammadi there was a discovery which might clarify the issue which Luke and John seem to be implying. Ancient documents were found, preserved by the dry Egyptian climate, among which were the Gospel of Truth, the Gospel of Philip, and the Gospel of Thomas, none of which is included in our present Bible. The Gospel of Thomas includes many of Jesus's words not found anywhere in our New Testament, some of which have been located in other ancient literature. The biblical gospels did not record all that Jesus said; at least one of his sayings is found in the book of Acts, as provided by the apostle Paul: "It is more blessèd to give than to receive" (20:35). Some biblical manuscripts have variant texts which include words spoken by Jesus not found in today's Bible. The literature of the church Fathers contains many other quotations of Jesus's words not found in the Bible.

Numerous other pieces of ancient Christian literature, some preserved to this day, others mentioned in ancient texts but now lost, are not part of our Bible. Among these are Paul's letter to the Laodiceans (mentioned in Colossians 4:16), another of Paul's letters to the Corinthians (mentioned in 1 Corinthians 5:9), the Acts of Paul and Thecla, the Protevangelium of James (tells of Mary's birth and unconsummated marriage to Joseph, a widower), the Infancy Story of Thomas (portrays Jesus as a child prodigy). We shall never know the totality of the vast collection of Christian literature available to the early church because of later selective preservation by the church. Those books which were not widely used were copied less, and since these were on perishable papyrus those few copies have vanished into dust.

Clearly, he who wrote in the biblical book of Ecclesiastes, "of making many books there is no end" (12:12), was not mistaken. But why was so much of this ancient Christian literature not included in the Bible? The answer lies in the concept of "canon."

The early Christian church looked to the Jews for an example of the limitation of Scripture to "the canon," that literature authorized as authentic by the leaders of the religious tradition. In the year A.D. 70 there occurred a cataclysmic event in Jewish history. After four years of outright revolt by Jewish religious radicals against Roman domination, Roman forces destroyed the Temple in Jerusalem which the Zealots had been using as their fortress. The Zealots continued fighting for another three years, eventually succumbing. But the Pharisees, concerned with the survival of Judaism, fled the city, taking with them the sacred Scripture of their tradition. With the establishment of the synagogue as a center of worship, Scripture replaced the Temple as the focal institution of the new Judaism of the diaspora.

Away from the historic geographical center of their faith, aware of the pull of the rising Christian belief among many Jews, the Pharisees knew that they must act quickly to prevent further losses to their religious tradition. A council of rabbis convened in Jamnia in A.D. 90 to decide which books should be included in the sacred canon of Scripture. Over the next decade a synod of Jewish religious leaders debated the issue. In the end the canon of Jewish Scripture included twenty-four books. These books comprise the Old Testament of the King James Version of the Christian Bible. The thirty-nine books of the Old Testament resulted when some of the original twenty-four were divided into shorter books.

The early Christian church Fathers, however, quoted from several *other* books of Jewish origin, seemingly as if they were Scripture. The earliest manuscripts of the Christian Bible that have come down to us containing almost the whole of our present Bible include books which are not found in the King James Old Testament. Where did these books come from? Why were they included, if they were not in the Jewish canon? Why are they in early manuscripts of the Christian Bible, but not in most modern Christian Bibles?

Because the early church had spread into the Greek-speaking world of the Gentiles, the form of Jewish Scripture used in the early church was a Greek translation known as the Septuagint, translated from the original Hebrew by Jews living in Greek-speaking areas some time before the birth of Jesus. This earlier Septuagint contained many more books than the twenty-four finally authorized by the Jews as canon after Jamnia. Jewish tradition says that after the Jews returned to Palestine from exile in Babylon in the sixth century B.C. God ordered the scribe Ezra to dictate the ninety-four sacred books which had been lost during the exile. When that work had been completed God commanded Ezra to make public the first twenty-four books, but to keep back the other seventy to be read only by "the wise."

There is no indication that the early Christian church accorded distinct status to those Jewish books included in the Septuagint but not in the official Jewish canon of Jamnia. As the years passed Hebrew came to be known less and less in the Greek Gentile environment so that only a few voices of dissent were raised, namely from scholarly Christians aware of the differences between the Septuagint and the more restricted Hebrew canon. Only in the fourth century when Jerome translated the Hebrew Scripture into Latin was a clear distinction made. The other books were included in his new Latin Bible but in his preface Jerome called these "edifying" as opposed to "canonical." Nevertheless these extra books continued to assume canonical status throughout the Middle Ages. It is said that Christopher Columbus was convinced that there were new lands to be discovered beyond the seas when he read in one of these "edifying" books that only one-seventh of the earth is covered in water, the remaining six-sevenths being dry land.

During the Renaissance scholars began to study ancient texts and the ancient languages, and the diverging Greek and Hebrew Jewish Scriptures again became an issue. When Martin Luther translated the Bible into German at the beginning of the Protestant Reformation in the sixteenth century he placed the "edifying" books in a separate section under the title "Apocrypha" (a Greek word meaning "hidden away," which goes back to the original Jewish idea of books not meant for regular public use) because the concepts of purgatory, prayers for the dead, and salvation through good works—Roman Catholic doctrine he rejected—he found only in these books. Reacting to Luther's comment that these books were not sacred Scripture, the Roman Catholic church for the first time officially declared the Apocrypha, with only a few exceptions, part of the canon. Despite this decision of the Council of Trent almost five hundred years ago, some within the Roman Catholic church have continued to view these books as somehow secondary, as "deuterocanonical."

Within the Protestant wing of Christianity the Church of England followed Luther in declaring the Apocrypha suitable for instruction but not a source of doctrine. Hence, Protestant Bibles in English up to and including the King James Bible included the Apocrypha but separated them off from the canonical books. After 1629, when Puritanism became a dominating force in England, English Protestant Bibles began to omit these books. In the Westminster Confession of 1648, reformed churches in the Calvinist tradition rejected the Apocrypha altogether. Only recently have a few English Bibles begun once again to include the Apocrypha.

Orthodox Christianity grew up with the Greek Bible, not the Latin Bible of the West. Hence its canon has always been more favorable toward the extra books found in the Septuagint. The authorized canon of Orthodox churches has varied over the years within its different denominations. The Russian Orthodox Church, for example, has proclaimed all books of the Apocrypha non-canonical.

The idea of an authoritative Bible, a canon of Scripture, was adopted from the Jews soon after Christianity split from its Jewish origins. At first this canon consisted strictly of the books of the Septuagint. But as time passed and Christian literature proliferated there developed threats to the uniformity and identity of the new faith. A major challenge came in the person of Marcion around the year 140. Marcion took seriously what he read about the apostle Paul's controversy with those in the early church who wished a more Judaized form of Christianity, and set about to reform the church toward a stricter Pauline stance. Part of this reform required ridding the Bible of anything Marcion regarded as specifically Jewish. That meant all of the Jewish Scripture.

Marcion's rejection of Jewish Scripture in favor of more recently written Christian literature was based on the concept of the new covenant. Had not Jesus, at his last supper with his disciples, spoken of a "new covenant"? Paul's mission to the Gentiles, which followed this concept in his rejection of Judaic law, had a focal point in the city of Antioch, third in importance behind Rome and Alexandria in the Roman empire. The significance of Paul's adoption of new-covenant theology is manifested in the fact that it was in Antioch that those who followed Jesus were first called Christians.

If God had instigated a new covenant in Christ, should not this new covenant, like the old, also have its specific canon of Scripture? Should not the writings of the apostles be considered Scripture? Hence Scripture was split into that of the old covenant and that of the new covenant — the Old Testament and the New Testament ("testament" from "testamentum," the Latin translation of the Greek word for "covenant," "diatheke").

The need for a specifically *Christian* canon became evident a generation after Marcion when a group of Christians in Asia Minor (now Turkey) led by a charismatic leader named Montanus began prophesying in the name of the Holy Spirit. Montanus secured an extensive following which threatened the unity of the Christian church. If such an open-ended attitude toward individual revelation were allowed to continue, where might it lead? What if individual revelation contradicted church doctrine? To prevent such a contingency it was decided that Scripture would be *the* authority of the new church. Revelation contrary to Christian Scripture would be considered heresy.

But what Christian writings would make up the canon of Christian Scripture? In the early days Christian writing was done on long pieces of papyrus which could be rolled up. The length of these scrolls was limited — Luke's gospel would have required an entire scroll. That, and the fact that most Christian writings originated in different locations, meant that each of the Christian writings circulated separately, if at all. All of this, plus the expense of scroll production, dictated that no particular individual church was likely to have more than one writing or a very limited number of writings. Many of these were literature not now in the Christian canon.

Late in the second century, after the Montanus debacle, several church leaders drew up lists of recommended Christian writings, but these were inconsistent. Even as late as the early years of the fourth century Eusebius of Caesarea in his *Ecclesiastical History* indicated that no authorized and consistent canon had been determined. He had researched the authors found in the library of the scholar Origen to see which Christian books they acknowledged. Eusebius then drew up several categories. Universally recognized were the gospels of Matthew, Mark, Luke, and John, the Acts of the Apostles, Paul's epistles (the number not certain), 1 John, 1 Peter. A second category Eusebius designated "disputed" but "familiar to the majority": the Epistle to the Hebrews, James, Jude, 2 Peter, 2 John, 3 John. The third category, "spurious," not generally read in the churches, consisted of the Acts of Paul, the Shepherd of Hermas, the Apocalypse of

Peter, the Epistle of Barnabas, the Revelation of John, the Gospel of the Hebrews. Eusebius's final category comprises books written by "heretics" under the pseudonyn of one of the apostles: the gospels ascribed to Peter, Thomas, Matthias, and others; the acts of Andrew, John, and others.

Then in 313 occurred an event that finally, after years of harassment and persecution, put the Christian church on a stable footing and offered it a secure position it would never surrender. The emperor Constantine accepted Christianity as a viable religion within the Roman empire and even promoted it. He got councils of bishops to resolve issues and disputes so that there would be unity and consistency of opinion throughout the empire. He ordered fifty copies of Christian Scripture for the churches of Constantinople, his newly designated capital (formerly named Byzantium). By this time Scripture was bound in a book such as we have today, called a codex. This form of presentation itself dictated the selection of writings to be included. Was the Codex Sinaiticus, a fourth century manuscript, one of those decreed by Constantine? If so, it includes books not found in today's canon: the Epistle of Barnabas and the Shepherd of Hermas.

Sometime during the fourth century the New Testament canon was fixed, although variants remained here and there. In 367 Athanasius, bishop of Alexandria, listed as Scripture the twenty-seven books found in today's New Testament. Just as the Jews had limited their canon to what was written before the end of the "prophetic period," it had been understood for some time that the Christian canon would be restricted to what was written before the death of the last apostle. The popular Shepherd of Hermas was written after this time, so Athanasius allowed it to be used for instruction only. In 393 the Council of Hippo confirmed Athanasius's list as authoritative canon. Four years later the Synod of Carthage proclaimed the books of both the Old and New Testaments, as they are today, the canon of the Christian church.

Although the majority of today's New Testament books were widely read in churches by the end of the second century, the history of its canon was a gradual process of ratification and rejection. No council made any particular book canonical. The various councils and synods simply affirmed those books which had the longest and widest usage throughout the Christian church.

One criterion assured a book's usage: if it was written by one of the apostles. This included Paul's letters. But there was considerable debate over which epistles were Pauline. The book of Hebrews was widely accepted in the East because it was thought to be written by Paul. The number of Paul's letters acknowledged by various church leaders ranged from ten to fourteen. Even today biblical scholars do not agree on a definitive set of New Testament books sure to have been written by Paul. As for the gospels, even the four in today's canon originally had no designated author. Matthew and John may have been apostles, but Mark and Luke were not. Many of the books later considered heretical had originally been popular because their authors wrote under the name of an apostle. So how was it decided whether a book was authentic or not?

A book was authentic if its content was consistent with the apostolic teaching well established throughout the church — the *regula fidei*, the "rule of faith." This was not written in some document, but was an acknowledged summation of the essential content of the Christian faith which gradually evolved over time. The Christian writings were a source for this faith, and this faith a basis for deciding which books were authentic. It was the old chicken-egg dilemma, a somewhat circular process in which Christian doctrine and Christian canon evolved hand in hand.

# 3

# Gothic

In the library of Sweden's Uppsala University there is a manuscript of fine parchment dyed a deep purple. It is known as Codex Argenteus — the Silver Codex — because, except for the first line in each section and the names of the evangelists which are written in gold letters, it is completely written in large silver letters. But these are not in a script found in most biblical manuscripts; they are not in Latin, or Greek, or Hebrew. Instead, they are in Gothic, an ancient Germanic dialect no longer spoken.

Several generations after Jesus's life on this earth the Goths rose from the backwaters of history to gain the spotlight as the most powerful people in Europe for a period of three hundred years. They sat on the throne of the Caesars and ruled half the continent — Italy, Spain, and southern France. Then suddenly the Gothic kingdoms were no more. The Goths blended in with other ethnic groups and their language disappeared. Today only a few remnants of their writing bear witness to a once proud people. The Silver Codex is one of these, the most complete surviving copy of the Gothic Bible. Of the original 336 pages, 188 remain.

This famous manuscript first attracted attention in the sixteenth century when Renaissance scholars discovered it in the monastery of Werden near Cologne. How it got there remains a mystery. It then became part of the emperor's collection in Prague. When Swedish armies conquered the city in 1648 they carried the manuscript off as part of the booty and presented it to their queen, Christina, who in turn ceded it to Holland to pay debts. But the Swedes had long been proud of their Gothic heritage — represented by one of the three crowns in the Swedish royal coat of arms. So a few years later a Swedish nobleman purchased the manuscript and presented it to Uppsala University, adding a solid silver binding.

If the Silver Codex could talk it would provide a fascinating window into a facet of early Christian history, a story long lost to the mists of time.

As it is, historians have had to piece this history together as best they can from a snippet here, a snippet there. The problem is that historical artifacts are preserved, and history itself written and preserved, by those who have survived political and cultural struggle and controversy.

The story behind the Silver Codex began about three hundred years after Jesus's time, in the city of Alexandria in Egypt, where a bishop and his presbyter, Arius, disputed a point of theology. Which might not have mattered but for one thing. Alexandria was one of the chief cities of the East, an important center for Christianity in an era when Rome had not yet come to dominate the church. The apostle Paul was not the only early missionary to carry the gospel message from its origin in Palestine. He was only one among many. It is said that Jesus's disciple Thomas, after getting beyond his initial doubts concerning the risen Lord, preached the good word as far east as India. The Coptic church in Africa to this day claims Jesus's disciple Philip as its founder. Alexandria was the beneficiary of this heritage.

Because Alexandria was such an important Christian city a controversy between two churchmen which might otherwise have been quickly forgotten took on more than local significance. Arius was a popular and trusted figure among the local populace, and attracted the support of important bishops outside Egypt. Soon this theological spat became a major theological controversy. Christianity split into two parties; feeling ran high. So urgent did the matter become, Emperor Constantine summoned the bishops of the empire to the first ecumenical council in Christian history.

But this ecumenical council was not able to resolve matters, nor were the several councils which followed. One of the most divisive and bitterly fought theological disputes in the history of the church, the "Arian controversy" lasted for generations and threatened to blow Christianity apart at the seams. And although Arianism eventually became a dead-end stream in the evolution of Christian theology, some of its genes have survived to this day. Today its tattered remains are woven into the fabric of the Christian faith: both the Nicene Creed and the Apostles' Creed, major statements of Christian doctrine, were devised in reaction to Arian theology.

As the Arian controversy gained momentum Arius himself was sadly forgotten. It is said that on his deathbed he had to plea with the emperor to be allowed the final sacraments because his powerful friends were now too busy to minister to a dying man. After his death uncomplimentary gossip began to circulate. His name was tarnished. But by now the Arians had found a new leader, Eusebius, bishop of Nicomedia (not the Eusebius famous for his history of the church). Nicomedia was an imperial residence, just across the channel from Constantinople. With great political dexterity Eusebius maneuvered key bishops of the opposing side into positions of ill favor with his imperial majesty. As they fell from grace, Eusebius rose in status. He was asked to baptize the emperor and was consecrated bishop of Constantinople. The increase in Arianism's influence and power in the East grew with that of its leading bishop, Eusebius. So established did Arianism become, it had the support of emperors for the next several generations.

At the peak of his power Eusebius appointed Wulfila (Little Wolf) Arian bishop of the Goths. Wulfila was a Goth, born outside the Roman empire. How he came to live within the empire is not known; early biographers are silent on this. But since movement from outside to inside the empire was no simple affair, he likely came as a slave. Slaves were among the most important commodities brought from outside by Roman traders. Coming with a trader as a slave would have made entry easy. There were many ways to become a slave in those harsh times. The economy was depressed in Wulfila's homeland; perhaps his parents sold him into slavery rather than see him starve to death; perhaps it was to pay a debt. Perhaps he had been kidnapped.

But could a slave become a bishop? Most certainly. Reading and writing were common occupations for slaves in the ancient world. Wulfila was not the first slave to rise to fame on his literary ability. The philosopher Epictetus had once been a slave. The New Testament book of Philemon tells of the slave Onesimus who was "useful" to Paul, perhaps as a literary secretary. Despite the fact that literacy was rare in the fourth century, Wulfila wrote both Latin and Greek. By the age of thirty he had attained the office of lector to the Goths. The office of lector (reader) was the oldest of the minor orders. Youths were educated for lector as the basis for further ordination.

As bishop to the Goths, Wulfila would be returning to his own people. Today the word "Gothic" has acquired connotations of evil. Second only to the Huns, the Goths were reputed to be the ultimate barbarians, outside the pale of civilization. Tradition holds that they spent their days eating, drinking, and fighting. Legend paints the Goths as unrestrained by rational thought, driven by demons, given up to violent passions leading to unspeakable acts. A bloodthirsty, axe-swinging bunch, constantly pillaging and at war, even their women enjoyed a good battle. They had no regard for personal hygiene, and a peculiar stench resulted from their strange custom of greasing their hair with rancid butter. Tall and blond, the Goths presented a striking figure. Vigorously healthy, they were renowned for their procreative powers—women continued to bear into their fifties. A hardy, brave bunch, even if they were driven back into the marshes and forests from whence they came, within a brief interval they were back in increased numbers.

Or so tradition had it. The first-century Roman historian Tacitus gets much of the credit for creating this mythic figure, both feared and admired. He praised the barbarians for their simple life, their vigor and strength of character, their moral polity — all men were equal except for the warlord, elected by all and ruling with the consent of all — a pristine version of democracy and liberty. Centuries later Cassiodorus gathered tales of the past and wove them into a history of the Goths. His account of the origins of the Gothic people written for the Ostrogothic king of Italy, Theodoric the Great, has disappeared. But it served as a source for Jordanes's Latin history of the Goths written in 550 which has survived.

Jordanes, himself a Goth, says the Goths originated in "the island of Scandza" (Scandinavia), which may account for modern Swedish pride in the Silver Codex. From Scandinavia the Goths migrated south and east across the Baltic to an area around the mouth of the Vistula (now Poland) where they conquered the Vandals and settled. Jordanes provided the Goths with ancient pedigree — 1500 B.C., before the founding of Rome — and linked them with such ancient peoples as the Scythians and Amazons.

Modern historians have evidence that the Goths were on the south shore of the Baltic around Jesus's time. From here, in search of more fertile lands to feed a growing population, they thrust south and east deep into the interior, following rivers which flow south — such as the Vistula and the Dniester — until by the year A.D. 200 they had reached the north shore of the Black Sea. Fifty years later they were making raids into the Roman empire.

By this time the mighty Roman empire was beginning to disintegrate. For years it had been ruled often by several emperors at a time. At one time in the third century it split into twenty fragments, each with its own succession of emperors. The center of imperial power was wherever these military leaders chose to make camp.

Late in the third century Roman legions withdrew from the exposed province of Dacia (includes Transylvania, roughly the Romania of today) to south of the river Danube, the traditional imperial boundary. The Goths who settled in this abandoned territory of Gothia came to be called Visigoths, as opposed to the Ostrogoths who settled to the north and east. Wulfila was a Visigoth.

Roman civilization did not leave with the legions. The Romans had built 120 cities in Dacia. It was no cultural backwater. Dacia had constant contact with Roman soldiers and diplomats, and had been settled to a great extent by Romans. Many Visigoths adopted Roman ways and carried on a vigorous trade with the empire; they were granted access to Roman cities on the frontier for this purpose. Considerable wealth in goods came into Gothia, raising the standard of living.

Great numbers of Visigoths served in the Roman army, for the Goths were reputed to be excellent warriors. They were said to eat considerably more meat (human flesh, some believed) and dairy products than the peoples around the Mediterranean. Because of this diet, observed a Roman doctor, they had more red blood in their veins and were not afraid of losing it. This reputation as warriors caused them to be feared, creating tension between Romans and Goths across the Danube. Emperor Constantine paid an annual subsidy — protection money — to insure the Goths stayed on their side of the river. Roman emperors who were Arian Christians promoted Arian Christianity in Gothia in an attempt to destabilize its people. Consequently, tribal leaders in Gothia came to see Christian Goths as a threat, a Romanizing influence. At times when tension between the two peoples grew unbearable these tribal leaders would persecute Christians, including Christian Goths, living in Gothia.

It was during one of these persecutions in 348 that the Roman emperor, an Arian Christian, granted Wulfila and his following of Christian Goths sanctuary south of the Danube within the Roman empire in what is now Bulgaria. For the remainder of his life Wulfila ministered to this small group of Christian Goths. Here he translated the Bible into Gothic from the Greek, but first he had to invent a Gothic alphabet. He didn't translate the books of Kings because they are filled with warfare; the Goths' passion for war needed no encouraging.

Years passed. Decades. Then out of the steppes of central Asia, moving rapidly on horseback over flat empty plains, came the first invasion of Huns. The Ostrogoths went out to meet this threat from the east and were quickly humbled. Word spread that these new conquerors were the offspring of witches and demons. Tradition said that hundreds of years earlier the Goths had driven witches into the solitude of the Scythian desert. Here they mated with evil spirits, resulting in a race of beings only half human. Now these creatures were returning for revenge.

The Huns' reputation preceded them: Their faces were seamed with gashes. They never changed their clothing; it simply rotted on their backs. Their helmets were patchworks of rats' skins. They didn't cook their food, but they did warm their meat — by carrying it between their thighs and the backs of their horses. They slew and ate their old men, drank blood, and slept on horseback. It was said that their country was the back of a horse.

When the Huns arrived at the borders of Dacia the Visigoths were terrified. They begged the Romans to admit them into the security of the empire. Wulfila brought their plight before the emperor, and in 376, in return for a promise to adopt the Arian Christian faith, a large portion of the Gothic population of Dacia was allowed to cross the Danube and take up residence within the Roman empire. It was the first time a large group of Germanic people settled within the boundaries of the empire.

Once inside Roman territory the Visigoths were severely mistreated. Women were seized, children enslaved, goods plundered. Bad food sold at outrageous prices. These injustices were not long tolerated. The Visigoths revolted. The emperor's attempt to crush the uprising was a disaster. He was killed, his army routed. The contemporary Roman historian Ammianus Marcellinus compared this military disaster to Hannibal's victory over the Romans at Cannae, the most famous of Roman military reverses.

The Visigoths now had a firm footing on Roman soil. The peace treaty permitted them to settle south of the Danube as a virtually independent nation within the borders of the empire. It was the first time that a people from outside the empire had been allowed to live under their own leaders within the empire. Their adoption of Arian Christianity allowed them to assimilate much of Roman civilization, while maintaining an identity separate from Latin Catholic Christians.

From here the Visigoths headed west, driven by fear of the Huns and a desire for better land. Within a generation they were at the gates of Rome. Under the able general Alaric they captured the city in 410. It was the first time in eight hundred years that the Eternal City had been conquered by outsiders. The proud Roman self-image suffered a devastating setback, but Roman civilization lived on. The Roman population scarcely noticed any change, except that the new masters were Arians, for Alaric was an Arian Christian. The Visigoth leader preserved Rome's administrative system, Roman civilization, and the ideal of the Roman empire.

The Visigoths quickly and eagerly became acculturated to Roman ways, a process which had begun years earlier in Gothia. Christianity was the gateway to this civilized life, so more and more Visigoths converted to Christianity. But in order to maintain their identity as a people within the Roman empire and to prevent their complete assimilation they converted to the Arian variety of Christianity rather than the Catholic. Had they become Catholic they would have lost much of their cherished freedom; and their priests, who had enjoyed independence, would have had to answer to an outside authority.

Within a few years the Visigoths spread into southern Gaul (now

France) and Spain. They were followed by the Ostrogoths, also on the move. The Visigoths set up their own nation in Spain. Through Visigothic influence Arianism was the predominating form of Christianity for much of the continent for quite some time.

Catholic Christians resented their Arian brothers and sisters. The Catholic church had much to lose to the immigrating peoples. As the establishment in Rome, it resented the interloper. Claiming to be the proper heir to Roman power, and hoping to keep the Arians at bay, the Catholic church labeled the Arians "barbarian." Although the word had traditionally meant no more than "foreigner"—anyone living beyond the borders of the Roman empire—in Catholic usage it took on a new and sinister meaning. When Alaric took over in 410, Catholic historians said that Rome had "fallen," "sacked" by barbarians. These Arian "barbarians," Catholics asserted, had brought an end to civilization and ushered in "the Dark Ages." Catholic propaganda insisted that these "barbarians" had risen from the muck and swamps of northern hinterlands with the singular purpose of destroying all that decent humanity held sacred, of causing the ultimate triumph of evil over good, darkness over light.

All of this, of course, was a blatant exercise in stretched semantics. Roman armies had long been manned and commanded by foreigners. There were not enough Romans to defend the empire's ten-thousand-mile frontier. For generations it had been foreigner defending against foreigner, and Arian Visigoths continued to defend the empire from marauding forces. By Wulfila's time the Latin word "barbarus" had become a synonym for "soldier."

Then, in 451, came Attila the Hun, burning cities to the ground. So horrendous was the memory of this figure that thirteen centuries later he was still depicted with horns growing from his head. Attila's devastating march into the heart of western Europe was halted by an army largely composed of Arian Visigoths. Within two years the Huns disappeared into the east as suddenly as they had arrived. The threat had ended. The "barbarian" Visigoths had preserved the Roman empire from untold depredation.

By the time Wulfila's Gothic Bible had been copied into the Codex Argenteus, early in sixth-century Italy, the Ostrogoths had moved into Italy. A century later Italy was ruled by the Lombards, another Germanic nation. Some Lombard kings were Catholic, others were Arian. The official religion varied from king to king until the late 600s when the Lombard Kingdom converted to Catholicism. In 587 the Visigothic king of Spain changed with the times, proclaiming his domain Catholic. Five hundred years later, in return for papal recognition as king of Spain, Alfonso VI eradicated Arian Visigothic texts from his domain.

At the hands of Catholic revisionists Wulfila's Bible fared no better than did the facts of history. The fifth-century Catholic priest Salvian claimed the Visigothic Bible was corrupt, full of passages biased in favor of Arianism. So the Gothic Bible was cleaned up by busy Catholic hands, any indication of Arian theology "corrected." Its text was altered to bring it into line with early Latin texts. Today no sign of Arianism can be found in the Silver Codex. A window to the past has been forever closed, a chapter of history forever lost. This beautiful manuscript which is our witness to Wulfila and the Visigoths—a people which played a great part in laying the ethnic foundation for the Europe of today—has been so altered that scholars find it virtually impossible to determine Wulfila's text.

In Wulfila's day the Arian controversy overshadowed everything Christian. Everyone took sides—Catholic or Arian. What had begun as debate over a point of theology within the church had turned into a war between two cultures, one to win out as orthodoxy, the other to be branded "heresy." Because the Catholic version of Christianity eventually won out, wherever possible all traces of the Arian "heresy" were erased from memory. History was rewritten to Catholic advantage, for history—the power of the pen—belongs to the victor. Arian literature was searched out and destroyed. Because Wulfila was Arian we know little about him. Had Arianism won out, Wulfila, as "the apostle of the Goths" (the first Germanic people to be converted to Christianity), would most certainly have been canonized as a leading saint and would be celebrated today as one of the giants of Christian history. That his name has survived at all, witnesses to the stature of the man and his contribution.

# 4

# Doctor Maximus

Doctor Maximus in Interpretandis Scripturis Sacris. Such was the grandiose title bestowed upon Saint Jerome by the Roman Catholic church during the Renaissance. A sixteenth-century woodcut shows Jerome in his study working on a manuscript. A peaceful-looking lion reclines near his feet. On the wall hangs a cardinal's hat. But Jerome had never been a cardinal, or even a bishop. Instead, as one of the four preeminent doctors of the Roman Catholic church, his fame rested upon his translation of the Bible into Latin. Yet it was not until 1592, almost twelve hundred years after his death, that the church of Rome decreed Jerome's Latin translation — which became known as the Vulgate ("vulgata editio," "the translation in common use") — the official Bible of the Roman Catholic church.

By the middle of the fourth century, when Jerome was a young student, Rome had passed the peak of its glory. But that did not matter to this small-town boy in the big city. His wide eyes everywhere beheld monuments of history. The Colosseum. The triumphal arches of the Caesars. The Forum: Was it not at this very site that the dulcet eloquence of the illustrious Cicero had charmed numerous audiences? The Eternal City. Young Jerome could not get enough of its classical culture. He developed refined tastes not common in one so young. He steeped his soul in Roman literature. Acquiring a love of books, he began to collect a library which eventually became one of the most important private collections of his day.

Jerome had the good fortune to be educated by the celebrated Aelius Donatus. Donatus was renowned for pouncing upon peccadilloes of style, for pedantic insistence on the finer points of grammar. His reputation as the most famous educator of his time did not die with him. His textbook on grammar was in demand throughout the Middle Ages and was among the first books to be printed. Donatus set Jerome upon a path to becoming one of the finest Latin Christian writers. For the rest of his days Jerome would remain a stickler for grammatical correctness, a fastidious judge of diction. He prided himself on the choice of clear effective words. The focal point of classical education was rhetoric — the ability to argue a point consistently, in debate to demolish an adversary, to smoothly convince and persuade, using all the tricks of verbal manipulation. Looking back on his early years, Jerome remembered his youthful enthusiasm for rhetorical study and erudition as "white-hot." He fondly recalled slicking back his hair, donning his toga, and declaiming before his teacher.

Jerome's interest in pagan literature was soon matched by an ardent religiosity. As a young man, he was naturally attracted to anything novel, and for the Romans Christianity was something new. Not too long before, Christians had been martyred in that city, fed to the lions. Then in 313 Emperor Constantine became a Christian. In an official edict he declared that all religions would be tolerated, but it was obvious that he favored Christianity. He gave Christian priests special privileges and supported the building of churches. Land which had been taken from churches during persecution under earlier emperors was restored. In 325 he called and presided over the Council of Nicea, where bishops formulated Christian doctrine. As a young man discovering a young religion — it would be another generation before Christianity was proclaimed the official religion of the Roman empire — Jerome found Christianity exciting.

Christians commonly postponed baptism until late in life — Constantine waited until his deathbed — to allow youthful lusts to cool and avoid risking serious sin after baptism. Not Jerome. Filled with a sense of commitment, he got baptized as a young man. He wanted to make public his desire to break with popular religious practices he thought too lax.

Flushed with religious enthusiasm, Jerome went to Aquileia, a major city at the northern tip of the Adriatic. Aquileia had acquired a reputation for the ascetic life, and Jerome was eager to investigate this new and somewhat faddish phenomenon. But it was not long before Jerome's overweening fanaticism, irascible temperament, and tactless tongue made enemies. On top of all this he was guilty of youthful indiscretion. Now the scandal-mongers had something to chew on; a whispering campaign against Jerome resulted in closed doors. Protesting loudly against such slanderous gossip while at the same time confessing error, young Jerome realized it was time to depart for greener fields.

Antioch, the cradle of Christianity ... surely here a young man brimming with a fanatical desire to live the pure Christian life would not be disappointed. In Antioch Jerome was greeted warmly by a rich and influential priest with a thorough command of Greek and Latin and a taste for ascetic ideals. The real ascetics, the priest informed Jerome, were found in the nearby desert. There Syrian anchorites were fast becoming notorious for feats of personal privation. One lived in a hole in the ground; another survived forty days on fifteen dried figs; another spent forty years with his eyes fixed on the ground, a chain around his neck and waist to prevent him from looking up. These recluses wore goatskins, plaited fronds, or nothing at all. Sun, wind, and rain aged their skin, stretching it tightly over visible bones. Their hair was long and scraggly, their beards matted; they badly needed a bath.

Jerome's imagination was aflame. This was the life he must live. The priest had been fine company and this sojourn at the priest's mansion had been pleasant, but Jerome now realized it was a mere temporary interlude before the real thing. It was time to move on. He donned the traditional sackcloth and headed for the desert. There he slept on the bare ground, and prayed. And prayed. His soul became tortured with visions of Roman dancing girls. He prayed some more.

But Jerome's stay in the desert was never completely isolated. The priest with whom he had stayed became a frequent visitor, relaying mail. Scorpions and wild beasts might be sufficient company for other ascetics, but Jerome needed his books. So he hauled his extensive library into the desert. When young ascetics gathered about he kept them occupied making copies of his books.

Jerome eventually tired of the desert and yearned to move on to other things. But his time in the East had not been wasted. While in the desert he read the Greek classics and came away with a genuine feel for the language. He learned some Syriac, and a converted Jew introduced him to the study of Hebrew. But after the subtlety of Quintilian, the flowing eloquence of Cicero, the dignified prose of Fronto, the smooth grace of Pliny, Jerome found Hebrew a rough and unaesthetic language.

Jerome returned to Antioch, then moved to Constantinople. There, because of his facility with the Greek language, he was asked to accompany clergymen to Rome on a mission of urgent church business. He would function as a translator between Eastern churchmen and their Latin colleagues. In Rome Jerome's linguistic skills, his familiarity with the affairs of the Eastern church, and his writing ability drew the attention of the pope. Would Jerome remain behind and serve the pontiff? Gladly. Soon Jerome was busy drafting church documents; his careful choice of words proved invaluable on numerous occasions. Through gifts and legacies the pope had recently become a figure of great wealth. His banquets surpassed in splendor those of the emperor. He had become the darling of fashionable women. But this new social prominence was only the beginning. The pope wanted to enhance the status of the papacy, and Jerome was to play a part.

The pope was a man of cultivated tastes. He organized and re-housed the papal archives. He wrote poetry. But he was particularly fascinated with Jerome's knowledge of all things biblical. He plied the younger man with questions, and was rewarded with miniature essays. On Palm Sunday the Jews had welcomed Jesus with the word "Hosanna"; what did it mean in Hebrew? Jerome knew, and delighted in showing off his knowledge. The pope realized that in Jerome he had captured a prize. How many other Christians could answer such questions?

One day the pope came to Jerome with a special request. The text of the Latin Bible was a mess. No two copies had the same words. The Latin Bible had originated in the second century in response to the need for a Bible for the Latin-speaking West. But the Latin Bible had never received official translation from the Greek; instead, there had been several translations in different parts of the empire. Over the years its text had succumbed to errors of copying, and over-zealous scribes had "corrected" the text by inserting material from one gospel into another or by bringing the text into line with current orthodoxy. And as if that were not enough, the Latin in many copies had a local flavor or represented only a stilted and stiff reflection of the Greek. Could Jerome sort all this out and provide a clean text?

The pope did not want Jerome to make a fresh translation from the Greek. If he could start with the gospels and provide a revision based on the Greek that would be a marvelous improvement. It was a daunting and unenviable task. For each and every phrase, Jerome would have to select from all the available competing manuscripts that which was most consistent with the Greek. Jerome was delighted with the trust placed in his abilities. But he had no illusions; the end result would win him no popularity. Nasty names would be heaped upon his head. He expected to be censured as a sacrilegious falsifier for adulterating a "pure" and familiar text. Moreover, would anyone adopt the new text, or would his efforts be in vain?

Aware of these pitfalls, Jerome was extremely conservative in his revision of the gospels. He restrained his natural literary impulses and made as few changes as possible. Unless the sense diverged from the Greek, or the translation before him was so slavishly literal as to be unintelligible, Jerome made no changes. Often he retained wording simply out of respect for tradition. In 384 Jerome presented his finished version of the gospels to the pope.

While Jerome was an accomplished master in the world of books, his social skills were too often found lacking. Characteristics which proved invaluable in the study did not always transfer smoothly into the salon. A personality which yielded dividends in his scholarly pursuits worked against his best interests on the social ledger. Jerome was strongly opinionated, headstrong, and tenacious as any terrier. Aggressive and tactless, when it came to pamphlet warfare he gave no quarter. In the heat of controversy he was likely to say almost anything. Impulsive and indiscrete, he did not always rein in his caustic wit. He told one individual he would make an excellent speaker if he kept his mouth shut. A proud man, confident of his knowledge and abilities, at times extraordinarily touchy, distrustful, resentful, and suspicious of others to the point of paranoia, Jerome exhibited a complex and ambivalent personality.

Jerome made no secret of the fact that he regarded the morals of many Christians in Rome, including many of the clergy, as substandard. His moralizing and constant campaigning for asceticism was not looked upon favorably in many circles. Too often he pointed the finger, too often he was blatantly outspoken, for his incriminations to go unnoticed. In blistering portrayals he satirized bogus Christianity. His devastatingly caustic vignettes amused some; others were outraged.

He insisted that, as compensation for the sins of marriage and childbearing, parents must consecrate their offspring as virgins. He recommended that one couple send their baby daughter to his monastery as soon as she was weaned, to study religion and associate with ascetic adults for the rest of her days. What a crippled and colorless existence, thought the parents. But Jerome meant well. He felt genuine concern for the little girl's Christian soul. Beneath his ascetic exterior Jerome was a loving and compassionate man. Despite his love of scholarship, he quickly abandoned his books to care for refugees who came to his door. Never ready to concede where strong principles were at stake, he demonstrated no hatred for the person, whatever his or her viewpoint. A formidable foe in debate, he attacked ideas, not the person who held them. A man of strong mind but sensitive heart, Jerome was always ready for personal reconciliation.

But his good points meant nothing to his critics. They bided their time until they saw an opportunity to strike. Jerome acted as spiritual guide and teacher of Scripture to Roman women of wealth and social rank. He would while away the time at their homes—one a mansion on the Aventine, the southernmost of Rome's seven hills, an envied and exclusive address—and paint tempting pictures of the ascetic life. These aristocratic ladies were all aflutter: such a brilliant scholar, such a model ascetic—he had struggled with demons in the Syrian desert. Soon women who would otherwise have graced the social circles with their beauty and charm were actively withdrawing from society, dressing in coarse unattractive clothing, neglecting their appearance, fasting, avoiding the bath, and abstaining from sex.

Things came to a head. A vivaciously beautiful young woman of the upper class had no sooner consummated her eagerly anticipated marriage than she was left a widow. Jerome told her this was God's punishment for her sins—her haughty appearance, her worldly life. Jerome badgered her on these counts, but his remonstrations fell on deaf ears. Then a severe fever filled the young widow with the fear of God, and she fell under Jerome's spell. This quintessential society woman transformed into a model ascetic. She surrendered her soul in prayer, mortified her physical being, paid penance, studied Scripture. Within four months she was dead. The emotional and physical strain of the sudden change had been too much. Jerome praised her as a paragon of excellence, and castigated her mother for her tears—she should set an example as a Christian and rejoice that her daughter was now with the Lord.

Jerome was blamed for the young woman's death. He was gaining critics everywhere. His ideals of virginity and the ascetic life—that women should eschew male companionship—set a large portion of the populace against him. Rumors spread about his close association with one particular widow. His revision of the Old Latin gospels and his censure of Christians and clergy were resented. Where once he had been praised as holy, humble, learned, and even worthy to become pope, Jerome was now reviled as a scoundrel, a trickster, a liar, and an agent of the devil.

Then Jerome's political capital vanished. The pope who had commissioned his biblical revisions died, and with his death Jerome lost his most prominent supporter. Rome had always captivated Jerome, and his years there had been happy ones, but a new pope and the changing of the guard at the papal palace meant a political climate less hospitable to his interests. His enemies rallied, and forced out by the local clergy, he had little choice but to leave Rome. Within a year after completing his edition of the gospels Jerome left for the Holy Land, there to remain for the rest of his life.

Jerome never bore a grudge for any of this. He was a forgiving man, as was demonstrated years later when monasteries to which he had devoted much of his life were burned to the ground. Virtually everyone knew who was responsible. The pope offered to take drastic judicial action if Jerome would only come forth with a specific accusation and name names. But Jerome refused to do so.

After leaving Rome, Jerome, along with some friends, toured the East. In Bethlehem they founded a monastery. Away from the hothouse of Roman society, Jerome was free to pursue his own goals. He continued biblical research and translation to the end of his days despite, in his later years, general ill health and poor eyesight which precluded writing and made reading difficult, necessitating an assistant. A visitor who stayed half a year at Bethlehem reported that Jerome was always reading and writing, always at this books, never resting day or night.

In Palestine Jerome visited the magnificent library at Caesarea — the greatest collection of Christian writing then available. There he examined the Hexapla, which presented in parallel columns the Hebrew text and variant Greek texts of the Old Testament. In Bethlehem he began to revise the Latin version of the Old Testament, based on the Greek of the Hexapla. So successful was his revision of the psalter — the so-called Gallican Psalter — that it became the psalter of the Vulgate and of the Roman Breviary. Only recently has Jerome's psalter been superseded by the New Latin Psalter.

But Jerome discovered a problem. The Greek translations in the Hexapla differed considerably. One of the Greek texts — the Septuagint — had privileged status in the Western Roman church, but Jerome discovered that there were at least three major forms of the Greek Old Testament circulating in the East — one in Asia, one in Syria, and one in Egypt. All of this convinced him that the text of the Greek Old Testament was in just as bad a state as that of the Latin Old Testament. Upon which Greek text, if any, should he base his Latin translation? Moreover, since the Greek Old Testament was just a translation of the Hebrew original, he would be translating a translation. Jerome saw no practical alternative but to go back and translate the Hebrew, the language in which the Old Testament had originally been written.

Learning Hebrew was no minor task. First, the study of Hebrew fell under a dark cloud. Jews were considered hostile to Christianity — hadn't the Jews killed Jesus? But Jerome was determined not to be deterred, and proved to be one of few Christians with the courage and independence of spirit to break loose from these popular biases.

Second, Hebrew was, and remains, a difficult language for Europeans. It is a Semitic language — an entirely different group of languages from that spoken in the West. In Jerome's time Hebrew was written only in consonants; the vowels were understood. This resulted in a rather bizarre error. In the Middle Ages Moses was commonly depicted with horns coming from his head — like the devil — because the Latin Bible had mistranslated the Hebrew word "qrn" in Exodus 34:29 as "horn." With a different selection of vowels "qrn" becomes "shine," yielding the translation "the skin of his face shone" — which our modern versions have adopted.

Jerome had no grammars, no dictionaries, and no concordances. But one of the Greek translations in the Hexapla matched Greek word with Hebrew word. So he was able to build up his own list of Hebrew words for reference. In addition, Jerome consulted Jews concerning the Hebrew Bible and the fine points of the Hebrew language — often at night to avoid the censure of other Jews.

Once he knew the meanings of the words, Jerome could proceed with his translation into Latin. His finished translation was an accomplished work of scholarship, especially for that time. But, unlike his revision of the gospels which had been sanctioned by the pope, Jerome's translation from the Hebrew suffered severe criticism. Augustine, the influential prima donna theologian of the Roman church, and Jerome's contemporary, castigated Jerome for presuming he could render a better translation than the learned translators who had produced the Septuagint. Augustine's criticism was influential for several centuries thereafter, and there were other doubts concerning Jerome's translation. Because he had consulted with Jews, wouldn't his translation be adulterated with Jewish theology?

With these considerations, the church did not quickly adopt Jerome's translation from the Hebrew. As late as the thirteenth century scribes continued to bypass Jerome's translation in favor of making copies of the Old Latin version. Jerome's reputation remained somewhat under a dark cloud until the Renaissance, when his status as a consummate biblical scholar and translator was resurrected and he became one of the most celebrated figures in the Roman Catholic church.

# 5

# Cloistered

It was 1952. The sunbathed coast of southern Italy would provide a splendid location for the construction of a private summer home. Gentle breezes from the Ionian Sea wafted over the workmen as they excavated for the foundation. Suddenly their digging met with resistance — a large object buried in the earth. The outside was inscribed with lettering which the workmen thought might be Greek. The civil authorities were notified, who in turn contacted an archaeologist. Indeed, the lettering was Greek; the words indicated that inside were located the bones of a saint. And inside were some bones. Archaeologists later determined that the coffin and bones dated from the sixth century.

In the sixth century a wealthy man with the imposing name Flavius Magnus Aurelius Cassiodorus Senator described his family's estate in the glowing terms of today's real estate ads. While Italy's extreme south features sunny winters and moderate summers, it is a terrain which not every eye would judge beautiful — visually striking perhaps, but barren. Despite this apparent disparity historians connected Cassiodorus's description to the site of the 1952 summer house, claiming the bones in the coffin were his.

No legends survive concerning Cassiodorus. Not a figure to excite the emotions, he nevertheless earned the respect of centuries of men and women. For almost one thousand years his name was mentioned respectfully in literate circles. He left behind no cult of dedicated followers and no hagiographer to sing his praises. Never a saint of great popular renown, his name nevertheless appears in the *Acta Sanctorum* under March 17. In studied understatement Cassiodorus has been characterized as a man intent on backing carefully into the future, an organizer rather than a charismatic leader. Cassiodorus would probably have acknowledged this portrayal with a subtle smile.

Cassiodorus was the very picture of the urbane and polished gentleman of late antiquity. He came from a proud and distinguished family. The name Cassiodorus conferred a sense of responsibility, trust, and honor. Although Cassiodorus Senator was not a senator, his friends and contemporaries called him Senator and Cassiodorus enjoyed making punning allusions to his name — a sense of humor was part of the accoutrement of the gentleman in those times. So too were prudence, restraint, flexibility, and patience — all traits possessed by Cassiodorus. A true gentleman, he cherished the finer things in life — the better aspects of Roman culture, letters, the humanities — and strived to keep these alive in an era when they might have been forgotten, when waves of foreign peoples swept over Italy. A responsible citizen of refinement and good breeding, he did his best to preserve the traditions of old.

Cassiodorus did not see himself as a lonely representative of a dying age, nor bemoan the loss of an idealized past. Instead, he rose to the challenge before him. Demonstrating a sense of practical wisdom, he kept his eye on the distant horizon, discreetly ignoring the bumps of everyday existence. In a time of turmoil and confusion, like the Cassiodori before him, he sought to insure some degree of stability and continuity between past and present, while maintaining the classic Roman culture. Like his forefathers, Cassiodorus was both pragmatic and politically astute. His father, his grandfather, and his great-grandfather had served successive Ostrogothic rulers of the former Roman empire in important offices. His father had been Odovacar's finance minister. Then, when the Ostrogothic conqueror Theodoric the Great slew Odovacar, he served the new leader. The son followed in the father's footsteps. Theodoric appointed him quaestor, head of administration. As quaestor, Cassiodorus was Theodoric's mouthpiece and ambassador of public relations. He conducted correspondence, received foreign dignitaries, put the finishing touches on the sovereign's decrees, and wrote his speeches. Theodoric considered himself the legitimate successor of the emperors of imperial Rome, and his kingdom the natural continuation of the Roman empire, but he never mastered Latin so he put great value on Cassiodorus's eloquent ministrations. Cassiodorus admired the conquering Goths. He wrote a history of the Goths in which he hoped to reconcile Romans to being ruled by those they regarded as barbarians, by showing the Goths worthy to be classed with Greeks and Romans.

In a time of bitter and divisive religious controversy — Arians versus Catholics — Cassiodorus faithfully served his emperor in a spirit of tolerance. He was against enforcing any particular set of beliefs because he knew that no one can think or believe against his will. Rather than emphasizing theological differences, Cassiodorus devoted himself to preserving that which Christians of all traditions share — the literature of the Bible. After a long career of public service, at a point in life when most men would be content to sit back and watch the grass grow, Cassiodorus embarked on what was virtually a second vocation. Retiring to the family estate in the south of Italy near Squillace in Calabria in 540, he founded a monastery. The scene was idyllic — looking out on the Ionian sea, backed by a range of mountains, set among flowering orchards, beside a gentle stream. But the task was serious — to preserve classical language, learning, and culture for the future.

Rooted in the ascetic movement of the East, monasticism had been around for some time. Those who thought Christianity was becoming too worldly sought remote locations where they could devote themselves to prayer, meditation, and fasting. This spontaneous counterculture, this grassroots movement, was an indirect criticism of the church, a challenge to normative Christianity. The holy men of the desert cast the wealthy bishop in bad light. Jesus's remarks had been uncompromising. The Christian must sell everything he owns and give to the poor (Matthew 19:21). The Master had called for nothing less than whole-hearted commitment (Matthew 10:37,38). But the reward was worth any sacrifice: to everyone who leaves his home and his family to follow him, Jesus had promised eternal life (Matthew 19:29).

By Cassidorus's time the ascetic spirit had spread to the West where it was expressed in communal form. Monks and nuns were cloistered within four walls under a religious rule. The church was quick to confirm this new form of Christian living, for here was a way to accommodate the religious free spirit, here was a safety valve for the zealous minority which might otherwise prove divisive. Here could be contained the active mind, the Christian who asked difficult questions, who otherwise might be troublesome. Here could be hidden unruly sons and unmarried daughters. Here was a place for rejects and failures. Just east of Rome Benedict had founded a monastery which would become the primary model for all monasteries, for Benedict was championed by one of the most powerful and ambitious popes of all time — Gregory I. Gregory "the Great" built up the papacy and placed his mark firmly upon the character of the church and its future direction. By the eighth and ninth centuries *The Rule of Saint Benedict* would win out over rival monastic rules, and set a pattern of life for Western cloisters.

*The Rule of Saint Benedict* made no mention of the copying of manuscripts. By contrast, Cassiodorus made the copying and preservation of manuscripts a priority within the cloister, and gave it a rationale consistent with the general ethos of monastic life. He made a systematic practice of what previously had been only a random and haphazard occurrence. His lead would prove invaluable for the preservation of Christian tradition as found in its written documents, particularly with regard to Scripture.

The copying of manuscripts assured sufficient copies of classical texts of the past, both secular and Christian, so that traditions of the past would be spread far and wide and transmitted to future generations. Copying manuscripts had personal religious value as a form of psychological discipline. It taught the monk patience and steadiness; it kept his mind occupied — his imagination had no time to wander in wild theological speculation.

Cassiodorus furnished his scriptorium with novel technical devices: lamps that burned brightly and did not require constant attention; a sundial and a water clock to tell time. He acquired a substantial collection of manuscripts, for reference and to be copied. Much of his library came from Constantinople, a center for Eastern scholarship and theological pursuits. Bilingual scholars from the East came to his secluded monastic site, where in peace and quiet they could indulge a passion for translating Greek classics into Latin.

To guide future generations Cassiodorus wrote several books on scribal practice. His *Institutiones* described the model scriptorium and provided a list of books to guide monasteries in establishing and organizing a library. Cassiodorus cautioned the scribe against too readily emending a text. The scribe needed to be aware that languages change over time. So that the scribe might recognize past orthographic practice and ancient inflections Cassiodorus, in his ninety-third year, wrote a book on orthography.

Cassiodorus's influence spread throughout Europe. The first Latin grammar written in Ireland, by the monk Asperius, already in 600 showed evidence of Cassiodorus's *Institutiones*. A survey of medieval library catalogues shows that his Latin translation of Josephus was the most copied historical work of the Middle Ages. His commentary on the Psalms was praised at York in England and listed in its library. His works are quoted in many medieval manuscripts.

Cassiodorus set the model for scribal activity but he could not oversee the work of every scribe. In the ensuing generations monasteries were often founded by secular nobles who provided the land, the building, the revenues, and the charter. The monks were to pray constantly for the benefactor and his family, even after they died, to assure their souls everlasting peace. Usually the monks came from the nobility. (The serfs remained on the land to till the soil.) Children who proved mentally or physically deficient were placed in the monastery, there to remain for the rest of their days. Some individuals sought escape from the strictures, duties, and unpleasantness of medieval secular life. In the monastery they hoped to find simplicity, solitude, privacy in meditation, spiritual and intellectual growth, and companionship of kindred spirits. Life in the monastery became a constant repetition of Psalms, responses, prayers.

Scribal work in such monasteries often functioned merely as a means of discipline, even penance. The story was told of a worldly and sinful monk. When he died the devil claimed his soul, but the angels appealed this decision before the Throne of Judgment: had not this monk done penance for his sins, dutifully copying manuscripts in the scriptorium? A revised decision was handed down: for every letter the monk had transcribed in the scriptorium during his former life one sin would be forgiven. But the monk's worldly pleasures were so numerous his scribal work turned out to be one letter short of absolution. The Lord in his mercy allowed the soul of the monk once again to enter an earthly body, so that he might make up the difference.

Where the primary purpose of scribal activity was not the production of an authentic transcript of Scripture, corrupt manuscripts were sure to accumulate. Peter the Venerable had written that the monk who did not wish to take up the plough should take up the pen, sowing the seeds of divine words and preaching the gospel. Cassiodorus would have replied that sloppy scribal work sowed unsound seeds and preached false words. Better that scribes not dedicated to their work remain at the plough.

Some scriptoria were motivated by profit. This did not negate the possibility of quality work, but some trade-off in quality for quantity was to be expected. When illiterate patrons from the secular nobility sought lavishly illuminated manuscripts as an emblem of wealth, this did not encourage special attention to textual accuracy. Nor did the tradition of the gift book. In places the production of manuscripts became a mini-industry, with workshops often staffed by lay people. There was specialization of task — production of ink, parchment, and gold leaf, copying of text, illumination, binding. Some scribes were more interested in manual dexterity than anything else. One scribe was reputed to have penned a complete copy of the Bible in such tiny script that the whole fitted within a walnut shell.

Even where accuracy of text was of primary importance, the transcription of manuscripts required more than a steady hand. The ideal scribe needed a sound knowledge of Latin grammar, syntax, and vocabulary, and extensive training not only in penmanship but in reading and comprehending the work of other scribes. But how many such monks existed? Even within the renowned monastery of St. Gall there was not a single literate monk at the end of the thirteenth century.

Even a model scribe, educated in all of Cassiodorus's precepts, disciplined, enthusiastic, and eager to serve was nevertheless beset with problems. The work was physically demanding. It was not unusual for a scribe to work six hours a day — all the daylight hours he was not engaged in prayer. Many scriptoria were unheated in the winter months. Suffering copyists sometimes indulged in marginal notes, complaining about exhaustion and the cold. One scribe told of a heavy snow storm raging outside; it was so cold that the ink froze and the pen fell from his numbed fingers. An abbot at a different monastery apologized to his bishop for not sending promised manuscripts — the winter had been so cold that the monks' fingers could not work the pen.

The model scribe had to contend with more than physical hardship. His exemplar (the manuscript he was copying) might be difficult to read and full of errors, omissions, and unintelligible abbreviations. He struggled to make silk out of a sow's ear. Often he thought there was an error where there was none, and corrected what did not warrant correcting — perhaps wording did not correspond with that of the local liturgy, or he thought Jesus could not possibly have said or done *that*. As well, the scribe was vulnerable to any of the numerous standard unintentional scribal errors. His finished copy then became the exemplar for the next generation of manuscripts. With each generation of copying, errors were compounded and the text became more and more corrupt.

Cassiodorus remarked that every word of Scripture written by the scribe was a wound inflicted on Satan. But he envisioned the model scribe operating under ideal conditions. He envisioned the scriptorium as a sanctuary for the perfect preservation of Holy Writ and other classical literature. He would have been appalled at what took place in the scriptoria of many monasteries.

Not many years after Cassiodorus's death the movement of Lombards southward rendered conditions for study at his monastery tenuous. His library was dispersed and its holdings scattered far and wide, to the great benefit of future generations.

# 6

# Magic Talisman

As the ancient era gave way to what later historians would refer to as the Dark Ages, the Bible may have been a respected artifact in the monasteries, but outside those cloistered walls it was almost as if the Bible did not exist. Not for practical purposes that it mattered, for few could read, even among the clergy. Individuals like Jerome and Cassiodorus were the rare exception; they inhabited the lofty rarified and exclusive world of the scholar. It was not for nothing that they were canonized. But outside their privileged existence in islands of classical civilization, was a far different world.

Late in the fourth century Christianity was proclaimed the official religion of the Roman empire, but shortly thereafter the empire was overrun by wave upon wave of peoples from outside its boundaries, peoples who were not Christian. The Roman "Catholic" church had to fight for survival, not only in the face of strong Arian competition within Christianity, but in this wider pagan world.

The pagan world was steeped in magic, ritual, and sorcery. Minor spirits were believed responsible for life's misfortunes—from poor harvests, floods, and fires, to illness and soured milk. In order to survive, early Christianity melded with the magic and superstition of the pagan world. Popular magic became Christian magic. Pagan deities continued to be worshiped alongside the Christian God. In an attempt to assimilate pagan religion, Christian churches were often built on the foundations of pagan temples, Christian holidays expropriated pagan festivals (Saturnalia became Christmas), and ancient rites were condoned, or transformed with Christian interpretation. Little changed but the names. Pagan idols were renamed Jesus and Mary. Popular religion traditionally combined demons, spirits, and gods of classical, pagan, and folklore origin. It was no trouble to add to these supernatural entities the Christian God. Jesus and God were simply included in the popular pagan pantheon.

Paganism continued to hold sway long after the West had been "Christianized." Christianization was often merely token, the people only nominally Christian. The emperor Charlemagne gave people a choice: they could be baptized, or they could be executed. On one occasion he had 4500 beheaded; they must have thought he was bluffing! Christianization in name only. It was skin-deep and did not take root. The Christianity of common folk was usually thinly disguised paganism. Despite the valorous efforts of Christian missionaries, monasteries and churches in the West were islands in a sea of religious eclecticism. True and complete conversion in most cases remained an ideal.

In its rivalry with pagan beliefs the church chose saints as its chief weapon, hoping thereby to displace the numerous pagan deities. Pagan deities were renamed as Christian saints. But people named local saints often without the church's approval. There were saints for cities, monasteries, regions, families. There was a saint for every purpose under the sun, one to heal each type of sickness. The church declared these folk-saints minions of Satan, but it could not suppress them.

In the early eighth century the renegade priest Adelbert successfully conned pagans and Christians, even some bishops. He claimed that the archangel Michael had given him a letter from Christ, bestowing almost unlimited powers. Of humble origins, Adelbert understood the needs of common folk. He raised crosses and said the liturgy at pagan holy sites in field and forest. People began to abandon priests and churches in droves. They sought samples of Adelbert's hair and nails, distributed as holy objects, so they would have access to the supernatural powers that controlled all of life. Every man and woman sought precautionary measures, incantations, auguries, divinations, magic to ward off bad luck and disaster; for life was tenuous, every step full of danger, everywhere demons and spirits. Adelbert was a godsend, and there were many like him. The city of Cologne counted over 27,000 such sacred intermediaries.

Most saints were local. A saint's influence and powers decreased with distance. The place where the saint had lived and worked his miracles, or the place where his remains rested, was the focal point of his powers. A woman suffering from fever wanted to know which of three saints would best serve her needs. She lighted a candle for each to see which would burn longest. The candle of the local saint won the contest. The woman prayed to that saint and was healed. People were extremely possessive of the local saint. When the mountain-dwellers of Umbria learned of St. Romuald's intention to move to another location they planned to murder him, so that he would be with them forever. Stories abound about the bodies of saints being stolen — dug up and moved to another location and community.

Saints answered a deep need within the human soul. God was all-powerful, but invisible and distant. Saints were accessible. Saints were human — they were cursed when they failed to grant wishes. A saint was a personal guardian angel, a companion, a partner in life, a dispenser of gifts, a messenger to the supernatural realm, an intermediary to God, a heavenly figure with special powers, almost a personal god.

The physical remains of a saint and all her/his possessions were considered holy relics. A splinter of wood, a swatch of cloth, took on sacred and magical powers. A relic was a potent connection to the supernatural realm, the most effective channel through which supernatural power was available to mere mortals. Want your enemies punished? Want a loved one healed? Want the woman or man of your dreams to be yours? Then visit the shrine where your favorite saint's relics are deposited. Christians made pilgrimages to shrines to tap the power of the saints. Throughout the Middle Ages Christianity was all about relics.

The Christian church in the West was built upon relics. The authority of the pope rested upon the assertion that he was the guardian of the body of St. Peter. Except for his claim to that special relic the pope might have remained just the bishop of Rome, one bishop among many. Early bishops centered their realm around the great urban shrines. In the late fourth century Ambrose, bishop of Milan, had the relics of Saint Gervasius and Saint Protasius moved from their original resting place and buried under the altar of his cathedral. In doing so, he set a precedent — from here on bishops would guarantee their power and that of the church by taking possession of holy relics.

Bishops were not always overly delicate in how they came to possess relics. The twelfth-century bishop Hugh of Lincoln, in his time one of the most beloved and renowned English bishops, asked to see one of the nearby monastery's relics — a bone from the body of Mary Magdalene. The bishop hurriedly cut through the several layers of cloth in which the relic was wrapped and gazed in wonder at the precious bone. He tried unsuccessfully to break a piece off, then to the horror of the monks thrust the bone into his mouth and gnawed at it like a dog, chipping off two fragments which he took away with him for his own personal treasure.

The stealing of relics was not uncommon. Monks were often the culprits, but there were professional relic thieves. The story of how a relic was stolen often accompanied the relic in its new location, adding to its prestige and value. Soon these stories formed a genre of literature with standard motifs and plots: the quest lasted years, even decades — the robber joined the local clergy or monks, gaining their trust over a long period of residence, and then one night stole the relic.

A stolen relic possessed more value than one purchased or received as a gift. A relic was equivalent to the living saint, just as the wafer and wine of the eucharist signified the presence of the living Lord. (The body and blood of Christ in the wafer and wine were often placed under the altar of a new church, along with other relics.) Stealing a relic was regarded as helping a willing saint move to a happier location, an act of love. The saint appeared to a monk in a vision, telling about his unhappy situation — neglected state of the relic, insufficient reverence by the local clergy and parishioners — and requesting transfer to a community where he/she would receive rightful devotion. A relic — and hence the saint — could not be moved if the saint did not want to be moved, for the saint, after all, possessed magical powers. If the new location of the relic resulted in miracles, the saint had clearly favored the move. As a particular monastery or church gained more relics, it became a center of power and prestige.

Kings kept relics in their crowns or around their necks to guarantee their sovereignty. The throne of the emperor Charlemagne was stuffed with relics. In the dying years of the Roman empire the mother of Emperor Constantine, later canonized as St. Helena, went to the Holy Land in search of the cross on which Jesus had been crucified. She found all three crosses of Calvary. Which one was Christ's? A cadavre was brought into contact with each of the crosses. One of the three brought the dead body back to life. Here was the relic of relics. Consequently this cross was cut into smaller and smaller pieces until mere slivers were being sold and traded all over Europe.

Individuals of independent thinking scoffed at the idolatry of relic worship. In the late Middle Ages Giovanni Boccaccio satirized relics: a finger of the Holy Spirit, rays of the star over Bethlehem, a phial containing the sound of the bells of Solomon's temple. During the Protestant Reformation in the 1500s some Christians began to look upon relics as pagan: they joked that there were enough pieces of Jesus's cross to fill a large ship. They remarked upon the copious supply of questionable relics collected by the Crusaders centuries earlier: Judas's pieces of silver, *two* heads of John the Baptist, *three* versions of the crown of thorns worn by Jesus, a great many of Jesus's foreskins, the seeds from Jesus's parable about the sower of wheat seeds, one of baby Jesus's molars — how had anyone thought to save it? Yet even the enlightened Frederick the Wise, a Renaissance man and staunch supporter of the Protestant Reformation, made a positive fetish of relics, accumulating over nineteen thousand.

Where was the Bible in all of this? In the early centuries of the Roman church common folk never saw a Bible, if indeed they knew such existed. Only in the larger urban areas, particularly where a bishop resided, was there likely to be a Bible, and then only a single copy. On special ceremonial occasions it would be paraded down the center of the cathedral with great pageantry, and placed upon the altar beneath which were buried all the other relics. There on the altar it remained, the center of awed attention, a visible specimen of the realm of the supernatural. A relic among relics.

But few would be the fortunate individuals to see such a specimen. In those dark times few laypersons had any reason to come in contact with the written word in any form. Virtually no laypersons could read. Indeed, it would be another eight hundred years — the high Middle Ages — before an appreciable number of laypersons could read. Even at that later time, in England there were only a few hundred literate laypersons in a population of two million. The proportion of clergy who could read was higher — our word "clerk" (implying someone who can read and write) comes from the word "cleric," a member of the clergy. But a great many clergy were illiterate. The few literate clergy looked down their noses at the illiterate, calling them "idiotae" (Latin). Even in the monasteries, where Scripture was most likely to be found, many monks could not read.

Because of this illiteracy the written word was approached with superstitious reverence and awe. Written words, and much later, as copies of books became more available, all books, not just Holy Scripture, were regarded as sacred objects. Healing was effected by placing a scrap of writing or a book upon the forehead. In the presence of a book fortunes were told and black magic practiced.

The Bible was written in words of Latin. To the unlettered, the written Latin word — Latin had by this time become less and less a spoken language — was not a vehicle of factual information, but of magic, ritual, sorcery (hocus-pocus). So Holy Scripture was considered especially magical. Christian clergy would dip a parchment bearing sacred text into some wine; anyone who drank the wine would have his or her secret desires granted. Medieval society was based upon a hierarchical system of lords and vassals. When a vassal promised to be loyal to and serve his lord, he swore upon a relic or upon a Bible.

Outside monastic walls very few regarded the Bible as anything but an instrument of magic. Those who were fortunate enough to enter a church where one of the clergy knew sufficient Latin to read from Holy Scripture during the liturgy, must have felt blessed beyond all blessings as the church was filled with the sonorous hum of Latin. Magic words. Hocus-pocus.

# 7

# The Emerald Isle

Magic and saints were the essence of early Christianity in Ireland. When Christian missionaries arrived in any new land they compromised with the pagan beliefs and practices of the local people. The cultures mixed. Christianity co-opted what it could not suppress, and wrapped it in Christian clothing. So it was in the emerald isle. Irish Christianity included a healthy dose of pagan Celtic tradition. In becoming Christian the Irish did not stop being Irish.

Saint Patrick. We think of him as the person who brought Christianity to Ireland. But there were Christians in Ireland when Patrick arrived in the 400s. He was sent by Rome to organize these Christians into a church on the Roman model, with the bishop as figure of authority. He was only partly successful. Bishops came to have their place and function in Ireland, but the leaders of the Irish church were abbots and learned monks. Irish Christianity was centered on the cloister, not on dioceses organized around major cities as in continental Europe. In Ireland there were no cities; in this thinly populated land the largest communities were monasteries.

Irish monastic culture differed from the mainstream monastic culture which flowered on the Roman continent. On the continent, and even in England, the monasteries and their abbots soon came under the jurisdiction of the bishops, through whom was felt the strong hand of Rome. But Ireland had never been part of the Roman empire. Separated historically from the flow of life in mainland Europe and geographically from its landmass, the emerald isle went its own way. Monastic culture in Ireland had a particularly Irish flavor. The monastery remained closely connected to the local tribe and was deeply rooted in the people and the land. By the time Patrick arrived Ireland was fast becoming the proverbial land of saints and scholars. Here the spoken, and later the written, word had great value and power.

The arbiters of the spoken word were the bards. The Irish were proud of their traditions, of their antiquity as a people, of local glories, so those who gave literary form to the essence of the Irish spirit, who made poetry of nationalist passions, who dramatized the chronicles of Ireland's misty past, found a warm place in the hearts of the people. The bards fulfilled all of these roles. They were poets, musicians, genealogists, and historians. They sang of religion and war. They recited ancient laws. They intoned the genealogies of Ireland's patriarchs, and enshrined in verse the exploits of her heroes.

The legacy of the bards with respect to Irish mythology was invaluable. So too was their contribution to Irish culture and Irish Christianity. Instead of rejecting the new religion they fostered a close association between the church and the literary and artistic spirit. In this way the bards brought a new dimension to Christianity in Ireland. The arts became a faithful handmaid of, and an essential ingredient in, the ethos of monasticism in the land of the green. As the bards were tamed to Christian purposes they brought to the new religion the element of magic.

The bards were greatly respected for their wisdom and learning. They came to acquire considerable influence, and their popularity conferred special power — they could make or break kings with a few words. Words took on an aura of magic when spoken by the bards — the incantation, the spell, the charm; they had inherited this priestly role from the druids before them. The bard was priest, wiseman, and poet, all rolled into one — a figure to be feared and respected.

The time came when the king thought the bards had too much power. He wanted them gone. A Christian monk, Columba, came to their rescue. In his youth Columba had resided with a bard to obtain special instruction. The bard had filled him with the poetry of Ireland's colorful past, and inspired him with a taste for the power and beauty of words. Columba understood the unique blend of paganism and Christianity in his native land. He realized that to destroy the bards was to undermine Irish culture and Irish Christianity. Every prince, every lord, every monastery had its bard. Irish monasteries had their origin with the bards, as an outgrowth of the colleges where bards and druids studied. The years of exacting and disciplined study required to become a bard easily translated into the discipline of monastic life. Columba insisted that the bards were a prized part of the separate ethnicity and identity of the Irish people, a distinctive feature of Irish pride. The bards could not be allowed to disappear into history. Columba argued their case with eloquent force, so eloquently and so forcefully that the bards were permitted to stay.

The bards returned the favor. They sang Columba's praises and made him a legendary figure. The Irish love a good story: how Saint Patrick chose the shamrock to illustrate the doctrine of the trinity; how he drove the snakes from Ireland. (An observant geographer had remarked years before that Ireland was devoid of snakes.) In like manner legends grew around Columba.

Many a delightful tale tells of miracles he worked and of his extraordinary powers. One time a monk came to him with a completed manuscript. Without examining the manuscript Columba turned to a particular page and pointed out the one single error in the whole work. Manuscripts which he himself penned had magical powers: one fell into a pond but the ink did not run; sick cattle drank the water and immediately recovered. Metal from a knife Columba blessed was melted and overlayed on iron tools so they could be used without fear of injury. The Loch Ness monster obeyed Columba's command not to touch a swimmer. Like Moses Columba drew water out of a rock. Like Jesus he turned water into wine, brought the dead back to life, healed the sick, calmed the sea, cast out demons, multiplied food, provided a catch of fish for his followers.

Into the cloth of fiction was woven many a thread of fact. The wisdom of Solomon with which Columba was reputedly blessed was really psychological insight. One day a man came to him complaining about his wife, a good wife in all ways except that she would not share his bed. Columba reminded the wife of Scripture — that the two shall become one flesh. The woman said she would do anything the monk commanded; she would be willing to spend her remaining years in a nunnery, rather than one night in bed with her husband. Columba told the woman to take a week and think about what she had just said. When she returned a week later he asked her if she was ready to enter the nunnery. No, the woman replied, her feeling for her husband had suddenly changed from repugnance to desire. No nunnery for her. She would be staying, and sleeping, with her husband. From that day forward she proved the most affectionate of wives.

From the beginning Columba was destined to greatness. Before his birth an angel appeared to his mother, just as the angel Gabriel had appeared to Jesus's mother Mary, to tell her that she would bear a son. Columba's mother and father came from royal lines, and with Columba's ability and talents he might one day have become king of all Ireland. But this was not his destiny. Instead, he chose to be a servant of Christ. He was sent to study with an elderly wise man. Seeing the boy had such an alert mind, the old man sought out a prophet. It was time that he read Holy Scripture, declared the prophet. The prophet placed an alphabet in a cake and fed it to young Columba, who hungrily ate up the cake, and the alphabet. Soon, like the young Jesus, Columba was astounding his teachers in his knowledge of Holy Scripture. When one of them stumbled over a psalm Columba completed it.

A young man of such clear ability does not long tarry unknown in some rural hamlet. Soon Columba was studying in succession under a bard and the two foremost scholars of the emerald isle, both named Finnian. The Finnians were traveled men, men renowned on the continent as leading intellectual lights in classical and biblical learning. They delighted in the unfolding genius of the young man before them, and he in turn revered and came to love his teachers. Columba became a monk and was soon transcribing Scripture so that its holy word might be multiplied and spread over the land. The joy of this work filled his soul and shone in his face.

Columba's cheerful earnestness made the other monks jealous. One young monk complained to his elder about the privileges Columba's abilities attracted. The elder man led the younger into a workshed. He took down from the shelves an axe, a plane, and a drill. You have no right to complain, said the elder monk, for as a carpenter's son these tools are all that you have sacrificed to become a monk. But Columba has passed up the kingship of this fair land.

Columba matured into a man of noble bearing, unusual physical strength, handsome face, melodious voice, and sound judgment. It was time to set his own course. He meditated on the possibilities for some time, then decided to establish a monastery. After traveling about he found the perfect setting on the bend of a gently flowing river in the midst of a thick forest of oaks. Once again, the subtle blend of pagan and Christian which was Ireland. Ancient pagan tradition held that oak-groves were holy. Columba made sure that not a single oak tree was cut down to make room for building, for he believed that under every leaf angels came and went. From this site he could see to the north the open sea. He delighted in taking a small craft onto the roaring surf. With sea-gulls circling overhead he would gaze longingly out over the briny deep, in the direction of his own future.

Once his monastery was established Columba traveled about collecting manuscripts. His passion for the written word was a legacy from his years with the bard and the Finnians. What he could not possess he sought to copy. Legend has it that he personally made three hundred copies of the Psalms. Manuscripts were magic talismans of extraordinary value, and highly prized. Those who owned manuscripts guarded them jealously. When Columba journeyed some distance to view the books of a noted recluse the old man refused to let him see them. Columba was so incensed that he put a curse on the books. Ever after no one was able to make sense of their contents. Their carefully formed letters had become unintelligible jottings.

Columba learned that his aged teacher Finnian had just come back from a journey to Rome where the pope had presented him with several manuscripts. With great excitement Columba hastened to his old friend to marvel at his new possessions, especially the latest edition of the Psalms—how he would like to make a copy! But Columba knew the old man was jealous of his books. If he asked, Finnian would refuse and hide the new book of Psalms. Finnian knew his former pupil. He suspected Columba's intentions. Figuring Columba would search for the psalter among the manuscripts of his library, he put the psalter in the nearby church with the books used for services. For some time Columba's desires were frustrated, until one day he discovered the book. Night after night he shut himself up in the church and copied the psalter. On one of those nights a man who happened by the church, was attracted by a strange glow emanating from the windows and the slit under the door. What could it be? Demons? An angel? He approached, and pressed up against the keyhole for a look. There he saw Columba at work. But something strange. There was no candle. Instead, light was radiating from Columba's left hand as he wrote with his right. Suddenly there came a screeching sound from above. The man looked up to see a crane swooping down from its perch high under the eaves. It was the last thing he saw, for the crane tore out the man's eyes.

Finnian eventually learned what Columba had been up to. He was furious. Give me your newly copied manuscript, he demanded, confronting the younger man. Columba refused. Both men complained of injustice. Tribal passions were aroused. In those times families and tribes were quick to go to war over the merest hint of injustice; even the women took up arms.

And so to war. Columba's tribe won a decisive victory which they credited to the magical powers of the psalter he had copied from Finnian's manuscript. Like the magic talisman of former pagan times, it had been paraded around the army three times before the battle, and so it would be before every future battle of the tribe. Today the earliest surviving manuscript of Irish origin is a psalter called the Cathach (from the Irish word for battle, "cath"). Used by the chiefs of the O'Donnell clan as a protective talisman on the field of battle, it is preserved as a relic in a wooden box enclosed in a silver case.

It was not unusual for monks to fight in battle; they fought with their tribe. Columba fought with his. The Irish came from a long line of fighters.

The Romans had called them Scots, based on the Irish verb "to plunder," because they knew the Irish as pirates and plunderers. To die in battle, the Irish believed, was the noblest way to die. Yet in Columba's heart this was no solace for the many that died at his hand in the battle over his beloved psalter. He was tormented with remorse over the men he had killed. Every monk had a soul-friend for confessions. Columba went to his. As penance he decided Columba must be exiled from Ireland and not return until he had saved as many souls as men had died in the battle over the psalter.

So in 563 Columba set out northward with a few kinsmen in a small craft of wicker and hide. They faced the ferocious forces of the Atlantic ocean amidst winds that gathered unbroken momentum over two thousand miles of open water. After several days they came to an island. Columba disembarked and climbed to its highest height. In the distance he could still see Ireland. This, he knew, he would not be able to endure. He could not stay here, for the sight of his beloved homeland would forever haunt him. His body would be here, his soul in the emerald isle. He needed to press on.

More open water. Transoceanic swells tossed the little craft at will. But the sailors persisted and soon spotted a tiny lonely island off the windswept western shores of Scotland. The men carefully maneuvered their craft into a cleft among rocky cliffs rising three hundred feet, timing their entrance between thundering surges of breakers which threatened to dash them to pieces. Columba set out to explore the island. With the exception of the rocky southern and western shores, battered by the heavy seas of the Atlantic, the land was dotted with patches of lush green grass and wild clovers alternating with marshland and lichen-covered rock. To the north the island was covered in dazzling white sand. To the east was a gently sloping hill. Columba climbed this hill and scanned the horizon to the south. He could see nothing but an unbroken expanse of sea. Ireland had disappeared from sight. Here, he realized, he would remain, until his days on this earth ended.

The tiny island, one and a half by three and a half miles, came to be called Iona — Hebrew for "Jonah," which in Latin is "Columba." Here, Columba and his men constructed simple buildings of wickerwork, turf, and straw for their new monastery. Isolated and barren, Iona translated the classic desert motif of asceticism into Celtic idiom. And although he would always yearn for his beloved Ireland, Columba soon came to love the stark beauty of his new home. In June kingcups and iris covered the plain with a carpet of gold. Orchis, tormentillas, primroses, gentian, hyacinths, pinguicula, and St. John's wort combined to form natural rock-gardens. In August the few low bushes and shrubs were surrounded by a palette of color — heather, daisies, buttercups. During long summer evenings Columba drank in the salty tang of the air and savored the gentle fragrance of clover. While above ... the ever-changing chameleon of the sky.

As Columba slowly joyfully copied the story of Jesus's life from manuscript to manuscript, glorifying his Lord with every scratch of the pen, he could hear the gentle lapping of the waves and see through the open door of his cell the beauty of the Father's creation — grassy pastures sloping down to the white sands of the beach.

In such idyllic mode the years passed quickly. Columba relished every moment of his communion with the Holy Word of Scripture, but the time came when he knew his remaining days were numbered. He retreated to his simple hut and requested that no one approach. For three days and nights he neither ate nor drank. The Holy Spirit poured upon this saintly figure, revealing secrets hidden since the beginning of time. Passages of Scripture difficult to understand were suddenly clear. Columba's hut was flooded in a heavenly glow; brilliant light radiating through the crevices was seen even at great distance.

Columba learned that he soon would depart this earthly realm to join his Lord above. The monks sensed this, for Columba was growing frail with age, and often mentioned that his end was near. One evening the old man, as was his custom, had come out part way to welcome his monks as they returned from a hard day of toiling in the fields. As they continued on he tarried with a favorite monk, needing to catch his breath. The younger man expressed his fears: was Columba's time approaching? Yes, my son, the saint replied, the time is tonight at midnight. Tears flowed from the young man's eyes. Then across the meadow came a white horse, an obedient servant who had faithfully carried its burden over the years. It went up to Columba and nuzzled into his chest. Large tears soon wet the saint's tunic, for this dumb animal knew ... he soon would see his master no more.

Columba climbed the gentle rise above the monastery and blessed his home of many years. Then he went on, to the work that was his greatest joy. He took up his pen and copied the last words of Scripture he would ever copy: They that seek the Lord shall not want for anything that is good. It would remain for another monk to continue the text. At midnight, as predicted, Columba's soul departed for its eternal abode.

With Columba began Ireland's Golden Age of learning and art, a few centuries when the emerald isle was the intellectual center of western Europe, a beacon of light in the midst of the Dark Ages. Irish monasteries would hereafter take central place not only in the history of western monasticism but in the history of Christianity in the West. Irish monasteries became noted for their production of biblical manuscripts, and as the tradents of classical culture in Western Europe.

Yet the Irish monks never took themselves too seriously. Always present, a spirit of joyful playfulness. And why not? Had Jesus decreed that Christians go about with long drawn faces? Monks lived as close to their heavenly Savior as possible in this earthly sphere. Should not their spirits be filled with joy in the presence of that greater Spirit? Was it not a fitting balance to the material austerity of Irish monasticism?—Columba himself had slept on a bed of bare rock with a large stone for his pillow.

Irish monks amused and delighted themselves with word-play. Because Ireland had never been part of the Roman empire the Latin of Scripture and other books was a completely foreign language. Strictly a written language, it had never been spoken by the people. Hence, in Ireland Latin retained its classical purity, whereas by the 400s on the continent spoken Latin had considerably changed from its classical form. Irish monks loved this classical Latin, and took great pleasure in its exotic words. They took these and other unusual words and obscure bits of language collected here and there and mixed them in frivolous and frothy play—puns, wit, allegory, cryptograms—an activity known as Hisperica Famina. Columba himself indulged in this pastime. As a member of the order of the bards, he had a love of words and poetry. Among the poems attributed to him is the *Altus Prosator* in which the initial letter of each stanza proceeds through the alphabet. The poem touches on biblical motifs from the creation through the fall of man and the coming of Christ to the end of time at Judgment Day. It abounds in Hisperica Famina, and uses rhyme. It is believed that the Irish were the first to use rhyme both at the end of lines and within lines.

Just as poetry had its bards, music had its own sacred order—the ollamhs. In the monasteries music was studied as one of the liberal arts, intended to move an audience to tears, laughter, and other deep emotion. The Irish monks left such extraordinarily moving hymns as the popular and beloved "Be Thou my Vision."

This playful use of the imagination, this exuberant creativity, found its way into the biblical realm. Irish biblical commentators were responsible for the three—they are not numbered in the Bible—wise men of the Christmas nativity story. Three, for the Irish were passionately fond of triads, representing the three "sacred languages": Greek, Hebrew, and Latin. The wise men were given the names Caspar, Melchior, and Balthasar. This little bit of creativity stuck, and became part of general Christian tradition.

The Irish monk's spirit of play abounded. One calculated that Jonah had spent 2880 minutes in the belly of the whale. Another invented the game of "gospel dice," a sort of medieval Monopoly, which used pieces from a biblical concordance. Virgilius Maro Grammaticus (the Grammarian) is a figure who has long puzzled somber scholars. Was he serious, or simply a clever satirist mocking the pompous and overly-serious, the very scholars who questioned his motives? The famous philosopher John Scotus Erigena ("the Irish-born") demonstrated both sides of the Irish imagination. This magisterial figure produced the first great philosophical system of thought in the West, in a conservative age which preferred simply disseminating tradition. Yet this austere philosopher heartily indulged in Irish playfulness, and saw the lighter side of things. One day he and the emperor Charles the Bald were engaged in a friendly drinking bout. Primed with nature's solace, the emperor saw his friend across the table not as the celebrated man of genius but as the proverbial drunken Irishman. Part jest, part serious, and thinking himself the consummate wit, as do many in their cups, the emperor posed to Scotus a riddle: What is there between a Scot and a sot? His wit the match of the emperor's any day, Scotus did not miss a beat. "The width of the table," he replied.

The Irish monks gathered material from diverse sources: Christian literature forbidden by the Roman church generations before, such as the *Gospel of Nicodemus* and the *Acts of Pilate*; and pagan literature. Because of the earlier pagan traditions of the bards the Irish had an appreciation for pagan literature of any lineage. English scribes at the time were warned, previous to a period of study in Ireland, about the dangers of pagan mythology.

Irish monks colorfully decorated biblical manuscripts in a process known as illumination. Biblical illumination was replete with bird motifs. Ravens and cranes abounded on the emerald isle, a constant reminder of the mystical powers of nature worshiped in paganism and reflected in Celtic bird superstition — Christianity did not erase fear of the Morrigan, the dreaded raven goddess, prophet of doom. The Irish monks did not abandon old beliefs for new. Rather, they used something from here, something from there, skillfully weaving together motifs from Irish paganism, classical Roman paganism, and Christianity. They felt it wise to remain open to all forms of spirituality, to show disrespect to none of the cosmic powers.

The illumination of biblical manuscripts manifests two modes of the Irish spirit: appreciation of the written word, and reverence for the magical — to this day the withered hand of one illuminator remains as a relic.

The Cathach is the earliest surviving illuminated Irish manuscript —

possibly penned by Columba. Each psalm begins with an enlarged initial letter, followed by letters progressively diminishing in size to normal script. Red and yellow are used in some of these initial letters, and they are often surrounded by red dots. Although in the Cathach illumination is restrained in style and imagination and gives little hint of what was to come, these decorated initials are a first in Western scribal work — an innovation of the Irish.

The Book of Durrow — named after a monastery founded by Columba and perhaps copied from a manuscript penned by him — is the first surviving example of full illumination. A palette of color, an arabesque tour de force, an explosion of delicate tracery intersected by nightmarish human and animal figures, crisscrossed with networks of filigreed reticulation, its artwork in places covers whole pages without a word of text.

The technical virtuosity of the artwork displayed in the Book of Durrow marks the culmination of a millennium of pagan Celtic ornamentation. The pagan predecessors of the monks had decorated swords, shields, vessels, and numerous other furnishings with images of fanciful beasts and with intricate geometric patterns. Here is the same fascination with artistic play that led the monks to elaborate biblical narrative through the imaginative use of themes from pagan philosophy and mythology. Classical Latin provided the monks with a treasury of monsters and pagan gods and goddesses.

If the Book of Durrow displays an almost infinite degree of intricacy, the Book of Kells plunges one into the fractal universe of modern chaos theory. Known as the Gospel Book of Columba, although almost certainly not by his hand, it probably originated at Iona, but was discovered at Kells. Kells had become the mother house of the monasteries founded by Columba, after the monks moved from the seclusion of Iona to be safe from Viking raids which began around 800. The most richly decorated Irish manuscript (only two of its 680 surviving pages lack colorful illumination), the Book of Kells in its endless inventiveness best exemplifies the Irish spirit. The detail of the complex intertwining fretwork lavishly spread throughout the Book of Kells can be truly appreciated only with a magnifying glass. (The artists may have used the lenses of eyes taken from freshly slaughtered cattle to magnify their work.) One curious individual counted 158 interlacements within the area of a square inch, and found that every one can be followed, not a single one breaking off or leading into an impossible knot. How much more glorious must have been this artwork before it weathered twelve hundred years of wear and tear.

The Book of Kells is considered by many the finest handwritten book in the world, and by all an art treasure. In rich colors and profusion and complexity of artwork the Book of Kells is unmatched. Its colors came from a vast variety of sources—plant, animal, mineral—from urine and ear wax to the exotic lapis lazuli, a precious stone from Afghanistan. Here is a book intended not for reading, but to occupy a sacred place in the liturgy at the altar.

Some of its letters have been so sculpted that it is difficult to find the words in the maze of design and color. Text has clearly been subordinated to artistic endeavor, yet here again the Irish were innovative: they introduced word separation (previously, texts appeared as one long list of letters), capitalization of initial letters, and punctuation.

We are fortunate that the Book of Kells has come down to us. It was stolen and stripped of the gold in which it was encased, and later found hidden in the turf. What other similar treasures have been lost forever?

The monastery at Iona developed such renown that monks traveled from England, Wales, and the continent to spend time studying with their Irish confreres. The special Irish approach to manuscript design was adopted by many and brought back to their homelands. At the same time missionaries from Irish monasteries were founding new monasteries in Scotland, England, and northern continental Europe. A monk from Iona founded a monastery on the island of Lindisfarne, Holy Island, off the northeast coast of England around the year 635. It was a forbidding place, one of the bleakest stretches of the coast. Flat and almost treeless, it felt the bitter sweep of north winds. But its very exposure to the elements reminded the monks that they were at God's mercy and must wait upon him for all that life could provide. They witnessed the beauty of his creation as the northern lights lighted up the winter sky and reflected on the leaden sea.

The influence of Celtic art was passed from Iona to Lindisfarne and exemplified in the Lindisfarne Gospels, based on the text of Jerome's 384 revision of the Latin gospels, and prefaced by a letter from Jerome to the pope. A tenth-century scribe claims this was the work of Bishop Eadfrith; hence, its date around 700. Eadfrith had studied for six years in Iona. The Irish spirit is somewhat tempered in the Lindisfarne Gospels. The reverse side of pages has prickings and rulings, giving evidence of the use of geometric instruments in the illumination. Such careful planning and design give the Lindisfarne Gospels a mathematical regularity, measured precision, and almost sobriety when contrasted with the lavishly free exhilaration of the native Irish manuscripts. But Eadfrith finely balanced his knowledge of geometry and skillful draughtsmanship with a keen aesthetic sense, knowing when to alter mathematical symmetry in favor of perception. He combined Irish motifs with a rich Anglo-Saxon decorative tradition (intertwining patterns on brooches, buckles, helmets), and these with the classical pictorial style of Rome — for Britain had been Christianized both from Ireland and from Rome. Each gospel of the Lindisfarne Gospels begins with three full pages of illumination. The first of these is a picture of the writer of the Gospel — Luke, for example. Next is a page of pure ornamentation, resembling an oriental carpet. The third page contains the first few words of the text: a sumptuously decorated initial letter, with following letters progressively less decorated.

Once again there is an element of magic. After a Viking raid destroyed the monastery at Lindisfarne the monks fled the island taking with them the Lindisfarne Gospels and the relics of the English Saint Cuthbert. The monks wandered about for some time, finally deciding to take their treasures to Ireland. No sooner had they put to sea when a fierce storm arose and the waves turned to blood. The Lindisfarne Gospels were washed overboard and, despite a lengthy search, could not be found. In a dream it was revealed to one of the monks that the storm resulted from the saint's displeasure: his relics and the beloved gospels were to remain in England. The next morning the sun shone brightly and the monks found the Lindisfarne Gospels washed up undamaged on the nearby shore.

The tradition of richly illuminating manuscripts followed Irish missionaries onto the European continent. Bishops and missionaries requested manuscripts in letters of gold on purple parchment to impress the pagan soul. Such lavishly decorated manuscripts, fashioned for the altar and placed among the relics, were valued for their physical presence. In the pagan world the written word had traditionally been reserved for brief talismanic inscriptions in Germanic runes and Celtic ogham. The marvelously illuminated Bible opened the pagan soul to the possibility of a Christian realm of magic. Richly illuminated manuscripts had a profound effect on those who viewed them — surely such detailed work could not have come from human hands.

A twelfth-century traveler, marveling at the intricate illumination of a biblical manuscript, declared that such artistry must have been the work, not of men, but of angels. Then he learned the story behind the manuscript. The night before he was to begin work the scribe was visited by an angel who showed him the design of the first page. The scribe was awed by its subtle intricacy, and protested that he lacked the requisite skills. The angel insisted. The hand of the scribe would receive supernatural guidance. Each night thereafter the angel appeared with the designs for more pages. The scribe committed their details to memory and executed the designs faithfully. The resulting manuscript was a masterpiece of exquisite beauty and, of course, a miracle.

# 8

# A Light in the Dark

Across the water from Ireland lay Britain. Although at one time part of the Roman empire, Britain was far removed from the center of civilized Europe, Rome. Around the year 600 Pope Gregory the Great described Britain as off in the corner of the world, its people worshipers of sticks and stones. It was a land not found on many maps. The narrow but tempestuous strip of water which separated Britain geographically from the main body of the continent magnified its isolation. It is not surprising that its people developed a culture independent from that of the continental mainland, for the last traces of Roman civilization had disappeared. The land was constantly harassed by new waves of foreigners. Indeed, it was a dark hour for all of Christendom. Muslim fleets had appeared before Constantinople in the East, and Muslim armies in the West had crossed the Pyrenees and entered Aquitaine in the south of France.

Yet in the northeast of Britain, in an area considered by Romans the edge of the world — a few miles away stood Hadrian's Wall, beyond which civilization was thought to cease — dwelt a humble monk whose work would light up the Dark Ages. He never became a bishop, nor an abbot. He worked no miracles, and influenced no kings. He never wandered more than a few miles from home base. He never accomplished any acts of public repute. He led a quiet and uneventful life. Yet, holed up in a monastery, he became the most learned man of his time. Throughout the Dark Ages his widely-read works inspired and influenced others. A century after his death he was revered by the leading scholars of the day as one of the five great doctors of the church along with Augustine, Ambrose, Jerome, and Gregory the Great — the only Englishman to be honored in this way — and a church council declared him authoritative as the ancient Fathers. He is today considered the most important and influential student of the Bible for the half millennium following his death. From a land which had no tradition of learning and which had only recently converted to Christianity, the learning of this quiet figure spread through much of western Europe. Two hundred years after his life had ended he would be recalled in words of tribute by a monk in the land of Charlemagne as a new sun ordained by God to illuminate all humankind. Four hundred years after that the renowned Italian poet Dante would include him among the souls of the wise.

The stonemason carving an inscription on the monk's tombstone paused. What adjective would most appropriately describe this beloved and learned man? He left a spot blank, planning to fill in the word the next day, but when he arose the following morning he found his task had been completed for him. There was the word "venerabilis," presumably written by an angel. For here lay the earthly remains of the man ensuing generations would know as "the Venerable Bede."

Bede entered the monastic school at Wearmouth in 680 at the age of seven. During the two centuries following the departure of the Roman legions from Britain to aid in the defense of Rome, Germanic tribes had invaded the undefended island, leaving the south populated mainly by Saxons and the north and east by Angles. The original people, the Britons, had been mostly forced into the nethermost westerly regions. But those troubled times were now safely in the past. Bede's life would be lived during a relatively peaceful interlude.

Wearmouth was in Northumbria, settled mainly by Angles (hence, "English") from the southern part of what is now Denmark. Northumbria was one of seven kingdoms comprising the land we now call England. Northumbria had been Christianized from two directions. First by the Irish, in their missionary push from Iona to Lindisfarne and the region thereabout, for Lindisfarne was only fifty miles north of Wearmouth. Then from the south by the church of Rome. Missionaries from the south had reached Northumbria only fifty years before Bede entered the monastery. Irish and Roman Christianity clashed in many aspects. Less than a decade before Bede was born the Roman branch of the faith had won out and Northumbria came under Roman domination. Nevertheless, Irish influence remained. Bede was heir to the Irish passion for learning, harnessed to the intellectual discipline of the Roman church. For Bede, Ireland was a land of magical purity. Reptiles and snakes—symbols of evil—could not exist in that fair land. Snakes on board British ships perished on approach to the emerald isle, killed by the scent of its clean wholesome air.

The monastery at Wearmouth was founded shortly after Bede's birth. Soon a sister monastery was under construction at Jarrow, a few miles north. Young Bede watched with great anticipation as the new buildings rose — sturdy buildings of stone, not like the modest wooden structure at Lindisfarne with its thatched roof. His excitement grew as he saw the dedication stone laid, for this would be his new home, his home for the remainder of his life. Today that stone can be seen above the entrance to St. Paul's church in Jarrow.

In the northern latitude of Northumbria summer days are cool. Bede, the man, would later note that it was not unusual for summer to be dominated by violent winds and wintry storms. But the days are long; twilight lingers almost till dawn. In winter things are reversed. Days are short and the dark of night lasts eighteen hours. As a boy Bede rose at two in the morning during the cold winter months, and clothed in a coarse woolen tunic with lantern in hand proceeded to the chapel to begin his long day. Some days he worked in the kitchen preparing vegetables and cleaning pots and pans; some days he tended the animals or churned milk into butter; in summer days he worked under the hot sun hoeing the garden. All this young Bede took in his stride, but he particularly enjoyed learning the psalms. He relished the flow of the Latin, and thrilled to studies other boys found tedious. When Bede was twelve the Yellow Plague hit the monastery. It left only two who could read and chant the psalms for the daily hours — the abbot and Bede. The abbot recited the entire psalter twice every day. Later in life he would increase this to three times a day.

Abbot Ceolfrid took Bede under his wing, for he soon learned that here was a kindred spirit — a lover of learning and books. Ceolfrid's brother had studied in Ireland and the abbot was filled with the intellectual passion of the Irish monks. The founder of the two monasteries, Benedict Biscop, a man of far-reaching literary interests, had set a tone of learning. He was an ardent collector of books, traveling widely, several times to Rome — probably the first person to do so from Britain since the Roman departure. Ceolfrid followed in his footsteps.

In later years Bede would describe the departure of his beloved abbot on a final trip to Rome when Ceolfrid was an old man of seventy-four. He wanted once again to visit in the eternal city the shrines and relics of the blessed apostles. He would take a gift to the pope, a treasured masterpiece, a product of years of dedicated labor — a copy of the whole Bible, a rare thing in those times. Early in the morning Ceolfrid presided over his last mass at the monastery. All the monks were in attendance as their abbot blessed them with holy incense and the kiss of peace. The sound of weeping heard during the mass grew louder as the retinue proceeded to the shore. A man of peace, Ceolfrid commanded the monks always to remember the love and forgiveness of their heavenly Savior and to live their lives in that spirit. A prayer was said and the abbot boarded the boat with his traveling companions. Deacons joined them with lighted candles and a gold cross. The boat moved quietly over the water and all too quickly reached the other side of the river. Horses were mounted, and the monks saw their spiritual father vanish into the distance.

But what of the copy of the whole Bible Ceolfrid intended as a gift for the pope? Was this just a fiction, an interesting feature of a mythical story? Today biblical scholars find evidence of Cassiodorus's emphasis on scribal activity in Codex Amiatinus — the earliest surviving complete Latin Bible — which takes its name from its place of discovery, the abbey of Monte Amiata. Because an inscription states its presenter was Peter of Lombardy, the manuscript was assumed to have originated in northern Italy. It was puzzling, though, that Peter's name did not fit the meter of the dedication verses. This anomaly was resolved when recent ultra-violet photography revealed that Peter's name had been written over an erasure. The original name had been Ceolfrid, the Venerable Bede's beloved abbot. The text of the dedication is remarkably similar to that cited in the anonymous *Life of Ceolfrid*. This, then, was the copy of the complete Bible which Ceolfrid had hoped to present to the pope. But Ceolfrid died en route and the manuscript ended up at Monte Amiata.

Codex Amiatinus was an enormous undertaking. It consists of over 2000 pages of heavy vellum — the hides of 1550 calves — and weighs 75 pounds. The size and expense precluded the production of such a work in most monasteries. Codex Amiatinus was a copy of Cassiodorus's Codex Grandior — the whole Bible collected in one volume — which Benedict Biscop and Ceolfrid had brought back to England from one of their trips to Italy. Bede said that two other similar copies were made, but these have been lost except for a few fragments: one leaf was found in a bookshop serving as a cover for a ledger, and others were used to wrap estate deeds.

At the beginning of Codex Amiatinus is a painting showing nine books arranged on shelves — Cassiodorus's scriptorium produced a nine-volume set of Scripture. The lettering on the nine books in the painting corresponds to the divisions of the Bible mentioned in Cassiodorus's writings. A similar illustration appeared in Codex Grandior, according to Cassiodorus.

Codex Amiatinus shows Cassiodorus's influence on the work of Anglo-Saxon monasteries. Codex Amiatinus uses a form of phrasing advocated by Cassiodorus, in which the length of lines correspond to the phrasing of the words, to aid the inexperienced reader. The same is found in the Lindisfarne Gospels. Here, as well, is a painting depicting St. Matthew, similar to the painting of Ezra the scribe in Codex Amiatinus depicted in front of the nine books of the Bible.

The books Benedict Biscop and Ceolfrid gathered furnished a library unrivalled in all England: two hundred volumes on a wide range of subjects by classical and Christian authors— Pliny, Virgil, Jerome, Augustine, Pope Gregory the Great. In later years Bede would mention Cassiodorus; he knew of his commentary on the Psalms and used Cassiodorus's Latin translation of Josephus. As a youth Bede was in heaven as he hungrily devoured Latin and Greek Bibles, biblical commentaries, the writings of the church Fathers. Meanwhile he was developing skill with the pen. How he yearned to pass on to others the wealth of his reading.

A simple man, Bede lacked the flamboyance of the Irish. He knew Eadfrith the skillful decorator of the Lindisfarne Gospels, but he never indulged himself in the visual arts. He found no temptation to fondle and caress words; his was not the spirit of Hisperic. It was not words as words which attracted him, but what they could communicate. He wrote in clear simple Latin. Bede saw himself primarily as a teacher, relying on the power of narrative and the force of argument to make his point.

As a teacher, Bede pored over the biblical commentaries of the preceding centuries, extracting passages, comparing and evaluating, explaining their meaning. In all he wrote forty-five biblical commentaries. A few years after his death they were being copied throughout France and Germany. Six hundred years later copies were still being made. Bede saw his task not as blazing a new trail, but as gathering the best from the past, preserving it, passing it on. And so he is recognized not so much for his original thought, as for his ability to synthesize and present material in a clear readable manner. The local bishop at the time praised Bede's work: Yes, Saint Ambrose's commentary on Luke's gospel is rightfully renowned as a masterpiece. But it is so subtle and deep that only scholars can understand it. Bede, by contrast, writes his biblical commentaries in a style easily comprehended, allowing for wider readership, and a greater spreading of biblical knowledge.

Today Bede is best known for his *Historia Ecclesiastica Gentis Anglorum*, the first history of the English people. It remains our finest source for early English history. But it doesn't read like a modern history. For Bede, brilliant scholar though he was, was a man of his time. His history and his other works are filled with miracle stories and he makes constant reference to the power of relics. For in those days miracle stories were not the monopoly of the simple-minded; the most sophisticated minds of the time told and believed them. For Bede, miracles were the sign that the Creator was ever watchful of, and working within, his Creation. Bede sees God's watchfulness in the story of Noah's ark. He notes that the eight men aboard could not possibly have fed such a multitude of birds and animals.

Moreover, the mess and stench of their droppings would have made the close quarters of the ark intolerable. Nor could the hull of the vessel have withstood the corrosive force of this waste matter. But, says Bede, the God who preserved the ark, clearly resolved all these problems. And as Lord of Creation his miracles did not end with Noah's ark, nor with all the other miracles mentioned in the Old and New Testaments; his miracles continued undiminished down into Bede's own time in the saints and, after they had passed on, in their relics. Many of the miracle stories Bede relates, like those about Columba, parallel those in the Bible: the blind are healed; water gushes from dry rock; water is turned into wine; storms are calmed.

Bede tells the story of a poetic monk named Caedmon. Caedmon didn't start out as a monk or a poet; for most of his life he was a simple cowherd. It was tradition at local feasts for all the guests to take their turn singing and entertaining. But Caedmon was a shy man. When he saw the harp coming his way he got up from the table and left, for he knew not a single song or poem. He went out to the stable to fulfill his duties and then fell asleep among the cattle. A voice came to him in a dream, requesting a song. Caedmon protested. Had he left the feast only to have to sing among the cattle? But suddenly Caedmon was filled with the spirit of song, and found himself singing — singing praises to God the creator. The next morning he went to see the local abbess to repeat his verses and tell about his dream. She conferred with some learned men. They decided to test Caedmon. They told him a story from the Bible and Caedmon rendered it into verse. It was a miracle. The learned men realized Caedmon had been specially marked out by the grace of God to compose religious songs in English. The abbess was delighted. Would Caedmon consider abandoning secular life and adopting the cowl? Caedmon became a monk and spent the rest of his days rendering into song and verse the stories of the Bible: Noah and the ark, Jesus's incarnation, passion, and resurrection. All in Old English — a language with strange words and different letters from the English of today, a language which would disappear after the Norman invasion of 1066, when it mixed with the Franco-Norman tongue.

Today there survives a collection of manuscripts called the Caedmonian poems. They are like those mentioned in Bede's story and probably date from somewhat later, perhaps the ninth or tenth centuries. Some are close paraphrases of Scripture while others draw upon extraneous material and bits of obscure learning to embellish the core plot. These songs were clearly the playthings of learned men, the diversion of the erudite. Their appreciation would have required a sophistication not shared by the unlettered. Nor would they have made easy or palatable listening for the popular ear.

Other than what he could glean by talking with other monks, all Bede's knowledge came from books. To estimate the length of Britain's coastline, for example, he drew from the ancient texts of classical topographers. Surprisingly, his estimate — 4875 miles — is remarkably accurate. (Today's geographers estimate 4900 miles, allowing for the movement of tides.)

While Bede spent his life happily poring over books in the quiet seclusion of a monastery, he was not unmindful of the plight of those outside its walls. He was well aware that many priests knew virtually no Latin. Indeed, throughout the Middle Ages the church was content if the local clergy merely memorized the Ten Commandments, the Creed, the Seven Sacraments, the Lord's Prayer, and the Seven Deadly Sins, or at least some of these, even if they did not understand what they memorized. The story was told of a priest who listened politely to a sermon in Latin by a traveling scholar. When the scholar had resumed his travels the priest told his servant about this strange madman who was traveling about babbling gibberish.

So Bede decided he would render a great service to the church if he translated the Creed and the Lord's Prayer into Old English. Legend has it that he also translated the first six chapters of the Gospel of John into Old English, continuing his translation with his last breath on this earth. It was, as far as we know, the first attempt to translate any part of the Bible into English. Unfortunately his translation has not survived.

Fifty years after Bede's death the Vikings invaded Britain. Churches and monasteries, with their obvious stores of wealth, were special targets for plunder and destruction. Priests and monks were driven away or simply slaughtered. The monasteries of Northumbria were sacked. Buildings were burned to the ground, taking with them most of the record of Anglo-Saxon culture. As a result precious few manuscripts have survived from this early period.

This was nearly the end of the monasteries in Britain. It is said that eventually there was only one monastery in all the land, one lonely light flickering amid the gloom of surrounding forests and the stench of pervasive marshlands. Anglo-Saxon culture hung by a thread. For the monasteries were not only centers of religious teaching; they preserved all the literature and learning of the past. In a time when Roman civilization was all but forgotten the monastery was an oasis of culture. And Bede was its epitome.

Bede's lifetime had been an island of peace in a sea of war. A half-century earlier the land had been a maelstrom of warring tribes. His own times were bloody enough — the local king, a vicious character renowned for raping nuns, died at nineteen of mysterious and suspicious circumstances. But cloistered within walls of stone, during a brief interlude of relative peace, one of the most learned teachers of the Middle Ages was able to accomplish his work, and keep a light burning in the dark, a light which was passed on to the continental mainland before the shadow of Viking ships darkened Britain's shores.

# 9

# Life in the Big City

Nothing changed quickly in the Middle Ages. As the years and centuries passed, the influence of Irish and British monks was felt more and more on the European mainland, but laypersons had virtually no exposure to the Bible. It remained the tightly held possession of Mother Church.

And then along came a man named Waldo. We don't know his first name. Later legend gives him the name Peter, after the biblical Peter—for like Peter he was the spark of a new Christian spirit which would bring Scripture to the people. The name Waldo, sometimes written as Valdes, probably indicated his place of birth or the region of origin.

The legend starts in the city of Lyons, in what is now southeastern France, in the year 1170. Cities in Waldo's day were rapidly expanding in population and size. Former towns and hamlets had grown into centers of trade and industry, innovation and wealth. So quickly, in fact, that their infrastructures had not kept up. In those days cities were crowded dirty unhealthy places. Streets were narrow, twisting, and dark — each story of the buildings jutted out over the next lower story so that structures on opposite sides of the street almost touched at the top, allowing little light to reach ground level. Pedestrians walked through an unholy stinking mixture of excrement and garbage that often came up to the knees. The contents of chamber pots were thrown from windows above in the general direction of the open sewers which ran down the center of every street. The call of nature was answered in the street, and at every doorstep was a steaming pile of human waste. Even the people stank, bathing being virtually unknown. An anecdote tells of a man who, passing a perfume shop, fainted at the unfamiliar odor and was only brought back to consciousness when a shovel of manure was held under his nostrils.

The marketplace of busy cities like Lyons was frequented by itinerant entertainers who sang and gave poetic recitations. One day Waldo decided to rest from his daily cares and listen for a few moments. He had arrived just in time to hear the end of the ballad of St. Alexis. He was so intrigued he invited the minstrel back to his home so that he might hear the whole tale.

The life of St. Alexis was a favorite among common folk. Originating in Latin literature and extolling monastic virtues, it was translated into the vernacular (the local language of the people) and reworked to give it the charm appealing to popular taste. Waldo listened attentively as the songster began his tale.

Alexis had grown up surrounded by wealth and plenty. His father was a prominent nobleman. The time came for Alexis to be married. In that time and place it was the custom for the rich to purchase a bride for their son, so that he might marry the most perfect specimen of womanhood. Alexis's father loved his son dearly, for he was his only son. Because money was no object, he spent some time making a suitable choice. Then he found her. His son would be thrilled; she was beautiful, and intelligent, and virtuous—a woman who would quicken the pulse of any young man. Alexis's father gladly paid the high asking price.

The wedding was a glorious affair and the marriage appeared to be off to a happy start. Then suddenly something deep in Alexis's heart told him that this was not the life for him. An inner voice said that he who had known so much luxury must now renounce earthly treasures. We are left to imagine the devastating effect on his parents, and especially on his new bride, when he took a vow of poverty and left them for a pilgrimage to Syria in the east.

While on his pilgrimage he gave all he had to the poor and he himself became a beggar. His parents allowed time to pass, thinking their son would soon tire of his youthful idealism. Then they sent servants to search for him. But the servants searched in vain. They were not looking for a beggar, and so searched in all the wrong places.

Eventually Alexis returned home of his own accord. His appearance was vastly changed and no one recognized him. Nor did Alexis wish to be recognized. He asked only to be allowed scraps from the table and a place to curl up under the stairs. This was his life for several years. He endured the insults of those who had once been his servants. Then one day his parents found him still curled up beneath the stairs at a time when he ought to have been up and about. These kind folk wondered if he might be ill and need attention. To their horror they found the sad figure dead.

Suddenly, miraculously, the beggar's true identity was revealed. But of course it was too late. Why, why, why? cried his mother, clinging desperately to her dead son. Why? the minstrel echoed at the conclusion of his tale.... It was because Alexis had received his reward, the reward of all true Christians who have forsaken human ties and worldly privileges. He had been taken up to dwell with his heavenly Father.

Waldo was profoundly disturbed by this tale, for he was a wealthy merchant. A friend of his had recently dropped dead at his side. What would become of his own soul should he himself suddenly die? The more he thought about it the more concerned he became.

The next morning, anxious for his soul, Waldo consulted a local clergyman. The cleric turned to Scripture, to Matthew 19:16, 21. Here Jesus answers the question, What is required to obtain eternal life?: He who sells all his worldly goods and gives to the poor will find his treasure in heaven.

Jesus's words were unambiguous. Waldo knew what he had to do and lost no time doing it. When he got home his wife couldn't believe what she was hearing. They were wealthy people. Most people would do anything to enjoy the life they enjoyed. Had he completely lost his senses? Was he mad? Waldo tried to explain, but his wife demanded to know what was to become of her. She had no intentions of being impoverished. Waldo was disappointed that she would not be joining him in the true Christian life, but to quiet her fears and to be fair he would give her all his vast real estate holdings. She would remain a lady of wealth and privilege. And he would provide for their two daughters. He would pay their dowry for a place in the Abbey of Fontevrault.

Waldo was impressed by the story behind the abbey. Fontevrault had been founded a few generations earlier by a member of the clergy who spent his later years as a wandering preacher. With his long hair and beard, barefoot and dressed in rags, he was the veritable reincarnation of the Old Testament prophets. He attracted a following of men and women who abandoned their families and possessions, and it was for them that he founded Fontevrault.

Having looked after the security of his wife and daughters, Waldo used the remainder of his wealth to feed the poor. When he was down to his last handful of money he threw it onto the street, to show his disdain for material possessions. Waldo had proven to himself that he could put his trust in God, rather than in worldly goods, but he felt that something more was required. He went to the local church hoping to find the answer, for it was a major church in a major city and on rare occasions there was a reading from Scripture along with the readings from the church Fathers.

The church was damp and downright cold on this late autumn day. Some people had handwarmers—metal spheres containing hot coals. Waldo remained standing, while many others sat on the straw-covered floor. He watched in awe as the ceremonial procession moved up the nave of the church. The Bible was held aloft for all to see. Its gold lettering and beautiful artwork inspired reverence. Truly, such a magnificent thing of beauty must be the Holy Word of God. A hush went over the crowd as the procession ended and the Bible was given its prominent place upon the altar. Then in lengthy ritual each member of the clergy kissed this sacred tome, this magic talisman, this holy relic.

Waldo waited patiently and his patience was rewarded. The lector approached the altar to read from the Bible. His back was to the people, which made it difficult to hear the reading. Waldo looked around. He knew most of the people could not understand a single word of the Latin reading. As the lector rambled on people were trading the latest gossip; young men and women exchanged meaningful glances; others fell asleep to the sonorous drone of Latin. Yet many seemed to derive meaning from the service. In a foreign language, the reading clearly was not meant to instruct. It was the ritual that mattered, the solemnity of the occasion, the ambiance, the connection to the holy. The reading was part of the mystery of the liturgy, the magic of the holy eucharist in which bread became the flesh of Christ. Here people were in the presence of the shrines of the saints, the holy relics beneath the altar, and the holy relic upon the altar—the Holy Bible.

On this day Waldo had come for something else; today he listened with renewed eagerness and attentiveness as the lector droned on in stylized recitation, sometimes chanting, sometimes singing. Like many well-to-do merchants of his time Waldo had received a smattering of education in Latin. He caught a word here, a phrase there, but not enough for him to understand the reading. His quest for the words of Holy Writ would have to be satisfied some other way.

What could he do? He had heard about two exceptionally learned priests in the city who were ardent students of Holy Scripture. Perhaps he could get them to translate the gospels and some other books of the Bible into the local dialect for his use.

Waldo hunted up the two priests and made his request. The priests agreed, but for a price. At this point Waldo regretted throwing away his last pennies. Fortunately, he was able to convince his wife to sell some of the property which was now hers—for although she thought his plan foolish and impractical, she still loved Waldo and wanted him to be happy.

Today in the Bibliothèque Nationale in Paris is preserved a manuscript penned by the Dominican friar Stephen of Bourbon several decades after Waldo's death. It tells how he learned from the priest Bernard Ydros, who grew up in Lyons and as a young man worked as a scribe in that city, that Waldo had hired Ydros and another priest to translate the gospels and several other books of the Bible into the local dialect for his use. Stephen's manuscript bears testimony to the earliest certain existence of significantly lengthy passages of the Bible in a French vernacular. We cannot be sure what dialect was used, as the text has been lost. Stephen says it was Romanum — probably Provençal.

Waldo eagerly read the pages of translation as they came from the pens of the two priests. Then one day he found what he was looking for. In the final verses of the Gospel of Mark Jesus commanded his apostles to go into all the world and preach the gospel. Waldo knew what he must do next.

Waldo was excited about the idea of preaching, of sharing the marvelous material he was reading, but also somewhat intimidated. He knew that preaching took place in the monasteries and in the bishops' cathedrals in big cities like Lyons where clergy preached to clergy. He learned that sermons were in Latin — long-winded disquisitions filled with theological subtleties, allegory, and biblical references, meant only for the most learned of clergy. Only on very rare occasions had Waldo heard a sermon read to the laity in the local dialect — read from what, Waldo guessed, was a collection of standard sermons.

Because preaching would be uncontrolled and could be a dangerous thing in the hands of the laity, the church reserved preaching for the clergy. The church interpreted Scripture allegorically. A literal understanding might prove inconvenient, awkward, and embarrassing for the church. It would be difficult, for example, to reconcile the worldly wealth of the church with the Master's wishes that all worldly goods be sold and the money given to the poor. What might a lay preacher make of this?

Nevertheless, Waldo summoned courage and went into the streets and began to preach. It wasn't easy at first. Many thought him mad. Others were shocked. Still others scoffed. His now-former friends were careful not to recognize him. But soon his words began to fall on receptive ears.

The social structure of human life was changing. Lyons, like many towns and cities, was rapidly expanding, thrusting together in close quarters people of diverse backgrounds. The peasant who fled the country for life in the big city found himself adrift in an alien and confusing environment. He had left behind a simple and static existence. The rural parish had furnished the boundaries of his world. There he had been born, baptized, and married. He had confessed his sins to the parish priest and, had he remained, would have received the last rites from him. Once of the parish, always of the parish. What would happen when he died, he didn't know, for it was unlawful to be buried outside the parish of one's birth.

Much more than a place of worship, the parish church was the center of the community. Often the only stone building around, it served as a refuge from bandits, invading armies, and other marauders. It was the locus of dances, fairs, religious drama, banquets, and drunken merry-making. It was not unusual for the local priest to make beer and store grain in the parish church.

Things were different in the city. Its dog-eat-dog ethos fostered little notion of community. Wealthy merchants scorned the poor and destitute. The blatant contrasts and injustices of urban and commercial life cried out for an ethic to meet the harsh environment of this novel social universe.

Just as city life differed from that in the country and the rural village, the city church differed from its rural version. In Waldo's day the physical presence of the big-city church was becoming more visible to laypersons. For this was the age of the giant gothic cathedrals: Notre Dame, Chartres, Rheims, Amiens, Bourges, Cologne, Ulm. City competed with city in a show of religious splendor, as guilds and wealthy citizens happily contributed to the construction of these monuments to civic pride — towering spires, lofty naves, stone tracery, wall paintings, magnificent stained-glass windows, and sculptured figures in stone, bronze, and marble.

In the midst of need and discontent stood this physical representation of the church. Here the illiterate could read "the people's Bible"—sculptures depicting episodes and characters from the biblical story: the creation, the Old Testament prophets and patriarchs, the life and crucifixion of Jesus, the evangelists. In resplendent glass religious lore mixed with temporal imagery to invite the gaze of the unlettered: the signs of the zodiac, the labors of the months, the cult of the Virgin, the lives of the saints, the seven wise and seven foolish virgins. Should the layperson fail to grasp the significance of the imagery and symbolism of these architectural marvels, the sheer magnitude and magnificence of these towering structures inspired awe. Christianity was thrust forth with an insistence difficult to ignore.

In the marketplace touring drama groups depicted scenes of Calvary and the empty tomb. Images of a bleeding Jesus struck a sympathetic chord with those suffering in the streets. The reality of Jesus's humanity took on new meaning within city walls. But where was this Jesus who breathed love, who healed the broken-hearted, who set at liberty the bruised, who preached deliverance to the captives, who promised that those who mourn shall be comforted and that the meek shall inherit the earth, and who finally died an agonizing death that all that he preached and promised might be fulfilled?

As the physical presence of the church was becoming more visible there was a growing disconnect between image and symbol and human life. A gulf was opening and widening between clergy and laity. The layperson experienced the mysteries of the liturgy as a foreigner in an exotic realm — at a distance, excluded. There was magic, but no flesh-and-blood human connection. The boundary differentiating church and clergy from the laity was hardening. The body politic and theological soul of the church was closing in upon itself, forming a closed system.

Latin was part of the problem. Latin was the language of the church and its clergy. The church's liturgy was in Latin. Its thought and beliefs were expressed in Latin. Its Bible was in Latin. Laypersons in Lyons were completely cut off from Latin Scripture. A Latin wall separated laypersons from the Bible. Even when Latin had been the spoken language of the populace — well into the eleventh century in some areas — it was a vulgar form of Latin, more and more adulterated with the local patois. The Latin of the church was classical Latin, virtually another language. As Latin was no longer the language of the people, Latin itself was a force for division between clergy and laity. Latin incapacitated and disempowered the laity. Only the clergy and those whose business was international in scale used Latin.

By Waldo's time national vernacular languages had begun to develop. Secular schools were founded to educate the rising commercial class in the vernacular. Some clergy realized that the flame of a new religious spirit kindled in urban centers, that change was in the air. The church would have to get into step with the times, or there would be trouble. Reformist popes encouraged higher standards.

Laypersons began to want more than the rare and poorly read sermon. In some places pastors were rejected by their flock. The time was ripe for a layperson like Waldo to take to the streets and preach in the local dialect. People were eager to hear the message of the gospels in their own language. Others joined Waldo in his work.

The local archbishop was not amused. He epitomized all that the church's reform movement castigated, all that the people criticized in the clergy. He was devoted to political and economic matters, to the virtual disregard of pastoral duties. He had recently put an end to a long and grueling dispute with the local secular authority, a count. In exchange for a sum of money and a few of his many castles the archbishop got the count to surrender all his local privileges and rights. The archbishop was now both ecclesiastical and secular authority, archbishop and count.

The archbishop took umbrage with Waldo for two reasons. First, despite all the money Waldo was throwing around the streets, he had given none to the church. Second, he was jealous of the popularity of Waldo's preaching. The archbishop summoned Waldo before him. Waldo insisted he had no argument with his lordship the archbishop, nor with the church or the clergy. He was merely following in the footsteps of the apostles. Not knowing how to reply, sensing that his authority was being undermined, the archbishop prohibited Waldo from preaching.

So Waldo went to the pope. It took courage, for this was a pope who had humbled the celebrated Emperor Frederick Barbarossa. To this day guides point to a red flagstone which marks the exact spot of imperial humiliation — the spot where the emperor kissed the pope's foot.

The pope found no problem with Waldo's preaching: his message was orthodox, and there was no evidence that he was out to make trouble, that he was a revolutionary. Following the expected bureaucratic ministrations Waldo got his answer. While canon law stipulated that only ordained clergy could preach, the pope made an exception. Waldo would be allowed to preach, but only at the express desire of, and at the authority of, the local clergy. Back in Lyons the archbishop smiled when he read the verdict.

But Waldo was not about to stop preaching. Stories should end happily. This one does. The archbishop ended his days in a monastery doing penance for his sins. It is said that he read Scripture devotedly. Those who followed in Waldo's footsteps— the Waldensians—flourished: there were eight thousand of them during his lifetime alone. They translated the gospels, the epistles of St. Paul, the psalter, and the book of Job into French. Eventually Waldo and the Waldensians were declared heretics, not because of their vernacular translations of Scripture, but because they criticized the wealth of the church in contrast with the gospel message. As for Waldo, we don't know what became of him, except that he died after a full lifetime, presumably preaching his belovèd gospel until the end.

# 10

# Birds of the Air, Lilies of the Field

The little town lay on a gentle rise surrounded by rolling hills and fertile valleys. Here and there tiny chapels indicated the presence of man amidst vibrant nature. The soft Umbrian sunlight warmed ripening wheat, groves of olives, and pastures of wildflowers. Languid breezes wafted heavy with the fresh fragrance of pine, cedar, cypress, tamarisk. The air resonated with the hum of bees, the twitter of larks, the burbling of tiny streams.

Assisi. Birthplace of Saint Francis of Assisi, who, we are told, preached to the birds, tamed a wolf, and spent a storybook life in one of the most picturesque areas of Italy. Eight centuries later this simple humble man is admired and respected by people of diverse faiths as the saint of saints, the model of Christian living. He is the subject of countless books, movies, paintings. Hundreds of thousands have embraced his way of life and sought to attain his spirituality. Here was the man who brought the Bible's message compellingly to the people, who exemplified the living gospel.

Francis's life was the reverse of the Horatio Alger story of rags to riches. Francis's father Pietro Bernardone was the most prosperous cloth merchant in all Umbria. He frequently traveled to Provence in southern France to purchase his wares, for here he found the finest of fabrics: woolens from the Low Countries, linen from Egypt, cotton from Syria, luxurious velvets from Lyons, dazzling brocades from Byzantium and Persia. From one of his trips he returned with a bride—the daughter of a knight from Provence.

A few years later, in 1182, Pietro returned from a business trip to a welcome surprise. His wife presented him with a new-born son, named Giovanni after John the Baptist. Pietro insisted the name be changed; he didn't want a son of his named after a hermit who dressed in sackcloth and ate wild honey and locusts. No, the infant's name would be Francesco—

the little Frenchman—a tribute to the land which had been so good to Pietro, providing him with business and a wife. And so it was.

Gifted with unusual grace and charm, Francis became the apple of his parents' eye, and was quickly forgiven for his many boyish pranks. His mother taught him to sing in Provençal, for her native Provence was the home of the troubadours—poets of knightly romance, who sang of Charlemagne, the knights of the Round Table, fair ladies, heroic knights, purest love, and celebrated the virtues of sacrifice, bravery, loyalty. His father regaled him with tales of faraway places with faraway names, which Francis's fertile imagination embellished with adventure and romance. His mind filled with images of exotic lands, the boy ran his hands over the bolts of cloth in his father's shop, luxuriating in the various textures— smooth silks, sturdy woolens, soft velvets. His eyes feasted on the rich colors—rose, saffron, burgundy, the whitest white. Pietro watched with pride, dreaming of the day his son would join him in business.

Perched on a hilltop above the city was the castle of the German duke who ruled Assisi. Although he was a demanding sovereign, what he took in taxes he gave back in entertainment: tournaments with charging horses and flashing lances, fountains flowing with ruby wine, musical festivals with troubadours. The songs of the troubadours filled young Francis with notions of knighthood. A dreamer, an idealist, a romantic, he imagined himself a knight capturing the hearts of ladies. As a youngster he had pretended to be a crusader. In those years the streets of Assisi had pulsated with the excitement of the Crusades. He had seen the glorious Count of Brienne passing through with his entourage on the way to Rome, beside him the fair lady he had rescued and for whose rescue he had won the land of Apulia. Ever since that time Francis had dreamed of being such a knight, a conquering hero cheered by crowds in the plaza, a beautiful noble lady at his side. Now, as a youth, it seemed his dreams were about to be fulfilled.

Pietro the hard-nosed businessman also had dreams. He hoped that some day his son would marry one of the duke's daughters and join the nobility. Hence, when Francis entertained his aristocratic friends his father happily indulged the young man. Francis lived the life of a rich man's son to the hilt. He wore fine silks and sumptuous velvets. His sense of style won the admiration of his fellows. Dapper youths sought his opinion on the latest fashions. He took pride in outdoing his wealthy friends at playing host, for he was a sophisticated connoisseur of fine wines, savory foods, sensual perfumes, delicate china, elaborate decoration, rich tapestries, seductive music. Young Francis surpassed all others in vanities and merrymaking, parties and song. Yes, he was a spendthrift—but generous, open-handed, magnanimous, liberal with his riches. Definitely a fop and a peacock, but affable, kindly, courteous, and charming. Everyone loved Francis. He never stooped to vulgarity. He never spoke an indecent or unkind word. He was the quintessence of the virtuous gentleman.

Italy in Francis's time was not the unified nation it is today, but a patchwork of kingdoms, duchies, and independent cities. The people of Umbria in central Italy had difficulty understanding the language spoken in the north, in Milan, Genoa, and Venice. The cities were enjoying new energy, pride, expansive commercial wealth. Scruples did not thwart ambition as the cities engaged in intense rivalry. Traditional loyalties yielded to new alliances. Old grievances were stoked; the flames of old hatreds, fanned. Italian city warred viciously against Italian city. Acts of cruelty and inhumanity and barbarity gave full meaning to the term "medieval." For those were violent times. The game kill-the-cat was a popular pastime. A cat was nailed to a post and each competitor tried to batter it to death with his head while the shrieking cat clawed viciously at his face and neck. Enemies captured during inter-city vendettas wished they had died on the field of battle. Paraded in the public square to the cruel amusement of the captor city, they were shoed like mules, their noses were cut off, their teeth wrenched out, their mouths stuffed with toads, their women violated before their eyes. Citizens of Italian cities bragged about such cruel inventiveness.

Between the cities of Assisi and Perugia waxed a bloodthirsty hatred. The two cities faced each other from opposite hillsides across the Tiber. In the struggle for power between pope and emperor one city took the imperial side, the other the papal. Because it possessed the relics of a bishop martyred for refusing to submit to pagan practices, Assisi had become the cathedral city. Proud of this heritage, her citizens saw themselves as defenders of the church of San Rufino.

Then war broke out with Perugia. Assisi's knights and leading merchants mustered before the cathedral church of San Rufino to receive the power of the relics of its patron saint, before parading to the city gate for battle. Swords, shields, lances, banners were everywhere. The plaza rang with shouts of men and neighing of horses. Among the military force was Francis. Glory and more glory would be his. His dreams of knights and ladies were surely about to come true.

But such was not to be. The reality of battle was everywhere in stark display. Fields were not filled with wildflowers and ripening wheat in those November days, but tainted with blood. The soft Umbrian sunlight looked down upon broken bodies: here a hand, there a foot, over there entrails and a battered head. The bees were not humming, nor the larks twittering. Assisi had been defeated. Francis was a prisoner.

Among the prisoners was a knight from Apulia. From him Francis once again heard glowing accounts of the Count of Brienne — how with a force of only two hundred he had routed more than five thousand imperial troops. Once more Francis's thoughts soared, his passions took new life.

Francis spent a year in the Perugian prison. When he got home he came down with a fever. His body, never robust, but delicate, small and thin, had succumbed to months of iron chains, filthy straw bedding, tepid water, mildewed bread, stale fish, and the blows of the guards. It was spring in Assisi. The hills were carpeted with the white, yellow, and red of wild flowers. Gentle rivulets gurgled their way into the valley below, where trees were aglow with pink almond blossoms; birds chirped from every branch. But Francis didn't notice. He stared blankly, with glazed empty eyes. It might as well have been winter, for such it seemed in his soul.

Then Francis met a young nobleman who told him more about the Count of Brienne. Everyone, it seemed, was telling him about this famous figure — surely a sign that his destiny would be found with the celebrated knight. Francis's spirit once more came alive. The two young men fired each other's imagination. They would join the count in his adventures. They would go to the fabled land of Apulia and by virtue of heroic deeds earn knighthood from the Count of Brienne himself. Vestments of unequaled splendor and armor of the finest craftsmanship were ordered. Only the best would do for the young knights-to-be. Finally all was ready and the two set out.

But soon after their departure Francis fell ill; the fever had returned. While confined to his bed he had a vision in which he heard a voice: Why serve the servant and not the Master? Why join a knight who served Jesus, when Francis could directly serve Jesus? The voice in the vision commanded him to return to Assisi where he would learn what he was to do.

Riding his horse one day Francis saw a leper on the road ahead. These wretches had always filled him with horror and disgust: oozing sores, putrefying flesh, and that stench! Francis held his nose. Why didn't they stay in their colonies? On other occasions he spotted them from afar and reversed his path. He was about to do so this time, had actually turned his horse about, when something stopped him. He dismounted and folded some coins into the leper's disfigured hand. Then impulsively he kissed the hand and embraced the astonished leper. What had always repelled him, now suffused him with joy. He asked the leper to lead him to his colony, where he gave each leper money and kissed each on the mouth.

Astonished by his own actions, Francis wandered about the countryside, unsure what direction his life should take. He came upon a little chapel, almost in ruins. The roof was rent with holes; the open door had let in rain, debris, and mud; giant weeds and bushes were growing in the wreckage; bats hung from the ceiling and every nook and corner. Francis found himself drawn compellingly to a lone crucifix. How gentle and serene was the painted face of Christ. Francis went to his knees, bowed down, and prayed for guidance. What was he to do with his life? Suddenly he was overwhelmed with contentment, peace, and certainty. He looked up at the crucifix. Had he seen its lips speak? The words— were they in his head, or had he actually heard them spoken?: "Restore my church, which is in ruins."

Francis stayed near the chapel for days, weeks, before returning to town. Word spread that he had gone mad. His beard scraggly and unkempt, his hair long and greasy, he was barely recognizable. He had lost weight and his clothes were filthy. Children threw clumps of dried mud at him. Adults laughed: here was wealthy Bernardone's son, looking every bit the beggar. How pleasurable to see the proud debased! Adults joined children in pelting stones at the sorry figure. Even beggars joined in. Hearing such commotion, Pietro looked out, stunned to see his son the focus of attention.

Pietro had had enough. Instead of making him proud, Francis was a disgrace, an embarrassment. He dragged his son before the local bishop. The bishop could decide what to do; Pietro was tired of his son throwing his hard-earned money to the lepers. The bishop ruled in Pietro's favor, whereupon Francis stripped off his clothes and threw them at his father's feet. "You are right. Your money is yours, and so are these clothes. But henceforth you are no longer my father. Instead, my father is He who was crucified for me, before whom I stand naked, putting in Him all my trust."

The bishop made haste to cover Francis with his robes. He led Francis inside, gave him an old tunic to wear, and sent him on his way. Francis returned to the leper colony, where he bathed the lepers' supurating sores and ate from their bowls. In addition, obedient to the mission he had received from the crucifix, he busied himself with restoring the little chapel. He begged for his food, and for materials for the chapel. People were surprisingly generous, for Francis had lost his fine raiments but none of his grace and charm.

On St. Matthew's Day Francis went to hear mass at another local chapel, which he also helped restore. The celebrant read from the Bible, from the book of Matthew. As the son of a wealthy merchant, Francis had been privileged to learn to read and write Latin, so he understood what was read. The Bible told how Jesus instructed his disciples as they were about to set out preaching: they were to announce Christ's coming, cleanse the lepers, and cast out demons; they were to take no money or provisions, but beg for their daily food.

Francis knew these words were meant for him. Here was the answer he had long awaited. The path before him was clear. He was to go into the streets, barefoot and without money, and preach. He would be the glorious knight he had always dreamed of being. He would do battle, but not with the sword. The virtues of knighthood—courage, faith, kindness, gentleness, generosity—he would practice in his life's mission. Like the knights he would take a lady, but his lady would be Lady Poverty, for Jesus had been born poor and had lived in poverty. Poverty for Francis would be more than just deprivation of material goods. It would be a radical act of faith—faith in the providence of the Father. For had not Jesus said in the Bible—in that beautiful passage about the birds of the air and the lilies of the field—that we ought not be concerned about our food and clothing, that the Father will provide?

Francis was twenty-six. His real life was beginning. He would live the words of the Bible. He would be a living gospel. He now knew that the church he was to restore was not simply the tiny chapels outside Assisi, but the church universal, Christ's kingdom in this world.

Francis went into the streets, the public square, to rural hamlets, fields, river banks. His preaching was simple, straightforward, and from the heart. There was no formal sermon, no judgment, just a simple message: Christ came to free us from our fears and our cares and our labors. God loves the world and every person. Trust in him to provide. Look around: God's gift to humanity—this world in all its beauty and wonder—is here to enjoy ... free. Instead of worrying about the morrow, savor the fresh breezes, the azure sky, the colors of field and forest.

Here was a joyful man, a man who wished to share his joy in God and God's creation. His joy was contagious; while a few persons scoffed, most listened and many followed, wishing to live as Francis lived.

Francis had no desire to overturn the church in any way, nor was he critical of the church in his preaching. Indeed, he had great respect for the clergy, for the power of the priest at the mass. Yet as time passed he came to realize that there were clergymen who mistook him for a rebel, and might some day brand him a heretic. It was time to receive official church approval for his preaching. He would go to the pope.

At that time the papacy was at the zenith of its power, and the pope was one of the most powerful of all popes. The pope knew that the church desperately needed reform. Heresy was breaking out everywhere—the Cathars, the Waldensians. Just last night he had dreamt that the church was leaning dangerously to one side, about to topple over, when a little man in simple garb pushed his shoulder against it and set it upright again. Could this simple fellow before him, who asked only to be allowed to live the gospel, be that man?

The pope was both wise and practical. The little man before him seemed sincere, and was certainly no rebel. Perhaps here was a solution to the problem of the Waldensians. Excommunication, inquisitions, and crusades against the Waldensians had failed to stop their criticism of the church in their preaching, and did nothing to win the hearts of the people to the church. This Francis seemed a Waldo-like figure. Perhaps he could be the church's authorized version of the wandering preacher. He could compete with the Waldensians for the loyalty of the people. Here was a man who might captivate the heart and engage the passions of the common man and woman, for clearly he was gifted with grace and charm.

So the pope granted Francis's wish. He and his followers would be permitted to preach, provided they limited their sermons to moral and practical exhortation and stayed away from theology and criticism of the church.

And so in Francis the church found its Waldo. The Waldensians had felt the pulse of the times: where was Christian passion, Christian love? The human spirit was crying out for real religious contact. Because people wanted contact with the human Jesus, the mother of the human Jesus, the Virgin Mary, gained new significance. She was fast becoming the saint of saints. Mary didn't avenge one's enemies, she brought salvation of the soul — the soul of the individual had taken on new meaning.

In Francis for the first time in the long history of the church the gospel message of love, humanity, and toleration was coming to the people. Instead of a godhead to be feared, there was the man Jesus, who had suffered as all human beings suffer. Men and women could, for the first time, truly relate to God, not in the abstract but in the concrete. Easter had always been the central Christian celebration because of the resurrection, and so it remained. But Francis emphasized the naked *human* Jesus on the cross, abandoned and in human agony.

Christmas took on new importance. In the little town of Greccio, fifteen days before Christmas, Francis asked a local man of good reputation and even better life to make haste to follow his instructions. The man did so and on the eve of that holy day celebrating Jesus's birth people from the local community along with Francis and his followers approached a designated place with the light of torches and candles. There, before their eyes, was duplicated the scene of the savior's birth — the manger, the animals, the holy mother, and the child represented by a doll (a living baby would be blasphemous). But as Francis approached the doll a miracle occurred. The doll came to life as a human child. Or such was the vision of those in attendance that night.

A miracle had taken place. People made haste the next day to gather the hay from the manger. They fed it to sick animals and the animals quickly recovered. The hay cured people of disease, and helped women through difficult childbirth. So that future generations might never forget the magic of that moment, a church was erected on the spot of Francis's manger scene.

The child Jesus, forgotten for centuries, had been brought back to life in all the humility and poverty of the manger. The humble scene of the baby Jesus in the manger underlined his humanity. Francis emphasized those passages in the Bible which recognized the worth of each and every human being — something extraordinary in the feudal culture of medieval times: that human beings are created in the image of God (Genesis 1:26), that whatever is done to the least of persons is done to Christ (Matthew 25:40, 45). Jesus's life would be a model for every man and woman. No longer would it be necessary to enter the cloister. Travelers began to journey to the Holy Land to see the places where Jesus was born, lived, preached, and died.

The years went by. Francis continued to preach, to live the gospel, to bring the human Jesus to the people. But long years out in the cold and heat, the rain and snow, with little to eat, had taken their toll. Francis was becoming an old man before his time. His body was wracked with pain; he could scarcely see or get around. Before his life ended he wanted to retreat to the peace of the countryside and be alone with his Lord in prayer, to meditate on the word of God in Scripture. So he took a copy of the gospels and three of his closest companions and journeyed to Mount La Verna, a majestic peak from which could be seen on one side the Mediterranean and on the other the Adriatic.

Once there, Francis asked to be left alone. He read over and over and meditated upon those passages in the gospels concerning Jesus's last days and his death on the cross— the Passion. In prayer he asked to experience and share Jesus's agony in those moments of supreme sacrifice, to feel the love embodied therein. A month passed. Francis lost all concept of time, all consciousness of his physical being. Then one morning just before the sun rose it happened. A cruciform figure with wings of fire. Blinding light. Excruciating pain and ecstatic joy. Then all was back to normal, except... Francis looked down and saw piercing his hands and feet what looked to be the nails of Calvary, in his side a deep bleeding wound.

Although it was only late September, snow was beginning to fall on the heights. The little group must depart for home, for soon the way would be impossible. When they got back to the chapel outside Assisi, the people were in an uproar. It was apparent that their saint would soon die; he must be brought within the town walls to avoid kidnapping — how the citizens of Perugia would like to possess his body, an invaluable source of holy relics! And so he was brought to the bishop's palace. His frail body clung to life for two more years, and then Francis passed on to his heavenly reward.

So great a hold did Francis gain on the emotions and imaginations of future generations that he became the most popular saint outside of St. Peter and the Virgin Mother herself. He captured the hearts and imagination of the people, for he was of the people — a layman. Unlike the institutional church, he was there, he was visible, he was active. He spoke to the people in their own language.

This intriguing and inspiring figure had taken the gospel message to the people. He taught by word and example — that Christians should follow Jesus's teachings and lead the life he exemplified: in the humility of his incarnation, and in the charity of his forgiveness and gift of life everlasting.

In a symbolic painting Rembrandt depicts Francis on his knees before an open Bible. From the beginning Francis based his life, his mission, and his message on the words of Scripture. Seeking guidance for the direction of their mission, Francis and his first associate asked a priest to consult the gospels. The priest made the sign of the cross over the gospels and opened them at random to three places. Here he read what the two men were to do. When Francis sought from the pope to form a religious order its rule was biblical in form and phrase, full of quotations from the Bible and allusions to it. Always respectful of the learned theologians who spent their lives studying Holy Writ, Francis nevertheless knew that this was not his path. He was content to leave to the theologians of the church the interpretation of Scripture's more difficult and esoteric passages. It was the wonderful yet simple message of the gospels he wanted to share, and the joy it provided.

The church did not allow laypersons to possess Scripture except for the Latin psalter. But Francis had put a taste in the mouths of the common man and woman. In Francis they were closer to Holy Writ than they had ever been. He had conveyed the essence of the gospels to the people. In Francis they beheld the living gospel. He had whetted their appetite; in the future they would want more.

# 11

# Clandestine Operation

Life in the fourteenth century was brief. It was a world of children; half the population was under age 21. Six-year-olds were betrothed and received ecclesiastical benefices. A man or woman of thirty years was considered a senior. Childbirth killed many women, and only one child in three survived to adulthood. The gift of fine cloth a young woman wore on her wedding day, a few years later became her shroud. With such dreary prospects it is no surprise people drank heavily. The English — including children and nuns — drank an average of a gallon of beer a day. Since grown men seldom exceeded five feet and 135 pounds that much alcohol meant rampant drunkenness.

Between 1315 and 1322 Europe was scourged with the Great Famine, the longest and most severe of a series of famines. People traded their possessions, even the clothes off their back, for food. They ate clay, grass, roots, and bark. Gallows were ransacked for human flesh. Travelers were attacked, killed, and eaten. People ate their own children. Crops failed for three years in a row, 1315–1317. Climatologists now know that this was the peak of a minor ice age — longer winters, more rain, shorter growing seasons.

Over the years an expanding population had outgrown the land's capacity to produce food. Land which once supported one, now had to support twenty. The frontier of workable land could be pushed back no further. There was little distribution of food from areas of surplus, except to regions near major waterways. There was no connected system of roads and bridges. The mule train was the major method of transport. So inland areas had to rely strictly on local resources. There the underpaid hired mercenaries of local lords plundered the countryside. Moreover, this was a time of rampant war, and warfare had adopted a new tactic — burning the enemy's granaries, barns, and fields. As a result rural byways were crowded with vagabonds. People fled to the cities, only to starve in the streets. Cartloads of the dead were thrown into open pits.

Then things got worse. In October 1347 a Genoese fleet returning from a trading post on the Black Sea docked at Messina harbor in Sicily. All the crewman were either dead or dying. Some had black swellings the size of an apple at the armpits and groin, oozing blood and pus. Others had boils and black blotches on their skin from internal bleeding. They would die, like their fellows, within a days.

Rumors of a lethal plague had reached Europe a year earlier. It was believed to have started in China and spread through most of Asia. The old maxim never to believe rumors unfortunately did not hold. An extremely deadly plague had, in fact, broken out in the Chinese province of Hupei in 1320, then moved slowly westward along commercial routes, carried by fleas on infected rats. What caused the bacillus *Pasturella Pestis* to change into a virulent form is unknown. In those times the plague was considered God's punishment for human waywardness. By early 1348 it had spread into Italy. In two months it was in England. It would come to be known as the bubonic plague or the Black Death.

The Black Death came in two forms. The one infecting the Genovese crews infected the bloodstream and was spread by contact. Their trading post had been under siege. Dead bodies infected with the plague had been catapulted over the walls by the besieging Tartars. A second type attacked the lungs and was spread in the air as the victims coughed. Death from this type came in less than 24 hours. A person went to bed healthy and was found dead at dawn. Doctors caught the disease from their patients and died before their eyes. Or so said the spreading horror stories.

Dead bodies rotted everywhere. Whole populations were wiped out. Using some form of abstruse arithmetic the pope had calculated 23,840,000 dead — six times the population of England. By any count the death toll was enormous. Paris lost 800 a day, for a total of 50,000 — one half of its population. Venice lost two out of three; Florence four out of five. The plague could be fickle — here and there populations were relatively spared. But within the closed walls of monasteries and prisons the death toll was often complete. Small villages became deserted; nature grew back over the streets. The English village of Noseley was burned to the ground to prevent the plague spreading to the local manor house. One out of three Europeans were lost to this plague — 20 million dead. To this day the truncated transept of Siena's cathedral bears silent witness to the plague — with the loss of one half of the skilled workers work was abandoned and never resumed on an edifice that was to have been the largest in existence.

Everywhere death and the fear of death. Notaries refused to come and make wills for the dying. Priests refused to hear last confessions and administer last rites. Was the soul of the dying man or woman doomed?—a terrifying thought moments from that last crossing. For this reason an English bishop gave permission for lay persons to hear last confessions. Eventually the pope granted remission of sins to everyone who died of the plague.

In the university town of Oxford, up the river Thames from London, a sickening stench hung in the air—the bloody urine and black feces of the dying, human excrement mounting as street-cleaning became infrequent, rotting corpses in the streets. Every morning doorways were filled with the newly dead. Where families buried their own in graves too shallow the cadavers were dragged out and devoured by starving dogs. The creaking wheels of carts carrying the dead to mass burial pits gave ceaseless din. A young student named John Wyclif watched as bodies were dumped unceremoniously into a long trench, heaped on top of one another as from some human avalanche.

John Wyclif had come to Oxford University only a few years earlier at age fifteen. He soon learned that university life was anything but the mythical ivory tower. The townspeople were openly hostile toward the students—in one riot they burned five buildings and killed sixty-three students. Yet neither riot nor famine nor plague was going to drive young Wyclif away. Although he was a quiet man who kept his emotions to himself, his love for Oxford University knew no bounds. For this young man the university was a dwelling place for gods, the gateway to heaven. This was to be his world, his life.

Oxford University had recently become one of the leading universities of western Europe, supplying leaders of church and state for all England. Yet Oxford University and universities in general were relatively new. Universities had developed from cathedral schools as the age of the specialist dawned.

It started in the monasteries. As services became ever more elaborate, poets and writers were needed. Without clocks detailed astronomical observation was needed to assure that the crowded schedule of services began on time—on January 1, when the bright star in the knee of Arcturus in the constellation of Boötes falls between the first and second windows of the dormitory, it is time for the lighting of the lamps. The business of the monastery meant the keeping of accounts—arithmetic. Monks intrigued by this study of arithmetic and astronomy left the monastery to seek knowledge wherever it might be found.

Teachers who taught for a fee had at first wandered in search of students, but soon came to rest in the collegiate schools, attached to the cathedrals. Here modest libraries and schools of a sort were already in place. The curriculum of cathedral schools was less restricted than in monasteries, and more reflected secular interests.

At the same time the management and operation of the complex organizational bureaucracy which the church had become by the high Middle Ages demanded large numbers of educated personnel — lawyers, theologians, administrators. New requirements meant new skills and new disciplines. With heresies on the rise the church needed scholars to butress the church's position.

Some cathedral schools, especially those in major cities with better teachers and books, acquired an international reputation for particular subjects. The cathedral school at Bologna was known for law, that at Paris for theology. Students came to these centers, confident that their studies would result in eminent administrative positions, serving secular and ecclesiastical lords. By 1200 these cathedral schools had become the University of Bologna and the University of Paris. Soon other universities, such as that at Oxford, came into existence.

The university scholar built his reputation on his ability to split hairs and make fine distinctions. The academy was a place of disputation and debate — one scholar versus another in a battle of words. Debate in the fourteenth century was what the laboratory is today — a place to test, to challenge, and to develop new ideas. John Wyclif thrived on debate. He possessed all the traits of the skilled debater. He was stubbornly opinionated to the point of assumed infallibility, confident to the point of being headstrong, yet subtle and ingenious. His pleasure in controversy and opposition — he preferred the contrarian position, the underdog against huge odds, David opposing Goliath — made him a bitter fighter and uncompromising opponent.

The years passed. By age forty-three Wyclif had become a doctor of theology, a program requiring eighteen years of study. His reputation in the academy grew; he was fast becoming the most eminent theologian and philosopher in the West, without rival in learning. When he mounted his box (he was short) to lecture, people listened to this slight, some said ugly, little man with the large hooked nose.

Wyclif's particular hobbyhorse was the church. He never tired of inveighing against the sins of the church and its clergy. His complaints were not new. More than six hundred years earlier the Venerable Bede had noted abuses of clerical privilege. The bogus monasteries, for example. Laymen secured documents from bishops and abbots to found monasteries and then entered these monasteries with their families so that they would be exempt from military duty and their land from secular taxation. Bede reviled bishops who spent their time drinking, feasting, jesting, and telling stories. Villagers who never saw their bishop from the beginning of the year to the end, still had to pay taxes to that bishop.

By Wyclif's time things had gotten considerably worse. The church had become an organized state. It had a developed body of laws, and ecclesiastical courts in which to exercise these. It levied taxes and had its own tax-collectors. It owned a large percentage of the land of Europe. It was ruled by an increasingly powerful pope who had at his disposal a mammoth administrative machine and a small but effective army.

Wyclif found the evidence against the church particularly incriminating. Bishops lived in magnificent palaces on large estates, surrounded by luxury. There was little to distinguish them, or the abbots of monasteries, from the secular nobility. They were often appointed by secular lords, they raised taxes, they maintained military forces. In military combat the preferred weapon of bishops and abbots was the mace—a club ending in a heavy steel ball with sharpened ridged edges—for this skirted the rule that clergy were not to smite with the edge of the sword. Bishops had stables of horses and packs of hunting hounds and large retinues. To be a guest at the bishop's table was to understand why gluttony was one of the seven deadly sins. The menu for one feast required 3 carcasses of beef, 5 pigs, 4 calves, 22 kids, 3 deer, 12 capons, 88 pigeons (a total of at least ten pounds of meat for every guest), 1400 eggs, plenty of bread and cheese, limitless beer, and 66 gallons of wine. Even without guests a seven day fare included 6 carcasses of beef, 5 pigs, 21 deer, 53 geese, 60 fowls, 49 partridges, and some duck and pigeons.

Many monasteries were business enterprises, selling their produce at good profits, their monks renowned for managerial expertise. Some owned mills with the right to grind all corn grown in the area; others levied tolls on nearby roads or rivers; still others owned mines or specialized in breeding horses or producing wool. Some cloisters were little more than residential country clubs. The monks wore jewels, silks, and furs and were outnumbered by their servants. Monks lived well, enjoying the pleasures of the palate. In addition to 24 pints of beer a day, every day, the monks competed with the bishops in regard to food: a sixteen course feast required 30 oxen, 200 sheep, 1000 ducks, 963 fowls, 200 pigs, and a great many mallard, partridge, and larks.

Many a man of the cloth sought only wealth and power. Ecclesiastical offices—called benefices—were purchased with cold cash. They often proved a wise investment. Bishops averaged incomes of over one million dollars in today's money, many making several times that amount. Not all offices were purchased. Sometimes a feudal lord would appoint a friend who had done him a favor, and could be counted on to do more. Sometimes the local potentate appointed a relative to the bishopric or the parish to keep things in the family.

Often benefices were shopped out to hired clergy who did all the work for a paltry fee, while the non-resident owner kept the rest of the money. This allowed one man to own several benefices at the same time, a common practice. One clergyman held twenty-nine positions simultaneously. His income in today's terms was millions of dollars, while those he hired to do his work for him received less than one tenth of 1% of this amount. Over the altar of one of his churches was a structure of cow-dung bespattered sticks, while he sent the queen of France, as a small pleasantry, a carriage made entirely of ivory and silver. Another individual, reputed to be the wealthiest man in the world, held three hundred benefices.

The laity might never see the man who owned the benefice, and the person hired to do the work for him might be totally unfit for the job. One such individual on examination did not know any of the divine office (the prayers and psalms supposedly offered daily) or understand the Latin of the liturgy. Nevertheless, his examiner passed him. Such ignorance was common, for many of the lower clergy were illiterate peasants. Any schooling in church doctrine and liturgy came from the local priest — the blind leading the blind. A great many men holding church offices were not priests, and therefore could not perform the duties most important to the laity. But they presented some security against the big darkness, so laypersons took whatever existential solace they could from the dreary chant mumbled in Latin.

Outside the larger towns and cities Christianity often meant no more than an additional burden of fees and tithes — the tenth of all produce or profit, owed to the church. The parishioner had better pay up, or be excommunicated — something greatly feared by the laity. Excommunication removed the individual from the church and stripped him of all rights to citizenship in the human community. The excommunicate was cast adrift, unprotected from the forces of evil, sentenced to eternal damnation.

The ritual of excommunication was grim. A constantly tolling bell provided an air of ultimate finality. Upon the head of the unfortunate miscreant was laid the curse of God, Christ, the Holy Mother, the heavenly host, the prophets, the apostles, the saints — every conceivable power and all of creation, nothing was left out. The curse would fall upon him while he was eating, sleeping, riding, walking, urinating, in field, in town.... He was to suffer all manner of pain, affliction, and torment in this world, to be followed by the fires of hell. When the bishop had completed the reading of the curses, twelve priests dashed candles to the ground and trampled them. The quenched flames gave full meaning to the quenched life of the individual here and beyond the grave. So the peasant paid his tithe.

Clergymen passed their offices to their sons. The church was a money machine. It commissioned pardoners who sold absolution from any sin. Penances were remitted for money. Children were legitimized for money. So were stolen goods. Franciscan friars had gone upscale. Many served in noble households and dined with lord and lady. When a sect of Franciscans wanted to return to the ascetic ideals of St. Francis, so great was the contrast between these ideals and the wealth of the church the pope declared the sect heretical. In 1318 four of its members were burned at the stake.

On top of all this the clergy was, with few exceptions, exempt from secular law and could be tried only in ecclesiastical courts. A man of the cloth could commit murder, rape, theft, or assault with impunity, knowing that church justice was notoriously lax.

Wyclif thought the hierarchical organization of the church an abomination. The whole mess, he believed, should be replaced. The Bible — and he emphasized that the final authority for Christian living should be the Bible — gave no warrant for the offices and paraphernalia of the church. Furthermore, at a time when the average rural clergyman had no access to Scripture, Wyclif claimed it was the right and duty of every Christian to examine the Bible at first hand. He demanded free and immediate access to Scripture for all believers. The Waldensians had said as much a century earlier, but they hadn't said it from the lecture halls of Oxford, and they hadn't written it in literature copied in centers of learning throughout Europe.

Wyclif's world of ideas allowed only black and white, no compromising shades of gray. He pounded out his ideas in some forty hefty volumes in Latin (still in existence), the tone often abusive, bitter, and cantankerous. Students at Oxford were exhilarated by his revolutionary ideas, compelled by his impeccable logic, infatuated with his intellectual arrogance. In their young breasts he kindled a blaze of religious passion, for the young like something new, something in opposition to authority. To students seeking identity and purpose Wyclif was avant-garde, a rebel, a father-figure, a guru.

Wyclif was not the stuff of popular legends. A stern and forbidding figure, he lacked the humanity of a Waldo, the compassion of a St. Francis. Thoroughly bankrupt of any appreciation of the lighter side of life, this arid philosopher, this impersonal and humorless moralist, had no heart for the people. Nor did he likely understand them, for his many opponents and critics, try as they would, found not a shred of evidence that he ever indulged in any of the common pleasures. Wyclif's primary concern was ideas, not people. His interest in religious themes was purely intellectual. He preferred the security of the lecture hall over the arena of political life. He was a thinker, not a doer.

Yet somehow—there is no evidence of a personal connection—he inspired the popular movement that preached under the banner of his name: the Lollards. Ideas have their season. The time was ripe and the political environment appropriate for Wyclif's ideas to seize the popular imagination. The pride, avarice, and sexual appetite of the bishops was drawing even papal attention, and what was apparent to the holy father was certainly obvious to the laity: under layers of bureaucracy and codification the church had fossilized. It no longer responded to the religious needs of the people.

Meanwhile, the plague was a constant—six blasts in the sixty years following the Black Death, reducing the overall population by nearly half. The poor moved into empty houses, and for the first time in their lives had plenty of good food to eat. They strutted about in the fine clothes they found abandoned. A glut of merchandise and a reduced population meant lower prices and an orgy of spending. A depopulated town and country led to an acute shortage of labor. To keep land cultivated landowners reduced or even eliminated rent. All of this translated into upward mobility for many among the lower classes. The common people knew a surge of confidence and inner strength never before experienced.

It was payback time for the wealthy clergy. What began as public jeering and harassment soon turned into violence. In Rome a cardinal on procession took an arrow in his red cap. Pale and shaken, he resolved to venture out henceforth with a knight's helmet under his hat and a suit of chainmail under his vestments. Many clergymen did not get off so lightly.

The chaos resulting from the Hundred Years' War with France and the Black Death had shaken the English psyche and undermined the social structure. The lower classes saw that the powers that be were no longer in control, that they could be challenged. The time for change had come. The populace was tired of the flagrant sins of the clergy. Englishmen were gaining a sense of nationhood and resented the fact that so much English money left the country to fatten Italian and French popes. The church owned one third of all the land in the realm. Wyclif's idea that land bequeathed to the church could be repossessed—because the clergy was an illegitimate mediation between the Christian and his God—supported notions of revolution.

In 1381 the English peasantry rebelled. One of the leaders was a tall priest with a flowing red beard, John Ball. Ball told the peasants that unless they were wealthier than the local clergyman they owed neither offering nor tithe; unworthy clergy were unworthy of the tithe. Church authorities assumed some connection with John Wyclif and ordered him to cease lecturing. So Wyclif left his favored university for the small town of Lutterworth where he continued to write until his death two years later.

Today Wyclif's name is best known for the first translation of the whole Latin Bible into English. Over two hundred and fifty manuscripts of the Wycliffite Bible remain. The designation "Wycliffite" pays homage to Wyclif's fervent belief that the Bible is the ultimate authority for Christian living, not priest, not bishop, not pope. His belief, so cogently argued, inspired others—likely some of his students—to undertake the translation.

There had been earlier translations of portions of the Bible into English. But these, including Bede's translation of part of the gospel of John, were in Old English—a German dialect brought in by the Angles and Saxons, and incomprehensible to the Englishman of Wyclif's time. Earlier in the fourteenth century Richard Rolle had provided the *English Psalter*. Each English word matched a Latin word. Even the Latin order of words was retained: "Lord governs me and nothing shall me want." There was no effort toward literary effect. Yet this remained the standard English psalter until the Reformation, and was popular among the Lollards. Just as many people today prefer the exalted English of the King James Version despite a plethora of more recent translations, many people in the Middle Ages preferred the sound of the Latin psalms. Rolle's *English Psalter* allowed the reader to understand the text while retaining the pleasing Latin verse.

The English of Wyclif's time was not the English of today, but what linguists call "Middle English." It was language in a state of flux. There were several regional dialects; no one dialect had yet assumed precedence. Words had several spellings. "Wyclif," for example, was spelled Wyclif, Wiclif, Wicluf, Wycleph, Wycliffe, Wykliff, Vikkeluf, etc.—more than thirty variations are known. Middle English had letters not found in our modern alphabet. English was just gaining recognition as the language of the land. Up to this time it had been primarily spoken only by the lower classes. The king and the nobility spoke a type of French—Anglo-Norman. Then, in 1362, it was decreed that English rather than French was to be used in the courts. King Richard II spoke English as his native tongue. The Wycliffite Bible and Chaucer's *Canterbury Tales* did much to consolidate English as a written language.

The Wycliffite Bibles come in two distinct text-types. Manuscripts of the first text-type are literal, stilted, and in places even unintelligible—

only understood by reference to the Latin. Like Rolle's psalter, the English translation in these manuscripts is word for word, keeping the order of the Latin, in places yielding a sense opposite to the Latin. For example, "dominum formidabunt adversarii eius" was rendered "the Lord should dread the adversaries of him," instead of "the adversaries of the Lord should fear him."

Manuscripts of the second text-type comprise a translation in the full sense of the word—fluent idiomatic English. Because it is more likely that a fluent idiomatic rendition proceed from a literal one than the reverse, manuscripts of the more literal text-type are considered an "early version" of the Wycliffite Bible, and those in more idiomatic English, the "later version."

One manuscript from the earlier literal category states that its translation is the work of Nicholas Hereford, although the words which ascribe the translation to Hereford are written in a different style of penmanship—a different "hand"—from the main text. Hereford was the strongest advocate of Wyclif's views at Oxford. A brash outspoken young man who went out of his way to challenge the church, he took the message to the people in English, castigating canons, monks, and friars for their wealth and avarice. Then came his open incitement to sedition: The king should confiscate the church's superfluous hoards of money.

The church lost no time responding. The archbishop contacted the chancellor of Oxford. Hereford must not be allowed to preach or teach. So the intractable Hereford took to the streets distributing hand bills. He was summoned before the archbishop, but in no mood to recant he didn't show up. He was promptly excommunicated. Hereford fled, hoping to appeal to the pope.

The manuscript attributed to Hereford ends abruptly one third of the way down a column in the middle of a verse. This suggests that it was, indeed, written by Hereford: he may have stopped translating in order to flee the authorities.

A second manuscript of the earlier more literal text-type ends in the middle of the same verse, but at the end of a page. As it is the most literal of the Wycliffite manuscripts, suggesting an early date, it was for some time assumed to be Hereford's original holograph. It was dated 1382 because this was when Hereford suddenly vanished. Opinion has since shifted. Close examination shows that this manuscript was penned by five different scribes, displaying at least two distinct dialects. There are a large number of mistakes of the type more characteristic of copyists than of those engaged in original work, and there are many corrections. Hence, this manuscript is probably a copy of Hereford's original translation.

The later more idiomatic translation was completed in 1395 by several Oxford scholars brought together for that purpose by John Purvey. Purvey was Wyclif's secretary after he left Oxford, and the individual closest to him. Royal commissions appointed by parliament ordered Purvey arrested and his works confiscated. Protected by the Lollards for almost twenty years, he eventually fell into the hands of his persecutors. He recanted and was awarded a benefice. Two years later he resigned and disappeared.

The prologue to this later translation provides details concerning the process of translation and gives evidence of considerable sophistication. Meaning was emphasized over wording. There was recognition that there existed no set text for the Latin Bible — one manuscript said this, another that. In quest of the original Latin text the works of early commentators on the Bible were examined.

The Lollards read the Wycliffite Bible, but we know little about them and their exact connection with the Wycliffite Bible. Who were the original translators? Who produced the numerous manuscripts? Where were they produced? Who financed their production? (A Bible cost the equivalent of an average farm.) How did they get distributed?

From the beginning the Lollards were a persecuted group, forced to become a clandestine operation. Here and there they surfaced — caught by some heresy-hunting bishop, or sighted on the run. Sympathetic secular authorities offered a place to hide, but persecution increased with the passing years. In 1401 a law was passed decreeing for the first time in English history that a heretic could be burnt at the stake, sending the Lollards underground.

No universal or absolute prohibition of Scripture in the vernacular languages was ever made by a general council of the church or by any pope. Nevertheless, those responsible for the day-to-day running of the church — bishops, inquisitors, and the like — worked on the principle that possession of such literature was in itself sufficient evidence to warrant the presumption of heresy. A thirteenth-century synod at Toulouse, for example, prohibited lay people from possessing any Scripture except the psalter or a breviary, which had to be in Latin. Hence, when the English archbishop made it unlawful to translate any portion of Scripture into English, or to read English translations, unless special permission was officially granted by the church, he was acting according to precedent.

What became of Hereford? His plea before the pope landed him in the papal prison. He might have remained there the rest of his life but for an uprising three years later in which a disgruntled Roman populace freed all prisoners. Hereford found his way back to England but soon his venturesome nature got him into the hands of the English authorities. When next we hear of him he is on the other side, taking great delight in harassing the Lollards. The church generously rewarded him for his efforts, and succeeding kings endowed him with fuel from the king's woods and an annual barrel of wine. But Hereford remained restless to the end. Eventually he gave up all his benefices and benefits to live the life of an ascetic in a monastery. He drank only water, ate only once a day from a diet restricted to vegetables, and slept in a pine box. He died an extremely old man, buried in the same box in which he had slept.

The cantankerous and anticlerical Wyclif, and the excessive and sometimes bizarre activities of the Lollards—an abortive attempt to capture the king and seize political power by force of arms—so unnerved church and state (which joined forces to insure the continuance of their mutual hierarchical systems) that the resultant reaction set any chance of reform back one giant step and made possession of the English Bible the mark of a heretic. To own any literature in English — biblical or otherwise —could be incriminating. The fact that there was nothing heretical in the Wycliffite translation — orthodox monks and even a later king owned copies— did not slow the church's hunt to destroy all Lollard Bibles.

Thirty years after his death Wyclif was declared a heretic. His bones were dug up, burned, and the ashes tossed into the River Swift.

# 12

# Archheretic

An expectant crowd of onlookers has gathered. The civil authorities drive a heavy stake, to which is fixed an iron chain, into the ground. Then a middle-aged man is brought forward, looking much younger than his years and of hopeful demeanor despite the gravity of the situation. The authorities moisten some rope in a pail of water, and wind it around the man from his ankles to his chest, securing him to the stake. They tie his hands behind his back, and loop the iron chain around his neck. They arrange kindling wood beneath and around his feet, and stack bundles of straw and two cartloads of wood up to his throat. They check everything, then check again; this individual must be made secure, for who knows what sinister powers might infuse his bodily presence. Finally they place upon the man's head a paper crown decorated with figures of demons and bearing the word "archheretic," for the Holy Roman Church has declared the man a heretic of heretics. Care is taken that his gaze cannot wander in the direction of the Holy Land and thus defile it.

A torch is applied to the straw and kindling wood. Instantly searing flames lick at human flesh. Yet no scream of agony is heard. Instead, from within the flames quiet words of prayer and lines from the Creed, choked out a few minutes later by the smoke.

Life flees the burning body. Those tending the fire pierce the corpse's heart with a sharp stake, ripping it from its cavity. They break the limbs and ribs of the smoldering corpse and bank the fire to hasten consumption. With a sickening plop the charred skull, no longer supported, falls to the ground. Assuming a new and spectral life, it rolls eerily toward the feet of the executioners. In horrified and superstitious panic they club the smoking monstrosity into fragments and hastily shovel these back into the flames.

The crowd begins to disperse, but the most important work remains.

The executioners fear that common folk might make of the man burnt at the stake a martyr. Nothing which might be cherished as a sacred relic can be left. A separate fire is kindled and the heart thoroughly incinerated. All of the ashes are carted away and dumped unceremoniously into the Rhine.

Despite these precautions, John Hus did become a martyr. For the two hundred years following that summer day in 1415, the date of his death (and one of those bitter ironies of human existence, also his birthday) was celebrated as a national holiday in Bohemia (now the Czech Republic).

Hus was a learned man, a university professor. He had taught at the University of Prague since his youth. Founded in 1348 as the first German university, by Hus's time it drew 30,000 students from all over Europe. Despite this fine local university, many students from Bohemia chose to go to England to attend the renowned and older Oxford University. Close relations between the two countries had begun when the sister of the king of Bohemia became queen of England through her marriage to the English king. This English queen took a liking to Wyclif's ideas and encouraged the English translation of the Bible. Many Bohemians who studied at Oxford became imbued with Wyclif's ideas, and brought them back to their native land. Soon Wyclif's writings began to be studied at the University of Prague. It was at this fine institution that John Hus became an eager student of Wyclif's ideas.

Wyclif's idea that Scripture was the final authority for Christians, above pope and prelates, greatly influenced Hus. He began to speak out against the wealth of the church — it owned half the land in Bohemia and heavily taxed the peasants. He contrasted this wealth with the poverty decreed by Jesus in the Bible. A mild-mannered man, Hus nevertheless soon acquired a reputation as a scholar and preacher. The queen of Bohemia came to hear him preach every Sunday, and made him her personal confessor.

Hus's preaching attracted the attention of the church hierarchy in Rome. A papal inquisitor was dispatched to Bohemia to attend Hus's sermons and to closely examine him on church doctrine, but he found none of Hus's ideas heretical. Nor did the local archbishop. Criticism of the church was not uncommon. Many churchmen had recently criticized local practices and desired reform.

The church was in chaos. With three popes — each with a strong following — the unity of the church was rift. It was time for action, before it was too late. So bishops and cardinals and other prelates gathered at the Council of Constance seeking reform. After these church leaders had met for some time they summoned John Hus before the Council. He was happy to appear. Perhaps his ideas would be given serious consideration.

But no ... some of his writing had been called into question, and Hus was accused of heresy. But hadn't his ideas already passed inspection? Apparently not. One churchman found forty-two offenses among Hus's writings. But the chief accusation was that Hus was a follower of Wyclif, for the Council had just declared Wyclif a heretic.

Witnesses against Hus went unnamed, identified simply by title — canon of such-and-such, priest of so-and-so, this Master of Arts, that Doctor of Theology. Proof of transgression was not necessary. It was against canon law to defend a suspected heretic. Not that anyone was likely to try — mere rumors, scant whisperings, and the defender too might find himself charged with heresy. So Hus had to speak in his own defense. He claimed the church often acted contrary to Scripture. It withheld the wine of communion from laypersons, yet in the Bible Jesus offers it freely. If the Council found anything he had written or taught contrary to Scripture or the teachings of the Fathers, Hus fervently wished to be enlightened concerning his error; he would gladly recant.

This was not an era which enshrined the rights of the individual. Hus found himself alone, pitted against the mighty grinding machine of the medieval church. The church was all-powerful — more powerful than princes, kings, and emperors. The church was everywhere, present in every facet of human life. Hus's home town of Prague had three cathedrals, forty-four churches, twenty-seven chapels, and twenty-three cloisters. The Council pointed out that only the church, not the individual, had the authority to interpret Scripture. Hus was wrong to elevate his personal interpretation of the Bible over church doctrine. Did he consider himself wiser than all the gathered members of the Council? Did he place his opinions above centuries of tradition?

If Hus had at first anticipated stimulating debate, he soon realized he was mistaken. Intellectual discussion was not what the Council had in mind. The Council was law, its decrees fact. One churchman, wishing to help Hus understand the grim reality of his situation, approached the besieged man one evening and told him that even if the Council said he had one eye he should bow to its opinion. This was wise advice. Imprisoned with Hus was an individual known as the "antipope" John XXIII. Unlike Hus, he made no attempt to defend himself, confessed to every accusation, and supplicated before the Council. As a reward he was made Dean of the Sacred College.

But Hus persisted. Though worn out and ill from long imprisonment, insulted, ridiculed, and threatened, he refused to recant, for to do so would be to perjure himself before God, to say that he had taught what he had not in fact taught, to sin against his conscience and against divine truth. When he claimed that the Council misinterpreted his writings, that he was being falsely accused of things he had not said and did not believe, when he demanded to be heard, the Council said he must answer with a simple "yea" or "nay." His dialectical skill, his quickness of mind, went untested. He was baited, shouted down. Please, sir, for the sake of your soul, recant. Say you are wrong, apologize and all will be forgiven. The Council wanted a confessed penitent, not a martyr. If Hus admitted to teaching heresy, he would lose his following among the people. Hus persisted. He would not recant. The Council became an angry mob. Burn him! Burn him!

Hus refused to submit to the total power and authority of the church. Insisting he be proved wrong by reference to Scripture, he put the authority of the Bible over that of the church. His challenge was snuffed out at the stake. But the flames made Hus a martyr, extinguishing the man but not his ideas.

John Hus had exposed the Bible to public cognizance. He drew attention to the words and message of the Bible. He provided a translation in Bohemian, the language of the people. He preached the ultimate authority of Scripture over the church. It was a major step in bringing the Bible to the public. Today, six centuries later, Scripture has been translated into more than a thousand different languages and dialects, bringing its words to the remote regions and peoples of the globe. The intervening generations have turned to this literature for wisdom and inspiration, have found in it guidance and strength. It has shaped our civilization and influenced lives. Thanks to John Hus, a new and public age was dawning for the Bible.

# 13

# Prison of Doubt

What Wyclif and Hus had begun — to free the Bible from the clutches of the church and bring it to the people — was accomplished by an obscure German monk, Martin Luther. Luther's actions would echo through the centuries as the beginning of the Reformation — a series of events in the early 1500s which shook the Christian church in the West to its foundation and altered its shape and texture forever after.

Martin Luther grew up in the backwaters of rural Saxony. His medieval world was filled with horrors, dominated by the forces of evil. A subtle blend of pagan and Christian mythology populated the cold and blackness of winter nights with demons too numerous to name. Woods, winds, and waters were filled with gnomes, fairies, witches, sprites, elves. Luther had heard that to toss a stone into the waters of a nearby lake was to disturb the demons dwelling therein, resulting in violent storms. Coffins were closely guarded so that no cat or dog might approach and change the corpse into a vampire. In a world of witchcraft, sorcery, and black magic even the Christian clergy fostered belief in incubi, sirens, and satyrs. Because fear was a better tool of control than preaching Jesus's love, they spread tales about ghouls eating the contents of graves, vampires sucking the blood from those foolish enough to stay out after dusk, the undead carrying little children off to their underground dwellings. Even as a grown man, and the most eminent religious leader in Christendom, Luther wasn't sure whether witches flew or not, but he most surely believed in their existence.

The distinguished English philosopher Thomas Hobbes observed that human life is nasty, brutish, and short. Hobbes at least had the benefit of arriving on this fair globe more than a century later than Luther; in Luther's time human life was nastier, more brutish, and shorter. Life was not all that wonderful in the castle, and downright desperate for the commoner. Plague and famine continued to ravage human life — stories abounded of hosts who chopped up their guests and served their flesh in meat pies. Violence was everywhere in this worldly hell. The niceties of civilization would have to wait until history caught up.

The medieval social structure was divided into three divinely ordained groups: one to pray (the clergy), one to maintain order (the nobility), and one to work (everyone else). Luther was in the third group, but he knew that the church held the keys to heaven, that the only sure way to salvation from the forces of evil was the monastic life.

Luther had heard about a monk who threw off his monastic garb in the heat of fever and then died. Without his cowl the monk was denied entry at the Pearly Gate. This wretched figure peered through the windows of Paradise and witnessed the joyful existence that never would be his. How his heart ached! Then one day a monk inside the walls took pity and interceded for him. The monk who lost his cowl was granted a reprieve to go back to earth and fetch the missing garment. He did, and ever after dwelt happily in Paradise.

In the streets Luther saw a prince who had forsaken all earthly wealth and luxury for the poverty and humility of a beggar's life. Through fasting and vigil the young prince had become an emaciated old man, mere skin and bone. It made Luther think. If this earthly life was God's test, it made sense to pass the test. Why suffer everlasting torment when this life was over? Why not enjoy an eternity of bliss? A little discomfort in this life bought happiness in Paradise forever. The price was cheap.

One summer day as Luther was traveling just outside the town wall a tremendous crack of lightning forced the young man to the ground. A message from God? In terror he pleaded for the intercession of St. Anne, promising to become a monk. Three weeks later he bid his friends farewell and presented himself to the Augustinians as a novice.

Release from the concerns and distractions of secular life at first seemed a blessing, but quickly became a curse. Time hung heavy in the monastery. There were so many many hours to fill. Luther felt he should devote each and every one to saving his soul. He observed his vows with zealous earnestness, preferring fasts to feasts of celebration, Lent to Easter. He went without a crumb of food for three-day intervals. In vigil and prayer he exceeded stipulated requirements. The monastery was cold in winter; he cast off his blankets. Years later this monastic austerity would take its toll on Luther's health.

Yet despite his diligent monkery Luther was filled with misgivings. He was haunted by fears, the product of his own imagination. Had he fasted enough? Absolution for sins was available provided they were confessed. So Luther spent up to six hours at confession. But he no sooner finished confessing than he recalled further trespasses. And what if he had forgotten something? Could he be sure he had not overlooked some small misdemeanor? Had he examined his memory with sufficient thoroughness? Had he recognized all his sins as sins? Perhaps the Great Deceiver had tricked him into whitewashing his motives and actions.

Luther experienced what the monks called the bath of Satan — the winter of one's discontent, severe depression. He could find no spiritual comfort. He began to lose hope that his soul could ever be redeemed. He felt God's wrath and came close to questioning God's goodness — a most serious sin. Had God abandoned him? Was he among the elect, or among the damned?

Cloistered life was supposed to provide spiritual rest, certainty of salvation. But it resulted in just the opposite for this reflective young man with more than average concern for the security of his soul. According to the Augustinian constitution, monks were to study theology, provided there was a nearby theological school. So Luther took up the study of theology at the University of Erfurt hoping to still his spiritual unrest. The curriculum consisted of the four books of Peter Lombard's *Sentences* which dealt with God and the holy trinity, creation, angels, the fall of humankind, grace, sin, the virtues, the sacraments. But none of this answered Luther's spiritual problems.

Luther's religious ordeal did not go unnoticed. His confessor and spiritual guide was an esteemed doctor of the church, Vicar of the Augustinian order, and the first dean of theology at the freshly minted University of Wittenberg. This gentle and spiritual man did not neglect the personal and existential aspects of religion for the rigors of scholarship. Often impatient with Luther's overweening punctiliousness, he nevertheless was deeply concerned. He gave the young monk's personal trauma a positive spin — it was a sign that God had chosen Luther for great things. Had not Christ himself suffered hell before he arose?

When that didn't do the trick Luther's confessor was puzzled. He thought and he prayed, concerning how he might relieve the sincere young monk of his private spiritual hell. Then he had an idea. If Luther were given the care of other souls, he would have less time to be concerned for his own. He needed something to completely occupy his attention. Finally the answer came. It involved a complete change of venue. He would recommend Luther to replace him as instructor in Bible at the University of Wittenberg, where Luther could study for the doctorate.

Wittenberg was the capital of Electoral Saxony, a principality in the Holy Roman Empire. Said to be neither holy, nor Roman, nor an empire, the Holy Roman Empire was a collection of some three hundred sovereignties covering what is now Germany and extensive territory beyond.

Electoral Saxony was ruled by Frederick the Wise — one of the empire's seven electors. A year before the beginning of Frederick's reign, Saxony had been split in two in an attempt to resolve differences between the Ernestine and Albertine branches of the ruling house of Wettin. As ruler of a new political entity, Frederick was determined to make Electoral Saxony worthy of its imperial status.

He had little to work with. Wittenberg hadn't the ambience of a capital city; it was a mere town. Its population numbered twenty-five hundred at most, and it took only ten minutes to walk from one end to the other. It was located on the German frontier far from the refined south and west, on the edge of civilization, isolated from the larger world. Travelers accustomed to cultured cities found this bucolic burg a rude awakening, its inhabitants drunken, crude, and quarrelsome.

But Frederick was undaunted. He liked a challenge. He might have turned the area into a leading mining or trade center. Instead, he decided to drag this sleepy backward hamlet kicking and screaming into the world of new ideas and learning. For this was the age of the Renaissance, an invigorating period of intellectual quest. Frederick had studied the classics and learned Latin. It smarted that his rival in Albertine Saxony was reputed to be a superior Latinist, and that Albertine Saxony was home to the esteemed University of Leipzig. Frederick's domain was the only electorate in the empire which could not boast a university, and this hurt the pride of its energetic ruler.

Frederick decided to remedy the situation. A few years before Luther arrived in Wittenberg, Frederick obtained from the emperor permission to establish a university and was granted a charter letter. Wittenberg was the first German university founded without consent of the church — a sign that times were changing, that medieval was shifting to modern, that the strictures and limitations of the church were yielding to secular freedom and independence.

Essentially a conservative man, Frederick was neither reactionary nor afraid of the future. His optimism and energy were in harmony with the spirit of the Renaissance. He determined from the beginning that his university would be open to recent innovations in scholarship. Not all scholars adopted the new interests and methods, or participated in this rebirth of classical culture. Those who had built their careers on the old way of doing things and acquired a reputation in traditional subjects saw the advocates of the new learning as troublesome upstarts. Throughout Europe the proverbially peaceful halls of academe convulsed with new upheaval and agitated controversy. Jockeying for position on the academic ladder gained fresh vigor. Former institutional politics and loyalties went out the window. Novel alliances sprouted; ambitions were nourished.

Frederick sought the best scholars for his faculty, and forward-looking scholars eagerly anticipated this fresh start. Several came from the University of Leipzig hoping to find a less sterile, more progressive, intellectual environment. This must have warmed the elector's heart.

The new university was neither an exclusive haven for the new intellectual spirit nor inimical to the old, but showed tolerance for experimentation and leeway for individual expression not always found in the more established schools. Ironclad traditionalists and unbending reactionaries began to feel uncomfortable and quietly left. Replacements were Renaissance men, attracted by the University of Wittenberg's growing reputation. While young Luther could hardly yet be called a Renaissance man, he had an open mind and a thirst for knowledge. He was taken on as a lecturer in Bible at the University of Wittenberg, and Frederick the Wise agreed to pay his doctoral fees.

Until Hus's time the Bible had been virtually the exclusive possession of the church. The few Bibles owned by laypersons belonged to royalty and the higher nobility. Produced by hand, they were extremely costly. Only the wealthiest could afford one — among the clergy, mostly bishops. The "Bible" was usually just a psalter (the book of Psalms), although in some cases several books of the Bible were bound together. Among the laity Bibles were prized less for their written content (few could read, and those who could often did not understand the Latin) than for their aesthetic and monetary value as objects. Bibles possessed by laypersons were profusely illuminated, veritable works of art. A sixth-century Lombard queen had a Bible bound between two plates of gold bearing a cross set with precious stones and cameos. A twelfth-century countess owned a psalter with ivory covers decorated with turquoises. Such Bibles were often stolen, then torn to pieces and the pieces sold.

The prospect of lecturing in and studying the Bible excited Luther. The Bible was something new to the young monk; he had not known it in the monastery. Monks were prohibited from private Bible study. Their reading was a restricted diet of church authorities on Scripture (St. Augustine on the Psalms, St. Jerome on the prophets), lives of the saints, church history, and theology (Thomas Aquinas, Duns Scotus). But one day, while Luther was studying at the University of Erfurt, he discovered a copy of the Latin Bible in the library, chained to a reading stand for security. In Luther's time a complete Bible was rare. Since the Bible comprises almost a million words, about six normal-sized books, to fit all of this manuscript material into one volume meant a very large volume indeed. Surely therein lay a goldmine of holy truth. Luther's heart must almost have burst with anticipation. At the University of Wittenberg he would have the opportunity to peruse the Bible's treasures.

But Luther's personal spiritual war continued unabated. Doctoral studies at the prestigious new university didn't change things. He remained the tortured monk. In praying the Psalms Luther's soul did not understand the words his lips spoke. Surely God knew he was simply going through the motions and would severely punish him. He must consciously intend every word he uttered in prayer, and to do so he must first understand the words he was praying.

As he prepared his lectures on the Psalms Luther consulted the traditional commentaries, but these did not resolve his personal spiritual troubles for they interpreted the Bible in terms of Aristotle's categories— a sophisticated theological procedure. Over the centuries interpretating the Bible had become an increasingly esoteric science involving a complicated system with several levels of meaning. For practical purposes the meaning of Scripture was no longer directly accessible. The text of the Bible had become tangled in a theological web, buried under layers of scholastic commentary and the weight of dogmatic tradition accumulated over the centuries— the exclusive domain of the most learned of university-trained theological scholars. Luther found that Scripture could not be separated from the mass of theological literature and its sophisticated technical paraphernalia: rules of exegesis, handbooks, allegorical equivalents.

Traditional theology did not address the existential issues nagging Luther's soul. It stood remote and aloof from such earthly struggle, a thick carapace over the biblical text. So Luther decided to bypass the medieval theologians and in the spirit of the Renaissance go directly to the naked text of the Bible. Any Renaissance scholar worth his salt was expected to go back to a time before the medieval scholastics and examine the ancient texts, the foundations upon which the medieval theological and philosophical edifices had been constructed.

The library at the University of Wittenberg was amenable to Luther's wishes, heaven for the young scholar. In the spirit of the times Frederick the Wise had acquired a reputation as a bibliophile. He had begun his personal collection of books while visiting the Holy Land. Because he was respected by all sectors of the academic spectrum, leading scholars sent him a copy of their work for his library. When the contents of eight monastic libraries were added to Frederick's collection he donated his private library to the university, designating his advisor and closest confidant Georg Spalatin librarian.

It was a wise decision. Spalatin soon became the rallying point at the university for the new learning. Under his direction the university library reflected Renaissance interests. Not a single work by Aristotle — whose philosophy formed the backbone of traditional theology — was purchased.

Instead, the works of leading figures of the new learning. There was a copious supply of Bibles and grammars, a generous sampling from the church Fathers and the Greek and Latin classics. Spalatin was a passionate book collector, traveling hither and yon. It was a labor of love: beautiful volumes in Latin, Greek, and Hebrew, books from the prestigious Renaissance press of the Venetian, Aldus Manutius. Because Frederick was a devoted reader of the continent's greatest Renaissance scholar, Erasmus, Spalatin collected all of the diva's publications.

Armed with the exciting material he discovered among Spalatin's collection, Luther adopted a novel approach in his lectures on the Bible at the University of Wittenberg. He continued the practice of other universities—summarizing what Doctor A, Doctor B, and Doctor C said about Scripture—but he compared their comments with those of Renaissance scholars. In addition to this, Luther did something altogether new. He went past the commentators directly to the words of Scripture. He examined the biblical text in detail—not just the Latin, but the Greek.

Fortunately for Luther, the study of Greek language and literature had become a central focus at the University of Wittenberg—a bold and daring step, an innovation that flew in the face of tradition and marked Frederick's university as a center of the new learning. A few centuries after Jesus's crucifixion Christianity began to split into a Western (Latin) church centered around Rome and an Eastern (Greek) church centered around Byzantium. The study of Greek became a rarity in the West. In Columba's time, and for a few centuries after, here and there a few Irish monks knew Greek—John Scotus Erigena was a renowned Greek scholar. From there the study of Greek passed to northern England where Bede had some acquaintance with the language. But Christianity in Britain became Romanized and Greek soon became a virtually forgotten language, as in most of the West. Then in 1054 there came a definite and final schism between Eastern and Western Christianity, with most of Europe falling under the auspices of the Roman Catholic church. Latin became the dominant religious language. Greek came to be considered by some churchmen in the West as the mother of all heresies. So when the Renaissance quest for ancient texts made the Greek New Testament available it was regarded by many with suspicion. Fortunately for Luther such was not the case at Wittenberg.

Among the books in the university library Luther discovered one which would free him from the prison of his personal religious doubt, and in turn open the gateway to a whole new perception of Christianity which would eventuate in the Protestant Reformation: Erasmus's edition of the Greek New Testament, printed by Froben in 1516.

# 14

# A Scholar and a Gentleman

He was a bastard. His mother and father had not married, for his father was a priest, and priests were not allowed to marry. Few students of history would recognize the name Gerrit Gerritszoon, but by his Latin name—Erasmus—he is even today praised as the most glorious figure of the Renaissance.

Erasmus was a vocal and articulate critic of the church with an ardent desire for reform. He said that every man behind the plough and every woman at the hearth should have the words of Scripture in the vernacular, a statement which set the stage for Luther's translations of Scripture. Later he became a key figure in protecting Luther from Rome. At first Luther had nothing but praise for this celebrated scholar of the new learning. But the bold and impetuous young monk eventually abandoned his erstwhile father-figure. When Erasmus hesitated to follow his lead, the brash and cocky younger reformer came to think the sober and prudent scholar equivocal and faint-hearted, a naïve dreamer. Once mutually supportive, the two men later found themselves at odds.

Unlike Luther, Erasmus was not the stuff of popular heroes. While peasants, lords, and townsfolk quickly rallied behind the headstrong and confident Luther, Erasmus failed to capture the imagination of the people. Both were scholars, but of widely divergent personalities. Luther was ruled by passion. Once in the depths of a personal hell, he came to believe that God had chosen him for a special task, emboldening him with the unwavering self-assurance of the dogmatist. In his monk's soul there were no grays, only black and white; no "if's" or "maybe's," just "yes" or "no"; no room for quibbling, everything cut-and-dried. Where Luther provided answers, Erasmus posed questions.

Not for Erasmus the obvious ploys of the soapbox rabble-rouser. Instead, the subtle nuances of the practiced polemicist, the studied phrase, the reasoned plea. The pragmatic Luther knew when to abandon refined academic disputation in favor of overstatement and bombast. In a Europe quickly dividing into opposing camps—traditional scholastics versus advocates of the new learning, conservative supporters of Rome versus loud enthusiasts for reform—Luther brandished a club. Erasmus clung to his pen.

Erasmus made a fundamental error: he wrongly assumed that most people possessed his acumen, his lofty sense of morality, his optimistic vision for Christianity. He believed he could sway the masses with erudition, daunting wit, and corrosive criticism. It irked Erasmus that tattered pieces of saints' clothing had been carefully preserved in gilded reliquaries, while their books were abandoned to bug, worm, and cockroach. He said there were sufficient chips of wood venerated as relics of the cross to build a cathedral. Such clever satire went unappreciated. Churchmen and scholars did not quickly laugh at their own shortcomings. Pride was pricked. Superstitions exposed. Pieties belied. Erasmus shone too bright a light on human frailties: vanity, greed, credulity, indolence. Instead of awakening sleeping consciences, Erasmus's wit aroused enmity. His finer points flew over the heads of less perceptive readers. Erasmus was forever overestimating his public. This tolerant and cultured gentleman expected his readers to reflect his own educated sense of humor. He was confident that they too would remember the words of the prophet Isaiah: "Come now, let us reason together." He was certain that reasoned dialogue and gentle insinuation between civilized human beings would answer all differences, that every person, like himself, wanted peace. Peace would come once people were shown the error of their ways, once they forsook the superfluous notions which divided them.

Much of Luther's success fed upon the divisions among people. For Germans he translated the Bible into German. Here he was in step with the new reality—that Europe was breaking up into smaller units along religious and national lines. Erasmus held to the past. He was Dutch but did all his writing in Latin, the traditional universal language of Europe. Ethnic and nationalistic patriotism had no place in his heart. All of Europe was his home: he lived in Holland, in England, in France, in Italy. To Erasmus national divisions between persons were immoral. Christendom must be unified under one king, one lord—Jesus Christ.

Erasmus conceded that the church was rife with sin and error. He criticized priestly greed and lechery: most church rites—shrines, miracles, relics—played upon lay superstition to garner money. But as the embodiment of Christ's sovereignty on earth, the church needed to be repaired, not abandoned. Hence, Erasmus was content to live and let live, providing church practice was not clearly at odds with Scripture. Christ must be the focus of the church and belief. Ecclesiology and the divisive minutia of dogma were strictly secondary.

As time passed the opposing factions in church and academe became more entrenched. Erasmus's facility for seeing both sides of an issue and his efforts to unite the continent under one language (Latin) and one lord (Christ) made him enemies on both sides. He observed with customary perspicuity (his opponents would say peevishness) that he was a Ghibelline to the Guelfs and a Guelf to the Ghibellines. Erasmus was an easy target. Those who backed Luther said Erasmus lacked the passionate virtues of courage and decisiveness. Because Erasmus was not a party man, because he always saw the negative along with the positive, he was labeled fastidious and pusillanimous. If Erasmus thought of his opponents as barbarians, as hypocrites, fanatics, and dogmatists, his opponents found him equivocating, ambivalent, ambiguous, compromising, uncommitted, captious. But the discernment and fastidiousness which kept Erasmus from being too partisan, were virtues in the scholarly domain. Characteristics disadvantageous in the rough and tumble world of sixteenth-century politics proved invaluable to Erasmus the scholar in the work for which his fame has been justly celebrated.

From his early years the artful phrase, the melodious rhythm of carefully wrought words, excited Erasmus's youthful imagination. He was a man of his time. He preferred good literature over the jejune and impoverished philosophical mumblings, the mental gymnastics, of medieval theologians. As one Renaissance scholar phrased it, the wisdom gained from medieval scholasticism was as the milk from a male goat.

An anecdote of the time pokes fun at the self-important scholastic. One day the pope awakes quite ill. He and the attending cardinals debate whether he should see anyone that day. The pope decides to see the first three persons who come, but that is all; he will rest for the remainder of the day. Three men arrive within a few minutes. They are told about the pope's ill health and warned to keep their supplications as brief as possible. The first is a grave and learned scholar who has no intention of cutting short his rehearsed speech. As this tiresome and seemingly unending monologue drones on, the pope finds it an effort to smile politely. At last the disquisition is over. And what, the pope inquires, are the wishes of the other two visitors? With one voice they insist that if their desires are not wholly fulfilled they wish the learned doctor to repeat his speech. This greatly amuses the pope. He instructs that their desires be fulfilled, without so much as inquiring what they might be.

Renaissance scholars eschewed the learned bombast and speculative theology of medieval scholastics and turned with passionate enthusiasm to antiquity, to the refined rhetoric of Cicero and the deft poetry of Virgil. Words and language took on new significance. In the heat of summer two thousand persons listened to a two-and-a-half-hour lecture on a third-rate Roman poet; even on the third day all seats were taken two hours before starting time.

Consistent with an age which looked to the literary sources of the ancient world and studied them in their original languages, Erasmus went back to the fourth century, to Jerome. Jerome treasured the well-turned phrase and valued the masterful writers of classical times. In an era that preferred literature which spoke to the soul over the sophistic subtleties of the learned doctors of the schools, Erasmus found in Jerome a model for the new Renaissance spirit, a figure with whom he could identify.

In Jerome's letters Erasmus found ammunition against the scholastic theologians of the high and late Middle Ages— Erasmus called them "barbarians"—who asked such artificial and impractical questions as, Could God assume the nature of the devil, or of an ass? In his first major treatise, *Antibarbari*, written when he was twenty years of age, Erasmus contrasted Jerome with such literary and theological barbarians: Jerome made no display of cleverness and false learning; he eschewed theological jargon.

Erasmus wanted to imitate only the best, and the best was Jerome. To bring Jerome back to life he collected and edited Jerome's letters and wrote his biography. Today, five centuries later, the available collection of Jerome's letters remains largely that which Erasmus established. It took him the better part of three decades, on and off, to complete the task but he developed and sharpened textual skills which later proved useful in his biblical studies.

Erasmus saw Jerome as a model for the Renaissance man, meriting study and emulation. Jerome didn't waste time on theological pursuits, but instead concentrated on the Bible. Who cited Scripture with greater frequency and propriety? Who treated Scripture with greater piety? Jerome was the original biblical scholar. Those who would study the Bible should follow his example—become fluent in many languages and develop the necessary ancillary skills. In Jerome Erasmus found the inspiration to study Greek, to improve the fluency and diction of his Latin.

Erasmus was sure that the Bible was the answer to the ecclesiastical troubles of his time. Production of the best possible text of the New Testament would clear the path toward God's kingdom through an earthly church.

Erasmus followed Jerome in making a detailed textual study of the Bible. A contemporary portrait shows Erasmus working in his study. In the picture are four books. On two the title is clear. One concerns Jerome, the other is the New Testament. Erasmus used Jerome's methods to arrive at a better text of the New Testament. He went back behind the Latin to the Greek text of the Bible, because he knew it was impossible for the Latin translation to be completely faithful to the Greek original. Erasmus was unrealistically optimistic about growing interest in the Greek language. He found it such a beautiful language that he envisioned a time when translations would be unnecessary, when everyone would know Greek. It was this mistaken idealism in the belief that such a Golden Age was just around the corner which spurred him to work on his Greek edition of the New Testament.

His close study of Jerome introduced Erasmus to the philological approach to Scripture. Literally "the love of words," philology is the study of the use and meaning of words, particularly in their comparative and historical aspects. Erasmus discovered in Lorenzo Valla's *Annotationes* an example of philological methods which he would use to make a careful comparison of the Greek and Latin texts of the New Testament. He began by editing Valla's notes on the Latin biblical text.

Erasmus encountered a problem which expanded his project to more than a decade of intensive study. Which Latin text would he use? The Latin text was in almost as bad a state as in Jerome's day. For over a thousand years scribes had been mingling passages from Jerome's Latin translation with passages from the Old Latin: this phrase pleasing to the ear; that, more consistent with standard theology; another, better reflecting local liturgy. Such mongrel texts mated with other mongrel texts in a cacaphony of scribal genetics. The biblical books most used in the liturgy — the psalter and parts of the New Testament — got copied more often, and were the most corrupt.

Important ecclesiastical centers — cathedral towns and major monasteries — had from the beginning been focal points for the collection and production of manuscripts. From these centers local texts went out with missionaries and eventually blended with other texts. The rare complete Bibles were collections of texts: gospels copied from here, the psalter from there, each with its own complex pedigree. The complete early Codex Amiatinus is a good example of such a mixed text.

Late in the eighth century under Charlemagne — who was illiterate — an official attempt was made to clean up the Latin text of the Bible. Variant texts were collated, and standards of grammar and orthography determined. But the texts used for collation were already severely mixed and corrupted. The new standardized manuscripts to some degree drove out other texts by numerical dominance. But the older texts continued to be copied and soon mongrel texts resulted from intercourse between the new standardized text and older texts.

By the thirteenth century perceptive individuals like Roger Bacon were commenting on the chaotic state of the Latin Bible. Some observed that the Latin in their Bible did not match the same passages quoted by Jerome in his letters and commentaries. The few who knew Hebrew could see that the Latin Bible deviated in many places from the Hebrew Bible. During the Renaissance the tempo of this discontent accelerated.

Erasmus had before him a veritable dog's breakfast of corrupt Latin texts. But he was aided by the early commentaries of Jerome and Augustine. These contained detailed analyses of the grammar and syntax of biblical passages and were useful in reconstructing the biblical texts of a time before the Latin text had been severely corrupted by constant copying.

At this point Erasmus went to Basel to see Johann Froben who was publishing an edition of Jerome's works. He joined Froben on the project. He was assigned the first four volumes, and provided advice and help on the rest of the endeavor. The partnership became a lasting and productive one.

Erasmus had at first intended to revise the Latin New Testament based on ancient Greek and Latin biblical manuscripts and evidence found in the church Fathers of East and West, and include with his revision copious notes on the text. But Froben had gotten wind of a rival project involving the Latin and Greek texts, so he persuaded Erasmus to include the Greek text. Thus came about the achievement for which Erasmus is most famous: his 1516 edition of the Greek New Testament — the first time the Greek text appeared in print.

Erasmus used several Greek manuscripts he believed to be ancient (actually all relatively recent, from the twelfth century). For the gospels he relied basically on one manuscript, emending the text in places after comparison with a few other Greek manuscripts. A second manuscript formed the basis for the text of Acts and the epistles, again emended in a few places. A third manuscript supplied the text for Revelation. This last manuscript lacked the final six verses so Erasmus translated these into Greek from the Latin. A hastily constructed patchwork full of typographical errors (Froben wanted to beat the competition to market), Erasmus's Greek New Testament was nevertheless heralded as an achievement of the new learning, assuring his fame. Soon kings, prelates, and scholars vied for his company. King Henry invited him to London; King Francis begged him to come to Paris. The pope beckoned from Rome.

Erasmus's text has given us a part of the Lord's Prayer: "For thine is the kingdom, the power, and the glory, forever. Amen." These words were not in any of Erasmus's Latin manuscripts, but he included them because they were in all of his Greek manuscripts. Erasmus strove for clarity and accuracy. Every time a word appeared in his exemplar he translated it with the same word, to avoid needless theological speculation. He added philological notes to help prevent misinterpretation.

Erasmus knew that he had not spent enough time to produce a good biblical text. What should have taken six years had been accomplished in eight months. So he improved and supplemented his work in further editions. He searched for older biblical manuscripts and scoured the writings of the church Fathers for biblical quotations and exegetical notes concerning the less corrupted texts of early centuries. He made few changes to the text itself, however, preferring simply to add to his already detailed philological notes. The fifth and final edition contained 783 pages of notes, of inestimable value for later biblical scholars such as Luther, Tyndale, and the editors of the King James Version. Erasmus's notes set a standard. Thereafter, translations without notes—Giannozzo Manetti's translation of the New Testament, for example—got little respect.

Erasmus's Greek New Testament had two major advantages over its rival, which was actually a better text. It was first to market, and was printed in a less expensive and more convenient form. Both of these advantages showed the application of business acumen to the new technology of print. Erasmus's Greek New Testament was launched as a successful business enterprise. It started ahead and stayed ahead. It quickly gained widespread influence as pirated editions (in those days there was no copyright) appeared in cities throughout Europe—Venice, Strassburg, Paris, Basle.

The value of Erasmus's textual work, especially his detailed notes, was soon appreciated by scholars of the time. As the horizons and libraries of individual scholars grew, so did an awareness that divergent and even conflicting texts existed for most of the literary classics, including the Bible. It soon became evident that the first step in the quest for any true text was to collect variant copies and editions of the same work. Renowned Parisian printer Robert Estienne's edition of Erasmus's Greek New Testament left the text essentially unchanged, but noted variant readings based upon a considerably larger number of Greek manuscripts than Erasmus had witnessed. Over the years scholars continued to add to the list of textual variants as more Greek manuscripts were discovered. But Erasmus's text of the Greek New Testament remained virtually unchanged.

Then in 1633, in the preface of one of the many editions of Erasmus's text appeared what we today would call a publisher's blurb: "This is the text which is now received by all." From this apparently innocuous phrase came the powerfully influential catchword "received text," which seemed to imply that this text had dropped from the heavens, directly from God himself. Regarded as "the only true text" of the New Testament, it was slavishly reproduced thereafter. Although full of errors, based on just a few haphazardly collected late manuscripts, it was regarded with superstitious reverence. It became sacrilegious to criticize or emend it. Erasmus would have been appalled. He had intended his text to be merely the first step in a long line of texts progressively approaching the original.

Despite this concept of a received text, scholars for the next few centuries continued to assiduously ransack libraries for biblical manuscripts. The list of variant texts grew as more and more manuscripts were discovered. But this relatively poor text remained unaltered, and served as the basis for most of the more celebrated vernacular translations, including the King James Version, for almost four hundred years after Erasmus had issued the work which made him famous.

# 15

# Hijacked

It was this same Greek text of the New Testament, patched hastily together by Erasmus to meet his publisher's business deadline, which provided the answer to Martin Luther's personal spiritual crisis.

For some time Luther had been noticing the many discrepancies between available manuscripts of the Latin and Greek New Testaments, so he welcomed Froben's printed edition of Erasmus's Greek New Testament. Here Luther noticed helpful shades of meaning not found in the Latin. The Latin Matthew 4:17 has "penitentiam agite," "do penance"—specific acts properly completed to avoid divine punishment. But that was what troubled Luther: Were his acts the right ones? Were they properly performed? Had penance been accomplished? The Greek text, on the other hand, commanded the individual to "be penitent"—a feeling of the heart, an attitude of contrition, rather than a specific act. Luther certainly *felt* contrite. He felt inadequate before his Lord and wished with all his heart to have his slate wiped clean.

Up to this point Luther had understood "the justice of God" in the Latin of Paul's epistles as God's just punishment of the sinner. In the Greek text "the justice of God" referred to God's justification/salvation of humankind through Christ. Christ justified, made clean, the individual's slate. The individual Christian was not required to do penance. Christ had done his penance for him. Only penitence of spirit was required. Had not Luther's father confessor constantly pleaded with Luther to trust in the forgiveness of Christ? The ancient Greek text of the Bible proved him to be right. Luther's joy knew no bounds. He was now freed from the prison of his own doubt and fear.

Confident that his soul rested in Jesus's loving hands, Luther could say good-bye to his personal spiritual agonies. He needed to share his discovery, to spread the good news to others. Had not his spiritual guide, his wise and learned father confessor, said Luther's spiritual troubles were part of a larger divine plan. If Luther was indeed chosen by God, who or what could stand in his way?

Emboldened by his discovery, Luther became the chief spokesman for the new spirit of the Renaissance at the University of Wittenberg. Under his leadership Scripture became the focus and foundation of theological study, and Wittenberg became the first German university to teach all three biblical languages—Latin, Greek, and Hebrew.

But Luther did not stop there. A fiercely devout Christian, Luther was troubled by much of what he found in the church. On October 31, 1517, he posted his concerns on the door of the castle church. This was the famous act which is said to have started the Protestant Reformation. But Luther was no hotheaded rebel. Posting concerns and ideas was standard university practice—an invitation to other academics to debate within university walls.

Luther insisted that the church was too concerned with money, and not enough with salvation of the human soul. Money was king. Even murderers could receive pardon, providing they paid cash. Church offices were sold, often for a good price. Alexander VI, of the notorious Borgia family, had become pope by buying off his opposition—he gave his closest rival four mules laden with gold ingots. It was worth the price. The popes in Luther's day were the richest men in Europe. They created new offices, sold them, and then received half of the income during the first year and one tenth thereafter. When a church official died all his possessions reverted to the papacy. As a result, the church owned half of the wealth of the Holy Roman Empire and three quarters of the wealth of France.

The popes used this money to fight wars. Pope Julius II, the Warrior Pope, made a dashing figure at the head of his troops, with his flowing white beard and shining armor. In his brief seven years as pope Leo X spent the equivalent of $125 million on war, leaving debts of over $20 million. When he died it was rumored that the papal treasurer couldn't find enough money in the vaults to buy candles for Leo's coffin. Had Leo lived, his contemporaries joked, he would have sold Rome, then Christ, then himself.

Leo did not die in the field of battle. He died after an all-night party. Leo was famous for his lavish parties: fireworks, music, theater, the finest wines and food, gambling, acrobats. Most notorious of the popes of Luther's time in this respect was Alexander VI. His parties were costly and decadent. The approach to the papal palace was lined with golden "statues" in erotic poses—naked men and women painted gold. Inside, nudity and lust prevailed. Guests danced with naked prostitutes, then took their pleasure while the pope looked on. Alexander awarded prizes to the most virile men.

Alexander's personal life was not beyond censure. With sexual mores at an all-time low in the fifteenth century, one might have expected His Holiness to provide a more exalted example. He did not. He slept with his daughter Lucrezia Borgia, who bore him a son. It was the norm in Luther's day for popes to take mistresses and sire offspring. Nepotism ran amok at the Holy See. Sixtus IV appointed five nephews cardinals, and named one boy of eight years archbishop of Lisbon, and another of eleven archbishop of Milan. Neither had any religious instruction.

Fun and games at the papal palace required money, but that was never a problem. Priests and friars collected money based on what they judged the forgiveness of a particular sin to be worth, and on the depth of the parishioner's pockets. They kept a commission and the rest went up the hierarchy of the church. The sins of the dead could be forgiven. Pay cash and reduce a dead relative's stay in purgatory. Where at one time the forgiveness of all *past* sins could be purchased, half a year before Luther posted his concerns this was extended to include all *future* as-yet-uncommitted sins. Sellers of these "indulgences" earned a tidy commission, and boldly declared that *any* sin — even violating the Virgin Mary — would be forgiven for a relatively modest fee. All of this was backed by the pope's infinite power to forgive.

Luther's posted concerns criticized this trade in indulgences. He argued that the pope's power to forgive did not go beyond the grave; no pope could release a soul from purgatory. But if Luther was wrong about this, he had a question: Why, out of Christian love, did the pope not simply empty purgatory of all the souls imprisoned there?

November 1 was All Saints' Day. On that day, once a year, Frederick publicly displayed his massive collection of 19,013 relics — including fragments of Jesus's beard, and bread from the Last Supper — to which were attached indulgences valued at 1,902,202 years and 270 days of release from purgatory. This display always drew a crowd, and there for the crowd to see was Luther's list of concerns. Within a month they were translated into German and published. Luther's ideas had moved from the halls of learning into the public domain.

Luther was suddenly a popular hero. The German people awaited a leader. They sensed a new national spirit. They resented the church's taxes, all that German money going to Rome. It irked the rising business class that competing monastic businesses went untaxed. Germans wanted less power for the clergy, who were immune from civil law, while the pope could dismiss any secular ruler.

## 15. Hijacked

Once meek, passive, and retiring, but now convinced that truth was on his side, Luther had become a bold, blunt, blustering bull of a man with an almost cocky ego. Confident that he was right, he let nothing stand in his way. The opportunity to publicize his views came when he was challenged to debate at the rival University of Leipzig. Medieval disputations were the football games of yesteryear. Young men released pent-up combative energies. Even intramural university debates resulted in fist fights. Positions in a debate were purposely overstated to liven things up. Amid cheering and jeering the victor was paraded through town on the shoulders of reveling students.

A controversial figure from the rival university, Luther sold out. No one was disappointed. Amidst colorful processions, banners, the sound of fife and drum, Luther and other Wittenberg faculty arrived, accompanied by two hundred students armed with battle-axes. Luther's debating opponent was protected from the Wittenbergers and any Hussites who might happen to be in town by a 76-man bodyguard provided by the town council. The large numbers forced a change of venue.

During the debate Luther's opponent skillfully maneuvered the discussion onto the topic of John Hus. Didn't Luther, like Hus, prefer his own interpretation of Scripture over that of popes, councils, and doctors of the universities? The question was an obvious set-up, but Luther saw it as the proverbial brass ring to be grasped. Where Hus had meekly sought instruction and correction, Luther flew boldly and blatantly against the face of ecclesiastical authority — he was soon signing his name as "the liberator." Luther was audacious, a strident challenge, a noisy noise. He did not mince words. The articles of faith must come from Scripture, not from the church or the pope. Luther had found in the Greek New Testament a fundamental truth about Christian faith not previously understood by the church — the full grace of Christ. He must get the biblical message out to the people. In spite of the church, if need be.

The whole affair lasted ten days. It put Frederick's young university on the map and won Luther many supporters, but the authority of the church and the pope had been openly challenged. The present pope, Leo X, like the three popes before him, was no angel. He shared some of their sins, but he was no Sixtus, no Alexander, no Julius. He was rapidly bankrupting the papacy, but some of the money went to sponsoring eminent painters and sculptors of the day. Leo was a patron of the Renaissance. He read Erasmus.

How should Leo respond to Luther's challenge? He knew better than to react with imprudent haste. Things had been changing quickly in the century between Hus and Luther. The church was losing its stranglehold.

Other powers were gaining force. Cities were becoming centers of civilization and culture, and with cities came a wealthy mercantile class. Large nation-states were replacing minor principalities. England had a strong king, of the long and stable Tudor line. The domain of the French king had recently been greatly expanded. Ferdinand and Isabella had freed Spain from the Muslims for the first time in seven hundred years. That same year they sent Christopher Columbus on his historic first voyage westward across the Atlantic.

As the 1400s slipped into the 1500s Europe breathed deeply of a fresher and cleaner air. A new spirit of independence flourished. The medieval world was passing into history; a new era was beginning. Artists were learning the science of perspective, as the world expanded to new vistas. For this was the age of discovery. Whereas heretofore the European world of commerce had been restricted to overland trade and trade to ports serving the Mediterranean, Portugal's Prince Henry the Navigator had boldly sent sailing vessels into the vast unknown waters to the south and west, waters that ancient myths peopled with demons and monstrosities. Henry's mariners discovered the Azores and the Cape Verde Islands—almost a thousand miles out into uncharted ocean—and rounded the infamous Cape Nothing, beyond which ... well, sailors up to that time had had no wish to find out. Within a generation the southern tip of Africa had been rounded, and in 1498 Vasco da Gama continued from there into the Indian Ocean and on to India. By the time Luther was teaching at Wittenberg Portuguese traders in Malacca on the Malayan Peninsula east of India were sending home the equivalent of $25 million in trade, and had reached the fabled Spice Islands (the Moluccas) south of the Philippines. Sugar cane planted on Portuagal's Madeira Islands became the rage among Europe's elite. Malagueta pepper, elephant tusks, and gold dust were among the products of the Portuguese maritime venture. What unheard treasures and delicacies to delight eye and palate might be found in the Orient? Sandalwood, diamonds, emeralds, topazes, cinnamon? What new spices? What new fruits, nuts, and beverages? Would explorers meet with the mythical Amazons whose tears were of silver, find the trees whose leaves yielded wool, the snakes with precious stones for eyes, the men with dogs' heads? Would they find the Garden of Eden—located on maps far to the east, cut off from the rest of the world by a great mountain range—where every flower grew, the air was sweet with scent and melodious with birds' songs, clear streams rippled over jeweled rock, where it was never too hot, too cold, rainy, or windy, where sickness, death, and decay were unknown?

The known world was expanding at mind-boggling pace. New lands,

## 15. Hijacked

new continents. Amerigo Vespucci sailed westward, as had Christopher Columbus, and was sure that instead of China he had discovered a "novo mondo." Indeed, a few years later in 1507 cartographers produced the first map of the New World and named it America. Just three years after Columbus's fourth voyage twenty-two ships made the trip to America from Spain alone. It was a time for hope, for dreams. Human life seemed liberated from the stringent boundaries which had so long limited it.

What had long been, was now undergoing rapid change. The Christian Byzantine empire of the East, a power since the time of the emperor Constantine, fell to the Ottoman Turks in 1453. Using the recently invented cannon, the Ottomans accomplished what no other enemy had in over a thousand years—they breached the heavy walls of the capital, Constantinople. Eastern Christianity was now even more alienated from its Western counterpart, and Byzantium's churches were converted to mosques.

In the West the Latin church was the one continuity whose lineage could be traced from biblical times, a preeminent part of the structure of the medieval worldview. Now that that worldview began to be challenged, the medieval church was in danger. With so much of human existence undergoing fundamental change, the religious dimension of that existence was threatened. The ground was ploughed and readied. The seed need only be dropped. Luther, it appeared, might be that seed.

Forces against the church were rallying around their new-found hero, to protect Luther from Hus's fate. Prelates whispered in Leo's ear: he must act, he must do something to quash Luther and he must do it soon. But Leo knew it would be a mistake to act rashly. So he temporized. He could not order Frederick the Wise to silence Luther, put him in prison, kill him if necessary, because Frederick clearly supported Luther. Moreover, Frederick was one of the seven electors who would decide the next emperor of the Holy Roman Empire. The balance of power between emperor and pope had long been delicate. Leo did not want any of the obvious candidates— Henry VIII of England, Francis I of France, or Charles I of Spain. Each was too powerful. Each could unite his monarchy with the empire to pose a formidable threat to the power of the papacy. Leo wanted a minor figure like Frederick the Wise to be emperor. The situation required a sensitive touch. Leo could not afford to alienate Frederick.

Even after Charles won the election Leo continued to temporize. The coronation was a year away, and much could happen in the interim. He would see what could be done. Perhaps a war, some sort of alliance. Maybe simply not ratify Charles as the electors' choice.

While Leo temporized, Luther's supporters were spreading dissent. A year passed. Leo had become reconciled to Charles's becoming emperor, so Frederick was no longer part of the puzzle. The voices in Leo's ear became louder and more urgent. At last, on June 15, 1520, Leo acted. He ordered Luther to recant and publicly renounce his position.

But by now Luther was confident in his political powers. He was ready for battle. He issued several pamphlets in German — for he meant this to be a war of the German people against the church — amongst which were the inflammatory titles *An Open Letter to the Christian Nobility of the German Nation Concerning the Reform of the Christian Estate* and *Of the Freedom of a Christian Man*. He recommended a new national German church, severing all ties with Rome. The Roman church was not scriptural; it was a weapon of Italian imperialism, out to suck Germany dry. Luther's pamphlets promulgated distinctly novel ideas: marriage was not a sacrament; a woman married to an impotent man was free to sleep around until she conceived.

Luther was summoned before the Holy Roman Emperor in Nuremberg and ruling princes and potentates. Like Hus, Luther, ominously, was promised safe conduct. The papal nuncio arrived in town to an unfriendly reception. He tried not to notice the ubiquitous poems ridiculing him, or Luther's picture and writings prominently displayed in bookstores. He found it difficult to secure lodging, despite a liberal supply of funds, and ended up in a small, unheated room — an insult to his status. People immediately recognized the nuncio on the street. He wished it were not so. They gnashed their teeth, and made gestures toward their swords. In a hasty note to Rome the nuncio informed his lord the pope that things did not look favorable — nine tenths of the people were shouting Luther's name; the remainder, Down with Rome.

By contrast, Luther arrived with great fanfare. He rode in a carriage, preceded by the imperial herald. Crowds of curious and admiring spectators gave the appearance of a triumphal march. The town watchman announced Luther's approach by trumpet, and a hundred horsemen hurried out to provide escort. The press of people swarming at the city gate made entry difficult. Streets, walls, windows, and trees — from every vantage point people caught a glimpse of the renowned doctor of the university. A monk embraced Luther as he alighted from his carriage, and stooped to touch the hem of his robe as if Christ himself were present. Luther had no concern regarding a place to stay. He was welcomed at the official residence of The Knights of St. John.

The setting at the hearing would have pleased any stage director: the prelates of the church in their embroidered finery, the nobility luxuriously dressed in fur, velvet, silk; and opposite, Luther in simple monk's garb. Luther held the spotlight. He followed the dictates of his conscience — he refused to recant unless he could be shown his errors in Scripture. The inquisitor was not surprised; this was the usual plea of heretics. The pope had forbidden discussion of Scripture and its interpretation lest the whole ecclesiastical institution come crashing down.

The inquisitor requested Luther to repudiate his writing with all its errors. Luther would not. Furious, the emperor rose to his feet. He would hear no more of such impudence. Surely a lone monk who went against the church's traditions of a thousand years must be wrong. With that the assembly broke up. As Luther was hastily being escorted out and down the stairs there were calls for his burning at the stake.

The emperor would have to proceed with caution. Not German, he was sensitive to the political tension resulting from a growing desire for German independence. He knew that the notorious knight Franz von Sickingen, who offered Luther safe haven should he need it, had a large force of armed men just outside the city walls. The emperor needed allies, not new enemies. French armies had just crossed into his domains in the Netherlands and Spain, and he hoped to get a promise of 4000 horsemen and 20,000 foot soldiers from the assembly. To publish an edict against this German monk, who had obvious nationalist support, would be counterproductive and impolitic.

The emperor waited until he got his promise of troops and the assembly had broken up to make his move. He called the princes, and bishops, and remaining electors together — Frederick the Wise was missing; he had gone home with a bad case of gout. They approved an edict against Luther, declaring him a heretic. He was put under imperial ban. No one was to provide him with sustenance or hospitality. It was the duty of every citizen to take Luther prisoner and deliver him to the emperor. Or kill him on sight. Anyone who supported or aided Luther in any way was to be turned over to the authorities and his property confiscated. The buying, selling, printing, reading, or possession of Luther's writings was forbidden. Those guilty of such acts could expect arrest and death.

It appeared that Luther was a marked man. But emblematic of a medieval polity which was fast setting with the sun, the edict lacked teeth, and the emperor knew it. Even princes who supported the papacy knew that enforcing the edict would result in a German civil war — something no one wanted. Frederick the Wise asked to be exempted from the edict. Even though this obviously implied that Frederick would support and protect Luther, the emperor complied rather than alienate one of the empire's most influential princes.

Messengers warned Luther that he should make preparations to leave the city forthwith. Luther lost no time. The next morning he and a few companions departed in a small wagon. He had come in glory through the main gate; he exited quietly through a tiny back gate. Sickingen supplied an escort of twenty horsemen.

In a small town along the way Luther was received with great honor. Would he preach at the local monastery? This was prohibited. The abbot was taking a risk. Not all churchmen shared the abbot's cavalier attitude. When Luther preached at another town the pastor filed protest before a notary.

Luther wanted to make a slight detour to visit relatives, so the small group split. Two remained with Luther and the others continued on the main road toward Wittenberg as a decoy to any who might be following. The three spent the night with Luther's grandmother and his uncle's family. The following morning Luther preached in the village. Then, accompanied by a few relatives, he and his two companions went on their way. It was almost nightfall when Luther bade a heartfelt farewell to his kinsmen. The thick Thuringian Forest crowded darkly upon them.

Suddenly, a rustling and crackling of twigs. Armed horsemen charged from the forest. One of the horsemen pulled up the wagon's horses and knocked the driver from his seat. Another demanded the identity of the occupants. Luther announced his name. Crossbows were pointed at him and he was ordered to surrender. At this, one of Luther's companions, a monk, leapt from the wagon and ran for his life into the woods. Luther was rudely yanked from the wagon and after some rough jostling was made to run alongside the horsemen. With every step he could hear his friend Amsdorf's angry screams of protest growing fainter in the distance.

Amsdorf continued to curse loudly. He helped the driver up and back into the wagon. The poor man felt his head. Both wondered aloud what would become of Luther, but had to admit that they were fortunate to be alive. There was nothing to be done but continue their journey and hope the ruffians did not return.

Amsdorf must have smiled to himself, for he had been in on the plot to kidnap Luther. His cursing and screaming was an act, meant to deceive the driver and the monk who had fled.

But Amsdorf did not know the whole story. He had not been told, for example, where Luther was to be taken. The actors in the kidnapping were informed only on a need-to-know basis. With each person involved knowing only his own small part, the plan as a whole remained secret.

So far everything had gone smoothly. The number traveling with Luther had been conveniently reduced, and Luther had said good-bye to his relatives. The persons who could possibly foil the plan had been minimized. The isolated site for the ambush had been carefully chosen. On

## 15. Hijacked

seeing the armed horsemen approach, Luther had whispered to Armsdorf that this must be it.

Luther had a sketchy idea of what was to ensue. The night before his departure Spalatin had gotten word to him that Frederick would have Luther taken to a safe hiding place at some undisclosed location — Frederick himself had not yet been informed exactly where. The driver was not aware of the plan. He and the monk who had fled into the woods would be doing them all a favor when they told their tale of Luther's hijacking: Those who opposed Luther would assume him dead or in the captivity of his enemies.

As soon as Luther and the horsemen were out of sight there was no longer any need for him to trot along beside the horses. Luther was dressed to look like a knight and given a mount. Taking no chances, the small group followed a long and circuitous route to the hideaway. By dusk of the next day Luther lifted his eyes to the hills. In the distance he could see the massive contours of Wartburg Castle looming up against the darkening sky. At eleven o'clock they passed through the castle gate. It would be good to rest.

But the drama was not over. His captors threw Luther into a locked cell and were none too gentle about it — even the guard must not suspect Luther's true identity. Owls and bats flitted about in the gloom. How long would Luther have to stay here, a virtual prisoner?

# 16

# Room with a View

It was important that Luther not be recognized by visitors to the castle. Until the hair on his head filled in his monk's tonsure and his beard was of sufficient length to hide his identity he was strictly confined. He was instructed in the forms and manners of knighthood, for his disguise would be that of a knight. He was dressed, and addressed, appropriately.

Through the window of his small chamber Luther's eyes feasted on a breathtaking view. High above the ground, he looked out over miles of rolling hills—the magnificent Thuringian Forest. This idyllic environment offered respite from the often meaningless busyness of human concourse, an opportunity to relax, to breathe deeply of fresh country air, to savor the open skies, the warm sunshine, the cool woodlands.

Many would find hiding out in a castle in the hills under disguise adventurous and romantic. But not Luther. He was restless. Spending days beside a gently meandering stream, listening to the rustling of the trees and watching the wildlife, was not for him. He was invited to join a hunting party, but failed to get into the spirit of it. Spying a rabbit, he hid it in the sleeve of his cloak, hoping to preserve its life. But the dogs sniffed it out and bit through the cloth killing it.

The garrulous and extroverted Luther took no pleasure in this lonely life. He wanted to get on with the serious business of religious reform. There was much to be done. The days weighed heavily upon him. His ambitious spirit chafed. His mind was elsewhere. He saw only three persons: the warden of the castle, who watched over Luther as if he were a prisoner, and the noble's sons who twice a day brought food and drink. The contrast between his present solitude and inactivity and his exciting public life only weeks previously was almost too much to bear. He had never been particularly in favor of this whole scheme. He began to regret following his friends' advice. He berated himself for not having been more aggressive before the assembly. Better had he continued preaching, even if it meant a martyr's death.

Alone, Luther was once again haunted by former doubts and fears. The Prince of Darkness prodded him with questions: Was he alone right, and centuries of pious Christians in error? How could he be sure he was right? Might he be leading others into eternal damnation? Unfamiliar sounds in the empty castle began to sound like the rustling of demons' wings. By himself, in a room in a vast castle out in the middle of nowhere, Luther felt a perfect target for all the forces Satan could muster.

Time passed, and Luther gradually settled into the slower pace of existence. His friend Spalatin acted as intermediary between Luther and the outside world. He supervised Luther's correspondence and manuscripts, at times suppressing those considered imprudent. He kept Luther informed of, and involved with, the initial events of the Reformation.

Luther made time move faster by immersing himself in hard work. Cut off from the joy of preaching, he began work on a book of model sermons. This period of solitude yielded some of his most effective writing. But none of it compared with his masterpiece. For it was cramped within this plain, 15-foot by 20-foot room, a room normally used to quarter prisoners, that Luther translated the New Testament into German.

Luther was not the first to translate Scripture into German. There already existed fourteen editions of the Bible in High German and four in Low German, but these translations were suppressed by the church and had little circulation. Luther's translation had special significance. Where earlier renditions were based on the Latin, Luther remained true to Renaissance ideals, and making the best use of his scholarly tools as a professor of Bible, translated from the Greek — the second edition of Erasmus's Greek New Testament.

Translating the New Testament was a labor of love for Luther. Here were the words which had liberated him from his spiritual dilemma. It was as though he had *discovered* Scripture, not only for himself but for all of Christendom. A liberated monk had become the liberator. By translating Scripture into the popular tongue Luther was giving back where he had received.

Luther soon discovered that translation is an art. He faced a monumental problem which confronts all translators. No two languages exactly mirror one another. Languages contain subtleties, peculiarities; each language has its own unique personality. He often found it almost impossible to find a single German word to translate a Greek word which had a range of meanings, an array of associated nuances and implications. What the Greek might say with great precision, Luther found in some cases virtually impossible to express as precisely in German. Where the Greek conveyed special emphasis or emotion, how should he duplicate this in German without considerable circumlocution? How could he duplicate the nuance of a Greek idiom, or capture a delightful play on words or a figure of speech peculiar to the Greek language? It was not always easy to accurately communicate the sense of the original Greek in German idiom without losing something.

Clearly, Luther realized, perfect translation is an ideal, something to aim for but impossible to achieve. He worked without break, completing his translation in only eleven weeks. No sooner was he finished than he set about revising his work. On September 25, 1522, Luther's German translation of the New Testament went on sale to the public.

When he had completed his translation of the New Testament Luther did not pause to admire the result of his labors, but immediately began to translate the Old Testament. Again he went back behind the Latin text, this time to the Hebrew text, using the 1494 Soncino edition as his source. He consulted other scholars, notably the Hebrew scholar Matthew Aurogallus.

The Old Testament was printed in installments to keep the price affordable. The translation of the first five books—from Genesis through Deuteronomy—went smoothly and was ready for publication by the middle of 1523. By the beginning of the next year the books from Joshua to Ester were published. The book of Job proved extremely difficult. At one point it took four days to translate three lines. Nevertheless, by the autumn of 1524 the books from Job to the Song of Solomon appeared. At this point Luther became so preoccupied with outside events that he had little time to devote to the consuming task of translation. Nevertheless, over the ensuing years he continued to translate, publishing individual books of the Old Testament as they were ready. It was not until September 1534 that Luther's complete Bible was published.

Luther's German translation of the Bible was a significant accomplishment. It was the first complete Bible—both Old and New Testaments—in a modern European language translated from the original Hebrew and Greek.

The Bible had been wrested from the church and given to the people. And the people were ready. The pump had been primed, for laypersons were not unfamiliar with Bible lore. It was fashionable for a person of wealth and status to possess a Book of Hours. Beautifully illustrated—often with the burlesque: bare-assed monks, devils, priests with goats' feet, imaginary creatures—these books contained daily devotions, biblical stories, and saints' lives.

Bible stories were presented in mystery plays put on by the guilds, consisting of up to fifty scenes. The mystery plays provided entertainment for noble, peasant, merchant, artisan, and cleric. Jesus rose into the clouds on a system of weights and pulleys. Devils came up through trapdoors. Thunder was created by turning barrels filled with stones. Spilled guts were supplied by the local butcher. A fake head of the beheaded John the Baptist dripped ox blood. When the donkey carrying Jesus into Jerusalem answered the call of nature the crowd howled with laughter. Devils in masks, horns, forked tails, and suits of black horsehair ran through the crowd pinching and scaring the audience. The crowd loved the stock characters: obese friars, heroic knights, adulterous ladies, pregnant abbesses, avaricious Jews, proud cardinals, drunken students, wealthy merchants. Tears, laughter, noise and violence. The plays had it all. Yet they portrayed vivid images of the humanity of Jesus and gave religion a concreteness and relevance that the institutionalized church failed to convey.

The plays were written by clergymen who knew that the best way to the layperson's heart was through entertainment. They drew not only from the Bible but from non-biblical sources—legend and folklore. The results are with us to this day. Those three kings from the east in the Christmas story? There is no mention in the Bible of the wise men being kings. Nor is there anything about Eve's "apple," Moses in the "bulrushes," or the "ox and ass" at the manger (the latter from the legend about Francis's manger at Greccio).

Public sermons offered by the friars were also a form of entertainment. They spoke the language of the people. In a time when few left the boundaries of their town or village, the friars provided some contact with the wider world — racy stories of faraway places and famous persons. The friars spiced their message with legends, jokes, profanity and vulgarity. Some sermons were in verse. There was plenty of heckling, witty repartee, applause, and back and forth dialogue between preacher and audience. It was truly a performance.

But now, thanks to Luther, Bible stories and message were available in hard print. People willingly purchased Luther's German Bible at considerable expense, even if they couldn't read. In terms of a carpenter's income, the New Testament alone cost one week's wages.

Luther is recognized as the most important single figure in the history of modern German, having contributed enormously to its development and refinement as a written language. In Luther's day there existed a great many local German dialects. Most people still lived in the country or in small villages. They lived their lives, married, reproduced, and died in one narrow valley or one tiny hamlet. That was the limit of their universe. The flow of commerce and of information about the wider world was down the major rivers, for there were few roads. Persons any distance from rivers and roads were isolated; local dialects often could not be understood by those living over the next hill. In more populous regions the national languages which we know today were just beginning to take shape from among these numerous local dialects, but they lacked sufficient vocabulary to express more than the most rudimentary ideas.

How could one individual like Luther virtually create a language? Luther's timing was right. German nationalism was on the rise. A German Bible was a boon to nationalistic pride, giving greater independence from the Latin church, and the Latin Bible.

The dialect Luther chose for his translation — that spoken in the royal court and chancery of Electoral Saxony, and similar to that of the imperial court (when it was not using Latin) — had the advantage of being broadly based geographically. Eighty to ninety percent of Luther's expressions could be understood in both southern and northern Germany, giving his translation more than merely local usage. This hadn't been the case with earlier German translations. As Luther's Bible spread among the people with the advantage of printing, its form of German gradually became the spoken language of an increasing proportion of the German people.

That there existed no standard German language proved an advantage, for Luther was able to enrich the language of the Saxon court with words and phrases from several other dialects. At times he had to invent words because there was no German equivalent. The names of birds and animals, for example. What was he to do with "taragelaphus," "pygargus," "oryx," "camelopard"? Sometimes he used the names of objects which were close at hand. He named the precious stones listed in Revelation 21 after Frederick's court jewels. For the coins of the Bible he consulted numismatic collections in Wittenberg. Trips to the local slaughterhouse helped him designate the parts for animal sacrifice found in the book of Leviticus. All of this gave Luther's translation local coloring, in the same way that biblical figures depicted in accompanying illustrations bore a remarkable likeness to Frederick the Wise and other noteworthy contemporary Germans. Luther's Moses seemed almost German.

Luther's Bible is considered to this day a magnificent literary monument. Its style has long been praised, for Luther did not aim simply at a translation but a fine piece of writing. He strived to provide a text easily comprehended and unambiguous, written in clean, clear language, easy on the reader, flowing smoothly. He wanted the wording to be memorable, musical and pleasing to the ear. He was an exacting — perhaps fussy — translator, never satisfied. Twenty-four years after the initial publication of his New Testament he was still making revisions. It is said that just before his death the last printed page before his eyes was a printer's proof of his most recent revision.

Luther's translation, as might be expected, raised the ire of those on the side of Rome. Duke George of rival Albertine Saxony rushed to prohibit Luther's published translation of the New Testament. The duke's secretary was one of Luther's sharpest critics. A lawyer and a theologian, Jerome Emser attacked Luther in a book the title of which says it all: *The Reason and Cause of Why Luther's Translation of the New Testament Has Been Justly Forbidden to the Common Man: With a Clear Description of How, Where, and in What Passages Luther Has Perverted the Text and Unfaithfully Rendered It, or with False Glosses and Prefaces Has Led People Away from the Ancient Christian Way to His Own Advantage and Delusion.*

Emser was right to find Luther's choice of wording in places theologically nuanced. It has long been recognized that it is impossible to translate without some degree of interpretation. In Luther's case the Bible — as he understood and transmitted it — had particular personal meaning. For here was a man who had been rescued from a personal religious hell by particular words of Scripture, and was afire to pass on what he had discovered.

A few years later Emser offered his own translation, ironically containing many of the illustrations found in Luther's Bible. Emser's translation also proved popular, running to thirty-eight editions and forming the basis for several later Roman Catholic New Testaments.

A generation later an exceedingly reactionary pope instituted the first official Roman Index of prohibited books. Included in the long list were all the works of Erasmus and all vernacular translations of the Bible. Books were burned. But, as modern censors are learning, banning a book is the surest way to make it popular. The pope might huff and puff, rant and rage, but there was no way to turn back the clock. Luther had given laypersons the Bible in their own tongue.

# 17

# The Gutenberg Bible

Neither Luther nor his Bible would have become well known to a wider public without the invention of printing. Publishers made Luther a public figure. In less than a month the ideas he posted on a chapel door in a backwater town were published in one of the largest cities in the empire. Ideas wrenched from the quiet world of academe were in German bookstalls within weeks. Three different editions were printed almost simultaneously in three cities. Luther had become famous.

Printing rapidly spread Luther's ideas to other scholars. In the days before printing, the restricted collections in individual libraries had severely limited the boundaries of scholarship. Some scholars, particularly during the Renaissance, got around this to some degree by traveling and collecting or copying manuscripts they found on their travels. By making books more widely available, printing expanded the horizon of the scholar. It was no longer necessary to travel to see other books; the books came to the scholar via printer's agents as they sought to expand markets. Soon it was possible to examine a great many books without leaving the study. As Luther's publications came to the scholar's study his ideas spread like wildfire among like-minded intelligentsia.

The advent of printing had broader cultural significance. It introduced a standardization into the diversity and discontinuity of human existence, conformity where there had been nonconformity, uniformity where there had been variation, the typical where there had been the irregular. The advent of printing and a more uniform vernacular language, such as that fostered by Luther's Bible, began to make obsolescent the multifariousness, the disorder, the chaos, the bewildering diversity of local customs within any ecclesiastical or secular jurisdiction which had been characteristic of the medieval world. The German dialect chosen by Luther was broadcast with the printed copies of his Bible, promoting this particular German dialect over others, fostering a linguistic uniformity hitherto unknown.

The paradigmatic artifact of the invention of printing in Europe was Johannes Gutenberg's Bible — traditionally acclaimed as the first printed book in the West. Forty-eight copies have survived, in whole or in part — one bears the date August 15/24, 1456. On all counts this work is a magnificent example of the craft and represents an advanced stage of technology. These Bibles are printed in a large gothic type to simulate hand-lettered Bibles, on large sheets approximately 12 by 16 inches. Each copy consists of two volumes, totaling 641 leaves, 1282 pages. The Gutenberg Bible was meant for institutional use — primarily to be kept at the lectern for reading in church — and was in Latin.

The Cologne Chronicle of 1499 gives full credit to Gutenberg (Gutenberg was his mother's name, which he preferred to his father's — Gensfleisch, meaning "gooseflesh") for having invented and perfected the technique of printing most widely used at that time. The charming story of its invention begins with an apprentice dropping a woodcut for a printed page. It shattered into many small pieces; some had whole words and phrases, others just parts of words. Gutenberg boxed the lad's ears and then sat down to the task of piecing together the woodcut, lining up the separated words and phrases. Suddenly he had an inspiration: Why not start with smaller pieces and then put these together to make the block for a page? Then he could reuse some words for other pages. This would avoid much duplication of work and make the whole process more efficient. And so was born the idea of movable type.

The idea of printing was not new. Wooden patterns had been used for textile prints in Egypt during the sixth century, and block-printed textiles were common in the Rhineland from at least as far back as the twelfth century. The Chinese had been using the process of wood block printing since the sixth century. Late in the tenth century a complete set of Buddhist scriptures — over five thousand volumes — was printed, using 130,000 wood blocks.

The Chinese knew how to make paper back in the first century. Returning in 1295 from his adventurous travels to the Orient, Marco Polo reported on the use of printed paper money. One hundred and fifty years earlier paper had been manufactured in Europe. A mill had been established in France by a man who had learned his skills in a forced labor camp in Damascus as a prisoner of the Saracens during the Second Crusade. It was some time before Europeans used paper for printing, however. The cost was prohibitive until the 1300s when linen began to replace wool in clothing, the discarded rags being an inexpensive source of material.

At first paper was used only for writing. Then playing cards were printed on paper using the wood-block technique.

Wood-block printing was one thing. The typography found in the Gutenberg Bible was something else; it involved separate, movable, interchangeable, cast-metal characters of exact dimensions which could be assembled into a rigid form for printing, and removed from the form for use in the composition of another page. Casting of the characters required great precision because once in the form the letters had to be in a straight line and their printing faces had to present an even plane. A special metal alloy had to be developed to form the characters, and a mold of very close specifications had to be designed and constructed. When all of these problems had been solved an ink of sufficient viscosity and adherence had to be concocted, and a suitable press fashioned. All in all, a mind-boggling accomplishment. It was many years before Gutenberg got satisfactory results.

The actual printing of the Gutenberg Bible was a monumental enterprise. Fashioning the type began five years before publication. There were six presses, of which two or three were in constant use for about six years. Each press required two or three pressmen and a compositor to set the next page to be printed. Some copies of the Gutenberg Bible were printed on paper, others on parchment. Parchment was expensive. The hide of one animal yielded parchment for two sheets. The sheets were folded to give two leaves. Each parchment copy of the Gutenberg Bible required the slaughter of one hundred and sixty animals—a veritable blood sacrifice.

During the late Middle Ages there was a growing and urgent demand for more copies of religious books. The number of monasteries had steadily increased with each passing century. In England there were a thousand monasteries by the year 1300, compared with only sixty three hundred years earlier. Multiply this over all of Europe—Gutenberg and his associates must have done the math—and it spells a healthy demand for Bibles, breviaries, and missals. Gutenberg chose the Bible for his first printing, rather than some other work, because it was sure of a ready market. Profit dictated its printing, not religious motives.

The Gutenberg Bible was printed mostly for the monasteries. But monasteries were not the only consumers of books. By 1400 the growth of commerce in the cities had led to a marked increase in literacy. Creative writers in the vernacular—Dante, Boccaccio, Petrarch, Chaucer—began to appear. The development of schools and universities led to a demand for grammars and the texts of noted authors. University towns began to sport bookshops.

Eager to reap greater profits, Gutenberg's business associate gathered up a dozen or so copies of the Bible and headed for what he believed to be a sure market — Paris. Here was located the largest university in Europe — ten thousand students. He was apparently doing a brisk business when the local book producers' guild — copyists and other assorted trades — caught wind of the competition, and chased him out of town.

Fed by a sure market, the technology and the business of printing grew apace. Less than two years after publication of the Gutenberg Bible a psalter was printed which displayed great refinement of the printing arts. It was printed in both black and red and in three type sizes. Decorative initials were printed in two colors by wood block. It was common in early printed books for the initial letters of a chapter and other illumination to be hand-painted. Some copies of the Gutenberg Bible, for example, had hand-painted illustrations added later by an artist commissioned by the purchaser of the Bible.

Printing is a business, and marketing is an essential ingredient of the successful commercial printing enterprise. Book buying habits were shaped by the manuscript market. Bibles had been a saleable item well before the advent of printing. Printing only made them more so. The Bible and other religious material provided the surest and least risky road to profit for printers. Returns proved worth the risk. The Bible turned out to be a judicious choice for early mass speculative print runs. By 1500 the Latin Bible had been printed ninety-four times, and some part of the Bible in some version had been printed on one hundred and fifty occasions. All was readied for Luther's translation of the Bible into German. Luther became famous, but the printers of Wittenberg grew rich. Erasmus got credit for the first printed Greek New Testament, but the idea originated with his printer. Yes, printing was a business; for some, a very lucrative business.

But the hand-written book was not dead. The monasteries, which had been the centers of book production heretofore, could not cope with the newfound demand for the written word. To fill the gap public copyists appeared — people who made a career of laboriously copying books by hand. But as the number of these public copyists increased and the fraction of book production under the scrutiny of the monastic orders subsequently grew smaller and smaller, the quality of manuscripts dropped. Some public copyists took great pride in their work and furnished magnificent examples of their craft, but too often pressure to meet the urgent demands of the market resulted in an attrition of standards. Calligraphy became downright shoddy in many cases. Unattractive to the eye and difficult to read, many manuscripts were full of errors. As the pace of production increased, so did the errors.

Printing seemed the perfect answer to the growing manuscript dilemma of the fifteenth century. Printing establishments multiplied like rabbits. A quarter of a century after Gutenberg's Bible there were printing presses in 110 European towns. Venice is reputed to have had 150 presses. The House of Koberger in Nuremberg maintained twenty-four presses and employed over one hundred workers. Half a century after Gutenberg's Bible eight million books had been printed — more than scribes had produced since the fall of the Roman empire. One man could print in a day what it had once taken several copyists a year to produce.

Those who copied manuscripts for a living could see the proverbial writing on the wall. Their days were obviously numbered. Even the celebrated Florentine manuscript dealer Vespasiano da Bisticci, whose forty-five copyists produced two hundred volumes in twenty-two months, could not compete. He had dutifully advised and supplied Europe's bibliophiles for decades, but within twenty-five years of the advent of print he was forced to close shop. It wasn't just price; it was numbers. A copyist might only charge one third of what a printer charged for duplicating the same work. But for the price the copyist furnished one copy to the printer's one thousand copies.

Copyists did not surrender easily. They talked up the beauty of the hand-crafted manuscript and appealed to elitist tastes, but this was whistling in the dark. The Abbot of Sponheim wrote a book praising scribes. Copying, he said, is a noble enterprise. It keeps idle hands busy. It encourages diligence and devotion. He exhorted his monks to persevere in their honorable profession despite the invention of printing. He told them their work would last one thousand years, for it was on parchment, not on paper like those cheap printed editions. He neglected to add, of course, that a large portion of printing was also on parchment. But when it came to making copies of his *Praise of Scribes* the venerable abbot didn't turn to the monastery. Instead he made haste to the local print shop, as he had with all his other writing.

Printing did not eliminate textual errors. Preservation of text remained the problem it had always been. As far back as A.D. 174 the Chinese were concerned with preserving official texts from the errors of the copyist. According to the annals of China's Han Dynasty, the Supervisor of the Imperial Archives ordered the texts of six canonical books engraved on large stone tablets. When this work had been completed he decreed that these tablets be placed in front of the state academy so that scholars and students could at any time make exact copies by rubbings. Nine centuries later China's prime minister Fêng Tao commissioned the printing of the Confucian classics. This wasn't to make these classics available to large numbers of the public (private printing of the classics was forbidden), but to establish in quantity a single text. Wood-block printing circumvented the virtually unavoidable errors involved in the copying of manuscripts.

Movable-type printing was touted to have the same advantage when it was first introduced. But not every copy of a book printed with movable cast characters was identical. (For example, no two copies of the eighty printed copies of the First Folio of Shakespeare's plays in the Folger Shakespeare Library in Washington are identical.) There were several sources of inconsistency. The greatest of these was in the composition of the page. Business exigencies often took priority over accuracy of text. Compositors were pushed to have the next page ready for the pressmen. Printing started before the proofreader had completed his work. He spotted errors after printing had occurred. If an error was not deemed significant pages already printed were allowed to pass—paper was too expensive to waste—and the error was corrected for future printings. As a result the same page varied for different printings.

Sheets were hung to dry here and there in the shop. When they were gathered for binding a further complication arose. All the sheets of a given printing did not necessarily end up bound together in one book. Page four might be from the fourth printing and page five from the third printing. Printers often employed several compositors, each working on different pages. Compositors had their own individual styles of spelling, punctuation, and abbreviation, since these had not yet been standardized. (Printing would eventually help standardize spelling, grammar, and vocabulary, but only over a period of several generations.) Hence, the pages of a single copy were often of uneven quality.

In the early years of printing, labor was inexpensive and materials were dear. Not all printers had their own type foundry; none kept large stocks of type on hand. Because there was usually only enough type to set a few dozen pages at most, as soon as some pages had been printed the forms for those pages were dispersed to obtain type for the next group of pages. If the book sold well enough to warrant another printing, the whole process had to begin again from scratch, resulting in a whole new set of errors.

Printers often scrimped on proofreading. They might hire unqualified readers; they might take on too few and push them too hard; or they might pay them too little to encourage any sense of pride in a job well done. Sometimes, to speed things up, one person would read the exemplar to another who checked the proof. This made it easy to confuse words that sounded the same. Or the proofreader might not hear correctly.

If a book was reprinted several times the text became steadily debased. The exemplar was usually a copy from the former printing, with all its errors. New errors were then added with each new printing. The gradual corruption of the text was comparable to that found in scribal transcription. Printed copies of the King James Version of the Bible from the seventeenth and eighteenth centuries give ample evidence of this unfortunate fact. To this day typographical errors continue to plague the printed page.

But this was of no concern for those printers who smelled money. And Martin Luther was money, a hot item, a publisher's dream-come-true. Within three years after Luther had nailed his theses to the chapel door, his thirty publications had sold over 300,000 copies. Before he had completed any of his biblical translations four thousand copies of one of his writings were sold in only five days. One book out of three printed in the first four decades of the sixteenth century was written by Luther. His *Address to the Christian Nobility of the German Nation* was reprinted thirteen times in two years, and his *Concerning Christian Liberty* eighteen times in six years. If church doors had long functioned as an agent of publicity, they had now been replaced by the printing press. The printing press could disseminate ideas on an unprecedented scale and at an unprecedented rate. Looking back in later life Luther saw the invention of printing as an act of God helping the gospel spread rapidly among the people.

The printing press spread Luther's ideas both quickly and broadly. Although the advent of printing did not by itself precipitate the Reformation, it gave Martin Luther's ideas a powerful advantage which Hus's ideas—in many respects remarkably similar—did not have a century earlier. In print Luther's ideas became indelible, permanent. They took on a life of their own.

When Luther's translations of Scripture became available the market was ready. Sales of Luther's New Testament were brisk—about 200,000 copies during the first dozen years. The printing presses in Wittenberg were kept busy. There were fourteen editions and 83 reprints of the complete Bible in High German and four editions and 19 reprints in Low German during Luther's lifetime. Luther made Wittenberg's booksellers and printers wealthy. Several printers published Luther's Bible. One Wittenberg printer published over 100,000 copies in a fifty year period.

In the few generations before Luther the reading public had greatly expanded. Before, schools attached to cathedrals and convents were mostly limited to those preparing for the priesthood, so few—even among the nobility—could read. Now, with the growth of cities and the merchant class, independent secular schools for the general public were being founded by enterprising businessmen. People were eager to learn, and wanted something to read. Luther's Bible furnished a quality text, and the printing press assured adequate quantity.

# 18

# Cloak and Dagger

While Luther was creating a stir on the continent with his German translation of the Bible England was ruled by King Henry VIII. The English people had immediately taken the young — he ascended the throne at eighteen — king to their hearts, for his good nature shone forth in an open ready laugh. Bluff King Hal was larger than life, a fit sovereign for an emerging nation. Over six feet in height and handsome of face, he was cultured and scholarly: he knew Latin, French, and Italian; he studied religion; he wrote poetry and composed music. He was gifted with extraordinary athleticism: he rode, jousted, fenced, and played tennis; at the hunt he reputedly wore out a dozen horses an outing.

This vigorous and prepossessing figure, full of energy and joie de vivre, ruled by his own definition of kingship. He knew what he wanted, and he intended to get it. Those who stood in his way quickly learned that he had a hot temper, that this proud and impulsively ambitious sovereign was a formidable foe. When "off with their heads" became a byword, it was prudent to remain in Henry's favor.

Convince the king that your fondest desire was to serve him well, and there was never a better time to be an Englishman. Stephen Vaughan knew this, and his career was moving steadily upward. A merchant adventurer in Antwerp, Vaughan had been appointed the king's factor in the Netherlands. Then one day the king summoned him to court and entrusted him with a delicate matter. He was to persuade William Tyndale to come back to England. Tyndale was one of many persons who had been on the wrong side of Henry's religious agenda and had consequently fled to the relative safety of continental Europe. Vaughan was to inform Tyndale that the king had had a change of heart, that he needed Tyndale's knowledge, education, and abilities, that Tyndale's ambitions and goals were complementary to his own.

Great would be the reward for a successful mission. But how to proceed? Tyndale was no fool. He had covered his tracks thoroughly. None among the king's men had the foggiest notion of his whereabouts. Vaughan started asking questions and following leads. Soon he learned of three locations where he might possibly find his man. He wrote to these addresses, promising Tyndale safe conduct in the name of the king. He got a reply: Thanks, but no thanks. Tyndale had received too much frightening news from his homeland to chance returning. Besides, he suspected a trap. Vaughan persisted. He continued to write to Tyndale, in order to maintain contact. But where was the man he sought? Perhaps he was only a few blocks away — Tyndale's network of friends and associates relayed and diverted his mail. At least Tyndale was still answering his letters.

Then Vaughan got a mysterious message. Someone would like to see him. He would be led to an appointed rendezvous. Who was this secret stranger? Vaughan wanted to know, but he got no reply to his many questions. All was hush-hush. Suppose the stranger was Tyndale. Vaughan would have to take a chance. The opportunity might never be repeated.

Vaughan wrote that he would comply. When the day arrived he followed his guide through the city gate to a nearby field. Here he met the secret someone, who did in fact turn out to be Tyndale. But Tyndale only wished to assure him that he remained a loyal subject of the king. Yes, his life was far from satisfactory on the continent: he was poor, hungry, thirsty, cold, and deeply regretted the absence of fond friends. But all this he gladly endured, for he hoped that his labors would some day prove pleasing to his God and his king. It was not, Tyndale explained to Vaughan, that he did not trust the king's promise of forgiveness. It was the scheming clergy that made him hesitate; he feared that once he was back in England they would convince the king that he was a heretic and deserved no mercy.

Vaughan pleaded, argued, but failed to convince Tyndale. Tyndale said his farewell and headed away from town, into the countryside. Should Vaughan follow Tyndale? No. He would risk death, and at the very least destroy the trust he had established over several months. Then his mission would surely be unsuccessful.

Vaughan's prudence was rewarded. Tyndale met with him on two further occasions. Vaughan was unable to get Tyndale to return with him to England, but he came to respect Tyndale's motivation and character. Here was a man who would gladly die or suffer any discomfort, provided he could provide the English people with Scripture in their native tongue.

Years before, as a young man, Tyndale had attended Oxford University. The curriculum was still under the spell of medieval scholasticism. Theology reigned. Subjects for debate ranged from the arcane to the ludi-

## 18. Cloak and Dagger

crous: Is the pope more merciful than Christ? Can the pope command angels? Can God make a harlot into a virgin? Tyndale was appalled.

While he was at Oxford the first fresh breath of Renaissance learning was beginning to make itself felt in the stodgy halls of Cambridge University. Erasmus, doyen of Renaissance scholars, paid a visit to Cambridge. There were lectures on the Greek language. So Tyndale transferred to Cambridge, but he soon learned that the new learning would not win the field without a fight. Luther's works were being burned.

Tyndale's first pastorate was in the countryside. He could hardly believe the ignorance of his fellow clergy regarding Scripture. It made him appreciate what Erasmus had written in the introduction to his Greek New Testament: that Christ wanted his word published as widely as possible, and therefore all men and women should have access to Scripture in their native language. Tyndale now knew that his life-task would be to translate the Bible from Greek into English.

It was not the most propitious time to translate Scripture into English. The decrees issued in reaction to Wyclif and the Lollards were still on the books. The printing press was available, but no one was willing to risk printing the Wycliffite Bible. Only a few years earlier seven individuals had been burnt at the stake for teaching the Lord's Prayer, the Ten Commandments, and the Apostles' Creed, in English to their own children. The pope had named King Henry "Defender of the Faith" for his spirited attack against Luther. Did anyone dare fly in the face of this stalwart king and declare himself the English Luther?

There was a way around the law, however. Translation of Scripture into English was prohibited, unless authorized by a bishop. If Tyndale could find a bishop…. He would need to choose carefully. Many bishops were against Luther and anything that hinted of Luther. But one stood out — the new bishop of London. Cuthbert Tonstall had a reputation as a scholar and a generous patron of scholarship. Moreover, it was said that he had a liberal outlook regarding the new learning, was favored by the king, and — what clinched it for young Tyndale — was praised by Erasmus. Here was a bishop who surely would understand and appreciate Tyndale's concerns, who would eagerly support a scholarly translation of Scripture from the Greek into English. Perhaps he might even offer to be Tyndale's patron.

Armed with a letter of introduction and a sample of his Greek translation, Tyndale bade farewell to his quiet bucolic existence at Little Sodbury Manor, with its pleasant countryside, its fresh breezes and distant vistas. He said good-bye to an uneventful life with few responsibilities, and headed off to the big city. Once in London, Tyndale was delighted to learn that Tonstall's servant was a previous acquaintance. But things did not go as he had hoped. While Tonstall was not discourteous, nevertheless he was cool, reserved, and evasive. He was a busy man, he said, and really had all he could manage at the moment. Had Tyndale tried so-and-so?

It wasn't that Tonstall was opposed to the idea of a translation. But he was a cautious man of worldly wisdom, a practical man, smoothly political, not about to take up a cause which might prove imprudent. Years later when the winds of political fortune shifted he would be in the vanguard of support for, and happily lend his name to the title page of, the fourth edition of the duly authorized English translation of the Bible — ironically almost completely dependent upon Tyndale's translation. But that was years in the future. Now was not the time for an English translation of Scripture. Vernacular translations had always been suspect by the church, moreso now with strong negative reaction to Luther's New Testament, considered a breeder of heresy. Tonstall had no desire to arouse the hostility of his peers; he had barely settled into his new office. It would be foolhardy to compromise himself for the sake of this total stranger. He had everything to lose and nothing to gain, for he was very definitely a man on the rise. One false step could end his advancement.

Rejected by Tonstall, Tyndale was soon under the protective wing of a wealthy London cloth merchant who told him that if his project was to succeed he must leave England, or perish at the stake before his work was complete. On the continent he would find a more conducive atmosphere. There Luther's ideas were quickly gaining popularity, and enterprising printers were willing to take chances. Through the cloth merchant Tyndale gained the support of a well organized network of friends and associates, persons who helped him get out of the country — it was illegal to leave England without official approval — and directed him to a safe destination on the continent.

Once there, Tyndale went incognito to safeguard his friends and associates. Historians are not certain where he did his translation, but Wittenberg seems the best bet. Here he could work in peace because the reformers were in control and had the backing of the elector of Saxony. The University of Wittenberg's extensive library provided the books Tyndale most needed, and he could consult with experts on Greek and Hebrew. Moreover, Luther himself was present in Wittenberg at the time Tyndale was translating the New Testament. He would have delighted in Tyndale's work and have provided him with support and assistance. A clue is found in the registers of the University of Wittenberg — the name William Daltici from England. Was this Tyndale? Had he disguised his name by reversing syllables — "Tindal" to "Daltin"?

## 18. Cloak and Dagger

Close to Daltici's name in the register is that of Matthias von Emersen of Hamburg. The von Emersens were one of Hamburg's great Lutheran families, closely related to Reformation leaders. Matthias was the nephew of the widow Margaret von Emersen at whose home Tyndale spent considerable time. Against the prohibition of the town's senate Margaret had sent two of her sons to the University of Wittenberg, by this time known as "the vipers' pit" of the Reformation. Her nephew Matthias was the secretary of the Steelyard in London.

The Steelyard took its name from the English adaptation of the old German word for "warehouse." It was the port through which much of London's merchandise arrived from the continent. For over five hundred years it had been under the control of Germans whose commercial skills had earned them special privileges in the city. At this time most of the Germans had come under Lutheran influence and were importing Lutheran books into England. Mention of the Steelyard came up in a heresy charge against the London cloth merchant who had protected Tyndale. The merchant testified that he kept money for Tyndale until he sent for it from Hamburg via the Steelyard.

In Antwerp English merchants had the equivalent of London's Steelyard — the English house of merchants. The authorities were anxious to be on good terms with English traders who brought considerable wealth to their city so they granted the house virtual diplomatic immunity; it was a piece of England in a foreign land. Many of its merchants were of Lutheran persuasion. Tyndale read Scripture to these merchants on Sundays. His host in Antwerp for nine months was Thomas Poyntz, a relative of the lady of the manor at Little Sodbury Manor, and years later buried at St. Dunstan's. It was at St. Dunstan's that Tyndale had met the London cloth merchant.

Here were many tempting clues and tenuous connections, a loose web linking Poyntz, the Steelyard, the Antwerp English house, the von Emersens, and Wittenberg. Yet Tyndale remained hidden from hostile authorities. At the hint of danger he slipped down back streets and moved furtively from one friendly domicile to another, meantime continuing his work of translation.

Part of Tyndale's story is filled in by John Cochlaeus, a bitter opponent of the Reformation on the continent, forced to flee from two cities. One day while he was at the Quentel publishing house in Cologne he heard that an English New Testament was being produced. Cochlaeus decided to learn more. He got on familiar terms with the printers who, in an intoxicated state one evening, boasted that soon the whole of England would be Lutheran. Cochlaeus's ears perked up. England was to be converted to

Luther's revolutionary ideas by means of an English translation of the Lutheran New Testament, three thousand copies of which were now in press. This enterprise was being financed by English merchants who would secretly transport the finished product to England under the cover of other merchandise and distribute it throughout the country before the church knew what was happening and had a chance to prohibit it.

The next day Cochlaeus hastened to tell his news to a senator of Cologne, a personal friend of both King Henry and the emperor. The senator made an investigation of his own, and then notified the senate and obtained an order against the printer prohibiting further work. Two Englishmen gathered up the printed copies and fled to Worms, a town sympathetic to Lutheranism. Meanwhile Cochlaeus and the senator dashed off letters to King Henry and the bishop of Rochester, warning them to keep a sharp lookout at all British ports.

Despite these actions printed copies of Tyndale's New Testament arrived in England in great quantity. The disastrous harvest of the summer of 1525 had left England in near famine conditions. The order came down that grain was not to be moved between counties. London was in panic; the mayor threatened to seize corn wherever it could be found. To the rescue the Steelyard, importing a plentiful supply of wheat — a marvelous opportunity to smuggle Tyndale's New Testament.

Today there remain three copies of Tyndale's New Testament. One, discovered by a London bookseller, covers only the first twenty-two chapters of Matthew and is bound together with a treatise by Oecolampadius. There is no title-page, no date, no place of publication, but the typeface suggests publication by Quentel of Cologne, and there is a woodcut found in other Bibles printed by Quentel between 1527 and 1529, and in a commentary on Matthew published by Quentel in June 1526. Comparison of the woodcuts indicates that Tyndale's Matthew was likely printed by Quentel in Cologne sometime before June 1526.

The second copy of Tyndale's New Testament is incomplete at the beginning and the end. The third, although lacking a title-page, is in good condition. Watermarks, woodcuts, and typeface indicate that these two copies came from the press of Peter Schoeffer of Worms. The Worms New Testament probably appeared in England around March 1526. In August of that year Luther's friend Spalatin accompanied the elector of Saxony at the imperial diet. In his diary he recorded the conversation of one of the guests at a supper party — that at Worms six thousand copies of the New Testament had been printed in English, and that the English translator, who was staying with two other Englishmen, was so skilled in Hebrew, Greek, Latin, Italian, Spanish, English, and French, that one would think each of these his native tongue.

## 18. Cloak and Dagger

Tyndale spent about nine months translating the New Testament into English. He did not aim at perfection or pedantic exactness, for his primary objective was to get it to the people. A note to the reader in the Worms edition acknowledges that it is little more than a rough draft, and promises a later edition in polished English.

The Cologne edition contains many marginal notations similar to those in Luther's New Testament, in substance if not always in language. The text is divided into paragraphs, for the most part following Luther's work. Tyndale's introductory remarks paraphrase the preface of Luther's New Testament. Tyndale clearly referred to Luther's New Testament, but a close examination of the text shows that he made an independent English translation from Erasmus's Greek New Testament—a decided advancement from the Wycliffite New Testament which relied on the Latin.

Tyndale was a master of the English language. His choice of word and the rhythm of his sentences was without equal. Generations later ninety percent of his wording would find its way into the King James Version of the New Testament.

But this fine style was not everywhere appreciated. Perceived as part of the Lutheran revolution, Tyndale's New Testament raised a yowl of protest among the English clergy. Tonstall led the onslaught, claiming to have found two thousand errors in Tyndale's work. He summoned London booksellers to the bishop's palace and warned them against importing such literature. In an injunction to his archdeacons he accused Tyndale of seductive interpretation which profaned the hitherto undefiled majesty of holy Scripture.

Tonstall solicited the help of Thomas More's silky smooth pen: More could play Demosthenes, the eloquent orator of ancient Greece. More accepted, and for five years launched a thousand-page war of words against Tyndale. Once known for his liberalism, his charm, his agreeable nature, More now wanted reformers burnt at the stake. More said Tyndale's New Testament was untrue to Christ's message and full of antichristian heresies. He accused Tyndale of being a servant of the antichrist, deliberately distorting the text—using the word "repentance" instead of "penance," "love" instead of "charity," "acknowledgment" instead of "confession," "senior" instead of "priest," "congregation" instead of "church." Tyndale countered that over time these words had acquired connotations not intended by the authors of the New Testament books, and that he was providing a more accurate and up-to-date rendition.

Prompted by anxious clergymen, King Henry decreed that Tyndale's New Testament be burned, and those who possessed or read it be punished. Copies were burned and people imprisoned, but the imports continued.

The archbishop came up with what he considered a sure solution. The bishops would share the cost of buying up all the available copies and so rid England of this pestilent poison. But the archbishop clearly did not understand the law of supply and demand — the more books were burned, the more they were printed, making the printers wealthier and wealthier.

His New Testament in circulation, Tyndale turned his hand to translating the Old Testament. When he had completed the first five books he set out for Hamburg to have them printed. On the way he was shipwrecked and all his work lost. So he started over with the assistance of Miles Coverdale at the home of the widow von Emersen. Within nine months the first five books of the Old Testament were again ready for publication. They circulated individually, the book of Genesis dated 1530. In marginal notes Tyndale gave vent to hitherto restrained emotions. Unsavory remarks about the church's persecution of reformers reflected his anguish at losing a personal friend to the stake. He chastised the church for persecuting people who were trying to return Christianity to its original ideals.

Tyndale went on to translate Jonah and passages of the Old Testament used in the liturgy of the church, along with the historical books from Joshua to 2 Chronicles. He put his finished work into the hands of his disciple John Rogers, at the English house for merchants in Antwerp. Tyndale translated from the Hebrew with the assistance of the Latin, Luther's German translation, and the Greek Old Testament. On occasion he was pressed to invent new words, particularly for the ancient Israelite rites. Just as he was responsible for "shewbread," "tendermercies," and "longsuffering" in the New Testament, he coined "passover," "scapegoat," and "mercy seat" for the Old. Tyndale's Old Testament was praised for its noble simplicity of style and its strength of rhythm.

In 1534 Tyndale made good his promise to issue a revised New Testament. It contained over four thousand changes both in substance and in style. A year later a third edition included further minor changes.

While concentrating on the precise work of translation and the details of revision, Tyndale knew he was a marked man. But in time he came to feel a modicum of security in the English house for merchants in Antwerp, and one day let his guard down. On the street he met an acquaintance from his university days. Unknown to Tyndale, this individual was in the employ of the bishop of London. Tyndale's whereabouts were finally known. The church dispatched Henry Phillips to the continent with instructions and a supply of money. Disguised as a university student, Phillips won Tyndale's trust and was often his guest at the Poyntz residence. Meanwhile Phillips had procured the assistance of agents of the emperor. The net was tightening.

Sensing that Poyntz was growing suspicious, Phillips waited until Poyntz was out of town on a prolonged business trip before striking. He then inquired of Poyntz's wife concerning Tyndale's plans for the day: Would he be available for lunch? She didn't know, but Phillips was welcome to wait until he arrived. It turned out that Tyndale had already made plans for lunch, but invited Phillips to join him. They headed out and came to a passage so narrow that only one could enter at a time. With a great show of deference Phillips insisted that the great translator precede him. Two imperial officers were waiting and Tyndale stepped into the trap. His days as a free man were over.

Tyndale spent one year and one hundred and thirty-five days in an impregnable prison just north of Brussels. He was held as an offender against the laws of the Low Countries. Because Tyndale was not a prisoner of the English crown, the efforts of Poyntz and other Englishmen pleading his release were in vain.

While Tyndale was a prisoner his nemesis Thomas More was executed for treason. Tyndale's own execution bears a tragic strain of irony. Unknown to Tyndale and shortly before his death, across the channel King Henry had granted permission for an English Bible — largely Tyndale's translation — to circulate among the people. The heartfelt wish Tyndale had confided to Vaughan years earlier had been fulfilled.

# 19

# The King James Bible

The Bible which King Henry permitted to circulate among the people was the first printed English Bible to contain the complete text of all the books of both the Old and New Testaments. The title-page bore the year 1535. By early the following year it was on the streets.

This was a sudden change in direction. Henry had a reputation for volatility — in one day he sent three reformers and three conservative Catholics to their death. But there was more to it than that. The English Bible during Henry's reign, and for the next few generations, was a pawn in a wider chess game — the evolution of the relationship between crown and church, and the protracted establishment of the Reformation in England. Henry wanted England to be a Catholic realm independent of the pope and Rome. He wished for an England neither Lutheran nor Roman Catholic.

The new archbishop looked with some favor upon the Reformation; he had married the niece of a leading figure of the Reformation in Germany. Arguing that the bishops were losing the battle to keep Lutheranism out of England, particularly with respect to the most blatant symbol and vanguard of the Reformation in England — Tyndale's translation of Scripture — the archbishop convinced the convocation of Canterbury that an English Bible for the people was inevitable. Hence, it was best that the bishops seize the initiative. The convocation resolved that the archbishop petition Henry to nominate a committee to translate Scripture into English.

Henry was agreeable, so the archbishop divided the task among several bishops and other learned men. It soon became clear that the hearts of these men were not in their work. Their efforts were so inferior the project was dropped. But there was at hand an English translation other than Tyndale's. It was presented to the king for his inspection and approval, and the king referred it to his advisors, as he was wont to do.

Time passed. Meanwhile Henry fell in love with the young, vivacious, and promiscuous Anne Boleyn. Anne's sister and mother had previously warmed the king's bed, much to his delight, but he found greater delight in Anne. So did many at the court. When a man roused Anne's desire — and it didn't take much by all accounts — she dropped a handkerchief at his feet as signal for a tryst.

Anne kept a luxurious vellum copy of an English translation of the New Testament in her bedchamber so that all who came might read. So enthralled was she with this new translation, she interceded with Henry to have it printed and placed in every church, that the people could read it. What Anne wished, the king was happy to grant.

Anne's New Testament and that which the king's advisors were inspecting for approval was one and the same. The king grew impatient. Why were they taking so long? What did they think of the translation? They found it full of faults. But was it heretical? Reluctant bishops answered with a grudging "no." With his customary impetuosity the king put an end to their dalliance: Then in God's name let it be given to the people, he said. The clergy had little choice but to comply. And so the English Bible went out to the people.

The man responsible for the new English translation was Miles Coverdale, who had helped Tyndale with his translation of the first five books of the Old Testament at the widow von Emersen's in Hamburg a few years earlier. In the preface to his Bible Coverdale acknowledged the work of five others, but wisely made no mention that Tyndale was one of these, for Henry was against Tyndale's translation. Coverdale dedicated his translation to the king, in terms sure to appeal to his ego. Henry ate it up.

The Coverdale Bible was printed on the continent, bound and distributed in England. Lacking sufficient knowledge of Greek and Hebrew, Coverdale made good use of other translations. For the New Testament, the book of Jonah, and the first five books of the Old Testament he used Tyndale's translation, making slight changes. For the remainder he used Luther's translation and a Swiss translation. As well, he had access to the Latin Vulgate and a new scholarly version of the Latin. Coverdale tended to stay with Luther for several books — here the English words he coined have a distinctly German flavor: "unoutspeakable," "handreaching," "righteousnessmaking," "deadburier." Then he stayed with the Swiss version for several books. Some sections show considerable original translation from the Latin. Despite this dog's breakfast approach, Coverdale's style was praised as smooth and melodious. His version of the Psalms was judged musical, its phrasing of great beauty, although in places awkward: "Thou shalt not need to be afraid for any bugs at night" (Psalm 91:5).

Anne Boleyn's days as queen were soon over. Henry was once again in love, but with another woman. With Anne's execution Coverdale's Bible ceased to be of great importance. Another English Bible, financed by London businessmen, was waiting in the wings. The archbishop requested this Bible be sold and read until the bishops presented a better translation, which, the archbishop quipped, would be the day after doomsday. The new Bible appeared in 1537 with the king's official license — an authorized edition of Scripture for the people.

This translation purported to be the work of Thomas Matthew, but "Thomas Matthew" was a pseudonym. The New Testament, the first five books of the Old Testament, Jonah, and Joshua to 2 Chronicles was Tyndale's. The rest of the Old Testament was Coverdale's. The whole was edited by John Rogers, a close associate of Tyndale at Antwerp. The manuscript for Joshua to 2 Chronicles had been in his custody since Tyndale's arrest, and Rogers felt obligated to get it to press as soon as possible. The initials "W.T." were printed at the end of Malachi, to give credit to Tyndale for the Old Testament.

Matthew's Bible was given an official revision, with Coverdale appointed editor. This so-called Great Bible was really still Tyndale's translation, with slight modification. Henry ordered the clergy to provide this Bible at a convenient place in churches for public reading. The clergy was to actively encourage reading, and was forbidden to discourage those who wished to read. The clergy dragged its heels. In remote areas where few parishioners could read the clergy kept the Bible out of sight. In central and prominent venues, however, there was no way to avoid the inevitable. London's bishop had six Bibles chained to pillars in his cathedral, over each of which was a placard exhorting people to read. And people did. In fact they often read aloud in competition with the ongoing church service. So this bishop and other clergymen petitioned the king to have the Bible removed from churches. Henry was getting on in years. He had gained weight and was in constant pain with an ulcerated leg. Becoming ever more paranoid and suspicious of those about him, the king was easily convinced that things were getting out of control. He had parliament ban the Old and New Testament in English, now known to be Tyndale's. Copies of the Great Bible were taken from churches and burned.

After Henry died the nation experienced a series of dizzying swings in religious climate. With each new monarch ships carrying reformers and reactionaries passed each other in the channel, as one group alternately fled to the continent while the other returned to safety in their native land. Immediately following Henry's reign, in Edward's first year as king the Bible was once again installed in every parish church. When Mary, Bloody

Mary, wore the crown the reformers' clock was set back. John Rogers was the first in a long line of three hundred to be martyred under her rule. Bibles were roasted at every corner. When Elizabeth became queen every church again had its Bible.

Meanwhile, a group of English exiles had gathered in Geneva to work on a new translation. In 1557 they produced a New Testament, and in 1560 a complete Bible, with many features of today's Bible. Unlike earlier Bibles, it was small and handy-sized, suitable for personal study. Earlier Bibles had been printed in a ponderous typeface known as black-letter (what we often mistakenly call "old English"), meant to imitate the hand lettering of manuscripts, but difficult to read. The Geneva Bible was printed in Roman type — used in books today — and was consequently much easier on the eyes. Words not found in the Greek, but added to make a smooth English translation, were printed in italics. (Italicized words we see in today's Bibles are not meant to be read with special emphasis — notice how often "is" and "are" appear in italics.) That strange mark found in many Bibles today, which looks like a reversed letter "P" with the head filled in, was used to designate paragraphs. Dividing the text into verses was something relatively new. The Hebrew Old Testament had been divided into verses by Rabbi Nathan in 1448. The first Bible to have the modern verse division in both testaments was Estienne's Vulgate of 1555. The Geneva Bible followed the verse division of the fourth edition of Robert Estienne's Greek New Testament published in Geneva six years earlier. One wit quipped that to get such awkward divisions Estienne must have marked his verses while bouncing around on horseback.

The Bible had been broken into chapters from very early times. The modern chapter-division — students and scholars needed a handy way of referring to specific passages — was reputedly the work of Stephen Langton, a scholar at the University of Paris and later archbishop of Canterbury and leader of the barons in the struggle which yielded the Magna Carta.

The text of the Geneva Old Testament was a decided improvement from what had gone before. Those parts not translated by Tyndale had not until this time been rendered into English directly from the Hebrew. The Geneva Bible became the Bible of preference in many English homes. It was the Bible of the Puritans; a copy used on the *Mayflower* by the Pilgrim Fathers has been preserved at Harvard University. An act of the Scottish parliament made it law for every household in that realm with a specified minimum income to own a copy. Homes were checked for compliance. Disobedience meant a fine of double the authorized subscription price. Borrowing a Bible ahead of the inspectors didn't work; Bibles had to bear the owner's name.

Observing the popularity of the Geneva Bible, the archbishop at that time, Matthew Parker, decided to replace the Great Bible with a new official Bible. Parker did much of the translation himself and acted as editor-in-chief to the bishops and scholars he assigned sections of the work. They retained the text of the Great Bible except where it deviated from the original Greek or Hebrew. Because the bishops' knowledge of Hebrew was minimal they used recent Latin translations of the Hebrew. The Bishops' Bible, as it came to be known, was not a popular success. Even the queen refused to give it special preference.

A few months after he became king of England James I summoned churchmen and theologians to Hampton Court to hear complaints concerning religious matters. A Puritan leader seized this opportunity to propose a new official Bible. The bishop of London demurred; at this rate, he quipped, every individual would soon have his own version of Scripture. But the king liked the proposal. James was well educated and had acquired a taste for languages, literature, and theology. Before the age of ten he could read the Latin Bible and translate it into French and English. A few years later he put thirty psalms into meter. The king insisted that all existing English translations of the Bible were unsatisfactory, and lest the Puritan leader think he had won the day, added that he found the Geneva Bible the least satisfactory of all.

With great enthusiasm the king set about organizing the project. Fifty-four learned men would be divided into six groups, each with a designated allotment of translation. The Bishops' Bible was the foundation text, to be as little altered as necessary. In places where they better agreed with the Greek and Hebrew originals the following translations were to be used: Tyndale's, Matthew's, Coverdale's, the Great Bible, the Geneva Bible.

Each individual within a group presented his own text. Then the group met and compared notes, eventually agreeing on a final draft. Once a book was completed the group sent their draft to the other groups for appraisal. The other groups noted any problems and returned the draft. If the group responsible for that book insisted upon their original translation the matter was referred to a special committee, consisting of two members from each of the six groups, which made the final revisions. If there was a persistent problem or an obscurity in the text an outside scholar was consulted. When a final draft was agreed upon, comments were solicited from learned members of the clergy.

The project was completed in 1611. The resulting King James Version of the Bible was a scholarly production. There is no record of a decree ordaining its use; it replaced the Bishops' Bible as the official Bible simply because the latter ceased to be printed. It has come to be known as the Authorized Version even though it was never authorized in any strict sense and never actually received King James's blessing. Although the King James Version did not immediately displace the Geneva Bible in the hearts of the people, it did so within a few generations. The majesty of its wording and the music of its rhythm have endeared it to Christians down through the centuries.

As the King James Version was reprinted embarrassing errors occurred. There was the so-called "Wicked Bible"—"Thou shalt commit adultery" (instead of "Thou shalt not commit adultery"). Another printing had "the unrighteous shall inherit the kingdom of God." In still others: "purge your conscience from good works" (instead of "dead works"); "Christ condemneth the poor widow" (instead of "commendeth"). As the years went by small points of spelling and punctuation were brought up to date, but the text remains a direct descendant of Tyndale's translation.

The King James Version was a tremendous accomplishment textually and politically. But it was suspect among English Catholics who remained loyal to Rome. Roman Catholics who fled to the continent from England during the reign of Queen Elizabeth founded a college at Douai. Here a Roman Catholic English translation was fashioned—the Rheims-Douai Bible—based on the Latin Vulgate, authorized by the Council of Trent.

The original Rheims-Douai Bible was full of latinisms. The attempt to render a literal translation of the Latin often resulted in sheer unintelligibility (the Latin "exinanivit" was rendered "he exinanited himself"); many words and phrases were meaningful only to those who knew the Latin. Such jarring wording grated on the ears of even the staunchest Roman Catholics. In the mid-eighteenth century the Rheims-Douai Bible was drastically revised by Richard Challoner, yielding a virtually new text. But critics shunned this version—it contained neither a shred of imagination, nor a trace of poetry. Little wonder English-speaking Roman Catholics were unenthusiastic Bible readers.

# 20

# Man on a Mission

The King James Bible was a wonderful accomplishment; but English and other vernacular translations of the New Testament were all based on Erasmus's Greek text of the New Testament, the so-called "received text." In the eighteenth century Edward Gibbon, author of the celebrated *The Decline and Fall of the Roman Empire*, raised the issue of the quality of Erasmus's text. He claimed that manuscripts Erasmus had used to derive his text were corrupt; they had long before been tampered with in order to win controversies with heretics. He cited 1 John 5:7–8, where Erasmus's text contained words from manuscripts supporting the doctrine of the trinity (Erasmus discussed this point in his notes), a doctrine evolved much later than the original text had been written. Issues of this nature had for some time been politely discussed within scholarly circles. But now a famous historian was bringing this delicate matter before the public with serious implications. What did this say about the authenticity of Scripture? If some passages were suspect, perhaps there were others. Where would it end?

It got worse. A few generations later German theologians claimed the Bible was not historically factual. This scandalized the devout. Among their number was a young lecturer at the University of Leipzig whose name, Lobegott Friedrich Constantin Tischendorf, reflected the piety of his Lutheran parents.

Tischendorf was a ball of energy. As a student he had won academic prizes, written poetry, and had a novel published. Once he set his mind on something he did not let up, and now he set his mind on a quest for the authentic biblical text. He was sure that somewhere in the dusty corners of old libraries were ancient and forgotten manuscripts which would silence the critics. He was determined to find them, and use them to reconstruct, if possible, the text of the Bible as it had originally been written.

It seemed incredible to Tischendorf that for three hundred years a text of the New Testament — based upon manuscripts which happened to be immediately available to one man — had been so often reprinted, as if it were somehow sacred. He insisted this no longer be tolerated. There was reason to doubt that the present text represented anything like what the apostles had written fifteen centuries previous to Erasmus's time. Newly discovered earlier biblical manuscripts, quotations of the church Fathers, and other evidence proved that the original text of the apostles' writings, copied, recopied, and multiplied over the centuries had been seriously altered.

A cursory examination of manuscripts like the Book of Durrow, the Cathach, and the Book of Kells illustrates Tischendorf's point. The Book of Kells is full of spelling and grammatical errors, suggesting that little care went into the textual aspects of its production. In places its text is sheer jumbled nonsense.

To find the authentic text — the words which the apostles had originally written or dictated — Tischendorf needed to collect early biblical manuscripts, the earlier the better, before the text had been so badly corrupted by scribal error and intentional changes. He began his quest by building a personal library which eventually counted over three thousand volumes. Included in his collection were copies of the first and second editions of Erasmus's Greek New Testament and a copy of the first edition of Luther's German translation of the New Testament. Tischendorf studied paleography and the history of the development of calligraphy in order to date manuscripts.

Scholars had recently come upon much earlier manuscripts than the few relatively recent manuscripts Erasmus had used. The fifth-century Codex Alexandrinus, once presented to King Charles 1 of England, was kept in the British Museum. The sixth-century Codex Claromontanus was housed in the Bibliothèque Nationale in Paris. Both manuscripts lacked considerable portions of text: Codex Alexandrinus, most of the book of Matthew and numerous other passages; Codex Claromontanus, the gospels and Acts and other books of the New Testament and all of the Old Testament.

Codex Ephraemi was a twelfth-century Greek transcription of treatises and sermons by Saint Ephraem. But close inspection revealed a barely visible impression of what appeared to be biblical text. In the Middle Ages, because vellum was scarce and costly, it was often reused. In this case a scribe had scraped off the words of Scripture in order to copy those of Ephraem. Tischendorf's first major accomplishment was to decipher the underlying biblical text of Codex Ephraemi. The story is told that Tischendorf's mother had seen a blind man while pregnant with Constantin. She entreated God not to allow her baby to be born blind. As a result his eyesight was keener than average — so keen that he was able to discern the washed-out writing of the famous codex. In fact, Tischendorf used a chemical reagent to bring out the original fifth-century biblical text. Unfortunately the medieval scribe who recorded the sermons of Ephraem wrote upon scattered leaves from the Bible, so much of the text was missing.

Codex Vaticanus dates from the middle of the fourth century. It had been catalogued in the Vatican library in 1475. Just a generation before Tischendorf's time, before its value was fully realized, Napoleon had carried it off to Paris. Now it was back in the Vatican library, but Vatican authorities refused to let anyone study it closely. Anyone. Even scholars like Tischendorf. After pleading, Tischendorf was allowed a six-hour peek at the treasured codex. Two years later a British scholar had his pockets searched for writing materials, then two clerics stood beside him and snatched the codex away if his eyes fastened upon any passage for too long.

Tischendorf decided to have another look two decades after his initial attempt. A few years previously a cardinal had published two editions of Codex Vaticanus, but they differed so much as to be virtually useless. This time Tischendorf was somewhat less than honest about his intentions. He was now a famous textual scholar. Riding on his reputation he secured permission to examine problematic passages. Left alone with the codex for three hours a day, he began feverishly to make a copy. On the eighth day he was caught in the act. But Tischendorf was a determined man. His flagrant breach of etiquette notwithstanding, he was able to procure another six days. The following year he published his own edition of the codex.

This incident speaks volumes about Tischendorf's character. He simply would not allow others to frustrate his efforts. Nor did he permit moral scruples to get in his way. This would soon be all too clear. Yet if Tischendorf's actions at times lacked propriety, in this he was not alone amongst those in quest of ancient biblical manuscripts. Stimulated by Erasmus's notes, individuals were ransacking monasteries everywhere, and their methods were not always beyond reproach. They often showed great disdain for the monks, even bragging about unsavory practices. An employee of the British Museum boasted that he had gotten a blind abbot drunk in order to steal his books.

In Egypt is a mountain believed to be the scene of Moses's reception of the Ten Commandments, the location of the burning bush, and Elijah's experience of the "still small voice." The Desert Fathers of Egypt, among the first Christian monks, were drawn to this holy site. To protect these monks from marauding Saracens the emperor Justinian built St. Catherine's monastery at the base of the mountain in the sixth century. This lonely bastion of Christianity deep in the heart of Muslim territory, even with its eighty-foot walls, would likely not have prevailed against the Muslim conquest of the Holy Land in the centuries just after the death of their prophet Mohammed had not its monks been politically astute and demonstrated great sophistication in the ways of their fellow men. They bent with the winds. Legend has it that they sent a delegation to Mohammed himself to beg for protection. He granted their request and even visited the monastery. To this day pilgrims are shown the imprint of his camel's hoof in a rock. At a time of great political tension the monks built a mosque within the walls of their institution, hoping that the sight of a minaret would discourage attack by militant Muslims. Over the years this mosque served as a place of worship for the monastery's Muslim servants.

Thanks to the foresight of the monks St. Catherine's is the oldest continuously inhabited cloister in the Christian world. The monastery has had its ups and downs. In the fourteenth century it supported four hundred monks. But a few centuries later a French visitor was hoisted over the walls by rope and pulley and descended to find only a single monk. And *he* was on the verge of starvation.

Over the centuries the monastery at the base of Mount Sinai accumulated treasures of great religious value. Within its walls at one time was a bush reputed to be that in which God had appeared to Moses, the bush which burned without being consumed. But by the thirteenth century Christian pilgrims had divided it up for relics. In the library were over three thousand ancient manuscripts, many of which were gifts, in Greek, Syriac, and other oriental languages. Only the Vatican library had a larger collection of this nature.

Ancient and renowned, the monastery at the base of Mount Sinai attracted attention. Surely upon its dusty shelves were undiscovered treasures. Yet the first reports were not auspicious. In the mid-eighteenth century a British bishop found nothing of value among St. Catherine's vast assortment of old manuscripts. Another visitor was told there were only three Bibles in the monastery, and came away empty-handed. Hearing this, many who might have gone to St. Catherine's were discouraged from making the long and arduous journey to the foot of Mount Sinai. Why go, only to be disappointed?

A few were not deterred. One visitor took away five manuscripts. By persevering and rummaging around he had found a library of two hundred volumes. Sentiment reversed, and once again St. Catherine's topped the list of monasteries to be searched. A few years later a visitor reported that the library held fifteen hundred Greek and seven hundred Arabic manuscripts, but added that the monks kept it closed to Westerners. Many felt that the treasures of the library were wasted upon the monks. Visitors were positively indignant when the monks refused to let them remove manuscripts without compensation. One woman was outraged that an Englishman's offer to purchase the oldest biblical manuscript in the monks' possession was refused. Such a ridiculously high amount (actually a mere 300 pounds), she fumed, would give these stupid monks the mistaken impression they had something of immense value.

The monastery at Mount Sinai would be Tischendorf's next destination. His port of landing in Egypt was the fabled city of Alexandria. From there he took a small ship up the Nile to Cairo where was located a daughter house of St. Catherine's. Tischendorf wasted no time on formalities: Did they have any manuscripts in Cairo? No, they were all in the library at Mount Sinai. Tischendorf persisted. What about this cupboard? What's in it? They'd have a look. It took half an hour to find the key. Finally the cupboard door swung open. The shelves were stuffed with manuscripts. What treasures must await at the real trove in Mount Sinai?

The burning sun of the desert made it necessary to set out before dawn each day. From ten in the morning until five in the afternoon the travelers rested in the shade of their tents. Then they journeyed on for another six hours. On the twelfth day a speck of lush green vegetation and the inviting sight of the monastery were visible in the distance amidst arid rocky wasteland. The camels were prodded to a run. When Tischendorf arrived at the monastery he placed a letter of introduction into a basket lowered over the wall by the monks. Time ticked slowly as he tensely awaited a response. At last the rope descended once more, this time with a crossbar attached to draw up the small group.

Tischendorf assumed the same religious superiority toward his hosts as had previous Western visitors— particularly Protestants— and like those before him made little effort to understand the religious perspective of the monks or to bridge the cultural gap between East and West. He thought the monks lazy and without serious intellectual endeavor. He disdained their ridiculous legends and empty meaningless existence. He would later write about his distrust: In their faces he read malice and evil. He was particularly suspicious of the superior, whose expression gave evidence of duplicity.

But practical judiciousness dictated that he at least demonstrate a tolerable respect for the librarian. He so wheedled his way into this man's good graces that the librarian allowed him to examine manuscripts at his leisure in his own room. Then one day it happened — the discovery which would guarantee his fame. In the middle of the great hall was a large wide basket full of old parchments. What was in the basket? asked Tischendorf. The librarian replied that these were papers that had mildewed and were to be burned. Two similar collections had already met the same fate. Could Tischendorf look among the papers in the basket? By all means, said the librarian. Tischendorf's eyes must have widened when he found among this refuse several pages of an Old Testament manuscript in Greek. The writing appeared to be quite ancient, perhaps older than anything Tischendorf had ever seen. Tischendorf was allowed to take home 43 of the 129 parchments he found. Would his show of interest awaken the monks to their potential value, and preclude further visits?

Tischendorf scurried back to Leipzig with his haul and rushed to publish his findings. But the cagey professor had no intention of giving away any secrets. He did not reveal where he had discovered the documents; nor did he disclose that there were more where they had come from. He knew the British had the finances to purchase any manuscripts they could lay their hands on. Tischendorf was not about to share. He wanted whatever might remain at Mount Sinai for himself. He wanted all the fame, and all the glory. When it came to scholarly rivalry Tischendorf pulled no punches.

As a result of his discovery Tischendorf was made extraordinary professor at Leipzig. He continued to publish. He was famous, but he still wanted to procure the remainder of the sacred parchments. Since attempts to purchase these documents from a distance failed, he would have to return to St. Catherine's.

A second trip proved fruitless. There was no sign of the remaining parchments. Had someone beaten him to it? Or were the monks holding out? Tischendorf came away with only a single fragment of manuscript which had been used as a bookmark. It had writing on both sides—lines from Genesis. He was sure that this was from the same manuscript as the other forty-three pieces.

Years passed before Tischendorf returned to Mount Sinai, this time funded by the czar of Russia. In return he promised all his discoveries to the czar. But his third stay at St. Catherine's showed every sign of being as unprofitable as the previous trip, and preparations had already been made for his return home when he went for a fortuitous walk with one of the monks. The monk had been reading the Greek Old Testament. Did Tischendorf want to have a look at it? The monk went to the corner of his cell and took down a package wrapped in red cloth. He unwrapped the cloth ... the missing parchments, and more!

Tischendorf assessed the contents of the package. Not only did it contain the complete Old Testament, but also the New Testament, and two pieces of early Christian literature unknown in the Greek. Here in his hand was what was probably the most precious biblical manuscript material in existence, documents older and more important than anything he had seen in his twenty years of study.

Clearly Tischendorf must have this manuscript. The world must have it. But how? Surely the abbot would refuse. The only recourse was to bribe the monk. But the monk wouldn't budge. It wasn't his to give. Tischendorf would have to resort to the abbot after all. But the abbot was not at Mount Sinai; he was in Cairo on his way to Constantinople. Tischendorf hastened to Cairo, caught up with the abbot before he left, and made his plea. If the manuscript was brought to Cairo could he copy it there? Yes, he could. A Bedouin was dispatched, and returned with the precious material in twelve days. Then, with the help of two other individuals, Tischendorf copied all of the 110,000 lines of the manuscript, including the 12,000 alterations of later correctors, in a bare two months' time. In stifling heat.

Tischendorf was still not satisfied. He wanted the manuscript. He saw an opening. The archbishop of Sinai had recently died and it was time to choose another archbishop. The monks had made their choice but their selection had to be consecrated by the patriarch of Jerusalem, who was proving stubborn. If Tischendorf could enlist the support of the czar, the most powerful figure in Orthodox Christendom, for the monks' favored candidate, would they let him take the manuscript to Russia as a present for the czar? The monks agreed, but their decision would have to be ratified by an archbishop and there wasn't one.

Tischendorf continued to press, so the monks said he could borrow the manuscript temporarily in order to produce a facsimile edition in Russia. He took the manuscript to Russia, presented it to the czar, and a facsimile edition was published. Meanwhile the favored archbishop was in place. Now the czar would be able to keep the manuscript, just as Tischendorf had planned. But wait. The new archbishop insisted that the manuscript had only been loaned. This put Tischendorf in an embarrassing position. The manuscript had brought him further fame and fortune — his daughter was now a godchild of the sister-in-law of the czar — and the manuscript was on exhibition in the Imperial Public Library. Now he had to ask for it back? After presenting it as a gift? How could he do that?

Then Lady Luck smiled on Tischendorf. The Russians offered to support the monks' choice for yet another new archbishop provided they could purchase the manuscript for a specified low price. The deal went through. Tischendorf was off the hook. But the monks were not pleased. They had lost the codex. In its place they had one of the facsimile copies, presented as a gift before the Russians were aware that their ownership of the original was dubious. Today on prominent display at St. Catherine's monastery is a photocopy of Tischendorf's letter stating that he had received the manuscript as a loan and would return it to the monastery "at its first request."

The monks got a modicum of temporary satisfaction from a rather amusing incident. A certain enterprising Greek had fashioned a career selling forged manuscripts. Not only was he a highly skilled forger, he mixed genuine documents with his forgeries to further confuse potential purchasers. The Greek proclaimed that Tischendorf had been duped, that the manuscript he had taken from St. Catherine's was one of the Greek's forgeries, and a monk was willing to testify that he had witnessed the forgery. People believed the Greek. They knew, often from bitter experience, of the Greek's reputation and his skill at calligraphy. Everyone had a laugh at Tischendorf's expense. Eventually the manuscript was proven to be authentic, but not before Tischendorf had endured extensive embarrassment.

Tischendorf's prized manuscript ended up in the British Museum — after the revolution of 1917 the Russians were in desperate need of money and were more than willing to unload the document. The British acquisition cost 100,000 pounds, half raised through public subscription.

Tischendorf had greatly advanced the quest for the authentic text of the Bible. He produced twenty improved editions of the Greek New Testament, and edited and published the texts of seventeen codices. Above all he is remembered for bringing to the light of day the oldest manuscript yet discovered of a fairly complete Bible. Designated manuscript #43725 in the British Library in London, Codex Sinaiticus contains the oldest known complete text of the Greek New Testament. Much of the Old Testament is lacking. The manuscript dates from the mid-fourth century. No one knows how it got to the monastery at Mount Sinai, nor where it originated. Was Codex Sinaiticus, perhaps, one of the fifty copies of the Bible in codex form ordered by the emperor Constantine in the year 331 to be produced in the scriptorium at Caesarea?

# 21

# A Young Photographer

February, 1948. As the two men from the Syrian Orthodox Monastery of St. Mark unrolled the cream-colored leather, John Trever might well have recalled the story of Tischendorf at St. Catherine's. He must have experienced Tischendorf's excitement and almost disbelief at what appeared to be ancient writing, while at the same time not revealing any suspicion that these might be immensely valuable documents.

Trevor was acting director of the American School of Oriental Research in Jerusalem for the two weeks the regular director was away. He had set up an appointment to see the men from the monastery in response to a request the day before. The monastery's librarian had been organizing its collection of rare books for cataloguing when he came upon some scrolls in ancient Hebrew which had been in the monastery for forty years. Would Trever supply some information concerning the scrolls?

After a cursory look at the four scrolls Trever cautioned that he couldn't give the men an immediate opinion. Could he photograph the scrolls? Perhaps, but that decision would have to be made by the monks' superior. They let Trever copy a few lines from the manuscripts, which he did.

After the men left, Trever compared the lines he had copied with examples of paleography from old Hebrew manuscripts. Not only were the scrolls in an ancient hand, the lines he had copied were from the biblical book of Isaiah. But there were many unanswered questions: Did the scroll contain the whole book of Isaiah, or just part? Was this manuscript as ancient as it appeared? Could an ancient manuscript possibly be in such pristine condition? Or was it a recent copy, even a forgery...?

The next day Trever hastened to visit St. Mark's. He was welcomed with customary local hospitality and then got down to business. Could he photograph the scrolls? The metropolitan (similar to a Western archbishop), Athanasius Yeshue Samuel, demurred. They didn't normally permit this; they'd had some unfortunate experiences. Trever explained why he thought photographing the scrolls was necessary: The opinion of one young unknown student concerning the age of the scrolls would carry little weight. Published photographs of the manuscripts would allow renowned scholars to assess their value.

The metropolitan wouldn't budge. Had the metropolitan heard the story of Tischendorf and Codex Sinaiticus, and how after publication it was worth half a million dollars? Trever asked. Indeed he had. As a promising and capable scholar the metropolitan had been sent as a young priest to search out the library of St. Catherine's monastery — the very locus of Tischendorf's discoveries — in the hope of finding ancient Syriac manuscripts. How soon could the scrolls be photographed? Samuel asked the young man.

Trever took another look at the manuscripts before leaving. Perhaps the monks had been fooled, and the manuscripts were forgeries. Trever looked for the corrections found in all genuine manuscripts. He found them. And even better, they were in different hands and in different inks, and many were in later forms of writing. He looked for more evidence, and found several places where the scrolls had been repaired, a patch here, a tear sewn up there. If the scrolls were forged, the forger was indeed a craftsman. Trever was convinced the manuscripts were genuine.

Trever was the right man in the right place at the right time. He was in the middle of a one-year fellowship with the American School of Oriental Research in Jerusalem. In competition with several others he had won the chance to study in the land of the Bible. Despite the increasingly tense political situation in the Middle East it was an opportunity a young man on the threshold of his career as American lecturer in Old Testament could not turn down. Trever's project was to study the flora of the Holy Land as preparation for a course in biblical backgrounds. His hobby of photography would prove extremely useful as he gathered information about the trees mentioned in the Bible. He had been introduced to the camera at age twelve; it was love at first sight. Techniques he developed for photographing printed matter both in black-and-white and in color (for professors' lecture slides) helped finance his college tuition. He would use these techniques to photograph the scrolls.

Trever was preparing to photograph the scrolls back at the American school when the power went out. This was a common occurrence. He spent many evenings in darkness watching tracer bullets silhouette nearby buildings. The British mandate over Palestine, set up after the First World War, was about to run out, and Jews and Arabs were engaged in pitched battle to stake out territory before the British departed. Trever had narrowly missed being killed while out walking; five minutes later a loaded bus was bombed at the same spot, killing more than a dozen people.

The political tension and military state of emergency in Jerusalem meant that all supplies were limited. Trever had to ration his materials; he could not waste film and chemicals on too many test shots. Electricians arrived. The lights went on, then off again. It was nerve-wracking. Finally the lights stayed on. Trever hoped everything would remain in order. He must finish the job before the metropolitan changed his mind. He worked feverishly, solving numerous technical problems. Floodlights gave results superior to natural light. Trever proved a master of his craft. To this day his photographs remain among the finest for such subject matter.

But his work was not done. The American doyen of Hebrew paleography William Foxwell Albright had written about a Hebrew manuscript from the second half of the second century B.C. Trever looked up the article; when he compared the handwriting of the scrolls to samples presented in Albright's article he believed he was in possession of the oldest biblical manuscript yet discovered. He dashed off some sample prints to Albright.

In a few weeks Trever's hopes were realized. Albright wrote back sending his heartiest congratulations. He confirmed that Trever's manuscript was the greatest discovery of modern times, a script perhaps as old as the third century B.C., although considering the embryonic state of Hebrew paleography he preferred the more conservative estimate of 100 B.C.

There was more good news. Trever had been told that the scrolls were purchased from Bedouin forty years earlier. The Bedouin had found the scrolls in a jar in a cave and had taken two jars from the cave to use for carrying water. Trever knew enough about archaeology to know that pottery was often used for dating a site. Was there any chance the Bedouin and the jars could be located? The monks would try. But first they had something to confess. They had been somewhat less than truthful up to this point because they were not sure how much Trever could be trusted. The time had come to make amends. That bit about the forty years was pure fabrication; the scrolls had been purchased the previous August. A priest from the monastery had seen the cave where the Bedouin had discovered the manuscripts. In it were fragments of jars and scrolls. The monks had been trying to locate the two jars which the Bedouin had removed, but with no success. Metropolitan Samuel proposed that Trever accompany them on a visit to the cave.

Meanwhile the political situation was becoming ever more tense. The American consul general advised those at the American school to leave the country while they still could. It was rumored that their water supply had been poisoned. Trever had a bad scare. Returning home from a visit to the metropolitan, he was crossing an open field when bullets began zinging over his head. A few days earlier a woman on her way to church had been shot at the same location. Trever ran to the nearest shelter with some boys, waited for things to subside, and with his heart in his throat made a dash for the American school. He made it. *This* time.

Metropolitan Samuel learned from the Bedouin that the area around the cave was occupied by the Jewish army. The expedition would have to be abandoned until peace was restored. The metropolitan deposited the scrolls in a bank vault in Beirut. St. Mark's was too vulnerable; it might be bombed and catch fire. Indeed, shortly thereafter it was badly damaged.

When the director of the American school returned, an agreement was reached. The American Schools of Oriental Research would have sole right to publish the scrolls for a limited time. The scrolls would remain the property of Metropolitan Samuel. In consultation with Samuel the director drafted a news release regarding the scrolls, and dispatched it to the United States.

Trever accepted a position in the United States and was soon on his way home. As the lumbering Middle East Airlines DC-3 gained altitude over the deep blue of the Mediterranean, and the Sea of Galilee and the mountain ranges of Lebanon passed into the distance, Trever must have felt the quiet satisfaction of a job well done.

# 22

# Discovery

Exactly two weeks after Trever's finding had been flashed around the world the papers carried the stunning report that more scrolls had turned up. Eleazar Sukenik, professor of Archaeology at the Hebrew University in Jerusalem, had purchased them on behalf of his institution.

Late in 1946 or early in the next year — accounts vary — three Bedouin moved their goats and sheep into an area at the northwestern corner of the Dead Sea, as they did every year. One day the youngest of the men tossed a stone into a cave high up on a rocky cliff and heard the tinkling of breaking earthenware. Later, while his elder cousins slept, his curiosity got the best of him and he decided to see what was in the cave. He climbed the craggy face of the cliff and squeezed through the narrow opening of the cave. As his eyes grew accustomed to the darkness he saw ten jars jutting out from a rubble of broken pottery and fallen rocks. All but two of the jars were empty. Of the two one contained reddish earth and some scrolls. The lad took three scrolls with him as he left the cave. His cousins were angry that he had sneaked off on his own. Had he found gold and hidden it? They dreamed that someday they would find an ancient cache of gold in the wilderness. The Bedouin returned to the cave. There was no gold but they took two of the jars.

The two elder Bedouin took the scrolls and the jars to an antiquities dealer in Bethlehem, hoping to sell them for a small sum. Another dealer he consulted suspected the scrolls had been stolen from a synagogue, so he purchased the jars but told the Bedouin they would have to market the scrolls elsewhere. The Bedouin went from dealer to dealer, but no one recognized the strange form of writing on the scrolls. Maybe it's Syriac; try to find a dealer who knows Syriac and can tell you if these scrolls have any value, one dealer suggested. Eventually they met a Syrian Orthodox Christian named Shaya who did business with Bedouin. Shaya took them to shop owner Khalil Iskander Shahin, better known as Kando. Shaya and Kando would try to sell the scrolls. The Bedouin would receive two-thirds of the proceeds.

The obvious place to start was the Syrian Orthodox Church which used Syriac in its liturgy. So Shaya and Kando tore some pieces off the scrolls and took them to Metropolitan Athanasius Yeshue Samuel. He was interested. Could he see the scrolls? Kando smelled money. He told Shaya to go out with the Bedouin and see if the cave held any more scrolls. Digging into the dirt on the bottom of the cave they found four more scrolls.

Samuel came close to missing out on the scrolls. When Shaya and the Bedouin arrived at the gate of St. Mark's monastery with three of the scrolls dug from the bottom of the cave — the wily Kando suggested they hold the others back for future bargaining — the priest who met them was so repulsed by the shabby appearance of the Bedouin he turned them away, not realizing that Samuel had arranged for them to come. Returning through town they met a Jewish dealer who wanted to buy the scrolls. Would they follow him to his shop where he could pay them? Shaya told the Bedouin it was a trick. The dealer was going to turn them over to government authorities and they would be put in jail, because it was illegal to sell antiquities without official sanction. But the Bedouin, miffed at their treatment at St. Mark's, were willing to take the risk. They sold the three scrolls to the Jewish antiquities dealer for about thirty dollars along with two jars at eighty cents apiece.

With the help of an intermediary the three scrolls and the two jars were purchased by Eleazar Sukenik. Unlike others before him, Sukenik was an expert in paleography and immediately recognized their value.

Meanwhile Metropolitan Samuel arranged another meeting with the Bedouin and Shaya. Samuel purchased one of the scrolls dug out from the bottom of the cave, along with the original three, for $250. The young man who had tossed the stone and discovered what would be known as the Dead Sea Scrolls ended up with a rifle and a wife as his share of the profit.

Samuel spent considerable time trying to get an accurate appraisal of his new possessions. He tirelessly showed the scrolls to people he expected would know the age and value of the manuscripts — professors, archaeologists, librarians, scholars. They told Samuel that the scrolls were only a few centuries old and of little value; one said they were not worth a shilling. Samuel thought that perhaps the manuscripts came from the time of Christ. If Samuel were right, the experts scoffed, a table loaded with pound notes could not purchase them. This image only whetted Samuel's appetite.

Samuel went to the United States, sure that in this land of plenty he would find a buyer. It was soon rumored that he wanted one million dollars. But did he have clear title to the scrolls? Sukenik claimed that they belonged to Israel as part of Jewish heritage, and according to antiquities laws must be returned to the country of origin. He launched a campaign of letters to any person or institution he thought a potential purchaser, warning that the transaction would be illegal. Sukenik was not alone. The director of the Department of Antiquities in the new nation of Jordan, where the scrolls had been discovered, wanted complete control of scrolls and fragments thereof. "Partners" of Samuel began to pop up, claiming part ownership. All of which made potential purchasers extremely nervous.

On June 1, 1954, an inconspicuous ad appeared in the classified section of *The Wall Street Journal* among advertisements for welding equipment and rental units. With the heading "miscellaneous for sale," it said that four Dead Sea Scrolls—biblical manuscripts dating back to at least 200 B.C.—were for sale, and suggested they would be an ideal gift to an educational or religious institution. There was a box number at *The Wall Street Journal* for replies. The ad had been submitted by Metropolitan Samuel. After several years of displaying the scrolls and finding no buyers he was getting desperate.

Sukenik's son—Sukenik himself had died a year earlier—happened to be in New York at the time and someone drew his attention to the ad. Through intermediaries—including a mysterious "Mr. Green," later revealed to be a Jewish professor—he secretly negotiated the purchase of the scrolls for the Hebrew University of Jerusalem and the state of Israel. The scrolls were removed from a vault in the basement of the Waldorf Astoria and sent to Israel one at a time, each with a special code for tracking. Details of the transaction were kept secret for some time. Samuel had finally gotten a good price for the scrolls—$250,000, one thousand times what he had paid for them. It was worth all the trouble he had taken.

The seventh scroll, part of the Mr. Green purchase, was described as a wet cigar in appearance. It was badly decayed and required special care and technique to unravel. Nevertheless, its contents were soon revealed to the scholarly community. Today all seven scrolls are on display at the Shrine of the Book in the Israel Museum. The elder Sukenik's commentary on the three scrolls he had purchased was published posthumously.

# 23

# Ancient Treasure

It was almost two full years after the first scrolls had been discovered that Gerald Lankester Harding read about it in the *Bulletin of the American Schools of Oriental Research*. News traveled slowly in the Middle East. It was November, and only now was the April issue available. As director of the Jordanian Department of Antiquities and curator of the Palestine Archaeological Museum (known locally as the Rockefeller), Harding was responsible for monitoring archaeological interests in a new political geography.

Harding reckoned there might be more scrolls, undiscovered or discovered. It was important to find these before they were broken up by shady and unscrupulous dealers or lost completely to scholarship through deterioration or private collections. Archaeological discoveries were the sole property of the state in which they occurred. This had been the law under the British mandate, and remained the law under the governments of the new nations of Jordan and Israel. But in the existing urgent and chaotic political situation this law was not of pressing concern. A black market had developed and would remain. Harding was a lean and practical man. He dealt with what was, not with what might or should be. He would deal with the market as it existed, meet its contacts, and offer a fair price, no questions asked. He needed to proclaim an open and orderly market, to encourage those with the goods to come forward and sell.

This was a wise decision. Things were happening which would make a man in Harding's position cry. It later came out that Kando, fearing discovery of his heretofore illegal dealings, buried some of the largest manuscript fragments from the cave in his back yard. Here the soil was much different from the dry dust of the cave in which they had lain for centuries. When Kando went to retrieve his fragments they had turned to lumps of sticky glue.

First Harding turned his attention to the cave where the seven scrolls had been found. The article he read did not specify its location so he sent Yusif Saad out to sniff around. Moving about in Jerusalem was almost suicidal; Saad had to dodge from point to point to avoid being hit with gunfire. Nevertheless, he persevered. He went to the American school, then to St. Mark's. Here he got no more than a hint of the location of the cave before Shaya stepped in and prevented further disclosure.

Saad decided Shaya was his man. He was certain Shaya could be bought for a price. Saad argued, cajoled, bullied. No luck. Shaya didn't budge. The last thing he needed was officials poking their noses into his private business. He had been mining the cave by night, and had removed an entire section of cliff face for easy access. To this day some insist that he found scrolls yet to be seen by the scholarly community.

Then out of the blue, some help. A well-educated officer of the United Nations Truce Supervision Organization who had read of the scrolls approached Father Roland de Vaux, director of the École Biblique et Archéologique in Jerusalem. If the officer could locate the cave would de Vaux assume the role of technical director of excavations, thereby making the enterprise legitimate? Yes, he would. The officer then contacted a military commander who in turn phoned Harding. With Harding's approval a military team which included some Bedouin was assembled. Using what little information Saad had gleaned as a starting point, they scouted the cliffs south from the end of the road to the Dead Sea. Three days later they met with success. In a few weeks de Vaux was on site and official excavation began.

They found pieces of pottery from more than forty jars, and fragments of about seventy manuscripts. The damage caused by illegal excavation was irreparable; proper stratification was impossible. The search would now be for whatever scrolls and fragments had been removed.

This was Saad's next assignment. A little bit of luck and much persistence yielded Kando's name. Kando could tell him what he needed to know. The journey to Kando in Bethlehem was half a day, by donkey. Saad took two museum guards with him. If anyone suspected he was connected with the authorities word would quickly spread and he would learn nothing, so at the outskirts of Bethlehem he left the other men with the animals and proceeded into town on foot by himself. In the narrow streets of a city cut off from the central government he must have felt very alone and unprotected. Bethlehem was a nest of shady characters, free from the hand of the law. Saad would have been aware that he was on their turf, with no easy retreat. He was interfering where there was fast money to be made; he could easily disappear and never be heard from again.

## 23. Ancient Treasure

Where might he find Kando? Saad pushed open the door pointed out to him. His eyes accustomed to the bright outdoors, he could see nothing at first. Then he spotted two men at the back watching him suspiciously. He approached the men and got straight to business: He'd been told he could find Kando here, that Kando knew about some scrolls found in a cave. At this, one of the men attacked him, shouting obscenities, calling him a traitor, a government spy. Meanwhile the other man, probably Kando, slipped out.

Saad could flee back to Jerusalem, setting a new Bethlehem-to-Jerusalem record by donkey — to remain could be dangerous. But Kando was his only reference point; he must stay and see if he could gain Kando's confidence.

He stayed and eventually was able to convince Kando that he could furnish a legal, safe, and reliable market for any scrolls or fragments that Kando might acquire. Better still, he would pay well. Kando said he'd be in touch. Several weeks later he showed up in Jerusalem with a small fragment. Was there more like this? Yes, but first he'd like to know who Saad was working for. An English professor. Then tell the professor to come to Jericho at such-and-such a time with plenty of money and Kando will deal.

Harding found someone to play the part of the professor. But how much money should he pay for the fragments? Radios all over Jordan blared the report that Metropolitan Samuel was asking a million dollars for his scrolls. That would drive prices up. Any available fragments would soon be bought up in hope of a quick profit. Harding decided to offer a good price — a pound per square centimeter — before prices escalated further. It was an outrageous sum for a piece of dirty old leather the size of a fingernail, but he had little choice. A price based on area would discourage those who might tear up larger pieces and sell the fragments at a mark-up, and encourage a search for more fragments. Each fragment would become more valuable to the museum as others from the same document accumulated. The last pieces of the puzzle would command the highest price, so it was imperative to flush out all the fragments as soon as possible.

The rendezvous with Kando in Jericho was at a seedy hotel in the tough part of town, accompanied by a cast of shifty-looking characters — Kando clearly suspected a trap and had brought some protection. Saad got right down to business. Did Kando have the fragments? Kando set a pile of wretched looking scraps on the table. The "professor" began to measure them; he could offer eight hundred pounds. (Harding had set a range of eight hundred to one thousand pounds.) Kando scowled. He started to gather up the fragments. Saad, too, could play hardball. He put his money back into his pocket and he and the "professor" headed for the door. Would they and their money be allowed to pass unmolested?

When Saad returned home Harding was supportive of his actions: Kando would be back. And he was. This time Saad negotiated a price of one thousand pounds. Kando winked, Give my greetings to Mr. Harding. Clearly he had known about the "professor," and realized that the authorities would deal fairly with him as long as he played along. Harding's strategy had been successful. He appeared to have cornered the market. And he had found a valuable middleman.

An exciting adventure had apparently come to an end. Archaeologists were resigned to the fact that the Bedouin had happened upon a chance hiding place, that the whole affair had resulted from a stroke of luck. The odds against another similar find were overwhelming. But the Bedouin believed otherwise. News of the discovery had quickly spread and large numbers of Bedouin were joining in the hunt for scrolls. The harsh wasteland for miles around the cave was scoured diligently and patiently for other caves which might bear ancient treasure. Caves were checked, their floors dug up. The Bedouin did not despair in the face of failure. The area is dotted with caves and the Bedouin were determined to search out virtually every one of them.

Nothing much happened for almost three years. Then early in 1952 some Bedouin arrived in Jerusalem with scroll fragments. Harding and de Vaux were away so they were directed to Saad. When Saad asked about the location of the cave where they had found the fragments the Bedouin fled. He got a jeep and some armed men and went searching for them. They spotted one of the Bedouin and forced him into the jeep. Saad got his information, and with some military reinforcements headed toward the site. They drove the jeep as far as possible and then walked for seven hours. A dozen miles south of the original cave they could see two caves far up on the cliff face. Dust was issuing from the openings indicating that Bedouin were hard at work inside. The soldiers fired shots in the air and the Bedouin emerged and dispersed. One of the two caves was immense — twenty feet wide, twelve feet high, extending one hundred and fifty feet back into the cliff. The Bedouin had labored for weeks, forty and fifty strong, in these hot dusty caverns digging for fragments. Sentinels were posted in the hills. At the approach of police, they signaled the workmen who then vanished into clefts in the rocks.

With the discovery of more scroll fragments archaeologists seized the initiative. From now on they and the Bedouin would work as a team. Archaeologists and twenty-four Bedouin searched five miles of cliff-face and found more caves worth excavating. It was not easy work. The roof of the entrance to one of the caves had collapsed. As the men worked to clear the entrance broken rocks were sent thundering down the face of the cliff. It was dangerous work — at any moment some of the overhanging rock might be dislodged and tumble onto the workers. Finally the entrance was cleared and the cave could be explored. A Bedouin lighting the way with a torch suddenly disappeared leaving the archaeologist behind in complete darkness. Was this a trap? Would he be killed? After a few moments the archaeologist heard a voice far below. The Bedouin had relighted his torch and was standing at the bottom of a pit into which he had fallen.

Only a small fraction of the documents recovered from these caves were well preserved. The precious manuscripts were used by rats to line their nests. Find a rat nest and there were almost certain to be pieces of manuscript — so much so that the expedition soon became a hunt for rat nests. The floors of caves were covered with bird and animal dung, dung which the Bedouin had for years been collecting and selling. De Vaux wryly remarked that the orange groves near Bethlehem were fertilized with the work of ancient scribes.

Almost three hundred caves were checked, fifteen percent of which contained pottery. Because the Bedouin did all the climbing it was suspected that they did not always notify the archaeologists of their findings. It seemed likely that some scrolls or fragments were going to the underground market.

Only one cave in this round of exploration produced significant manuscript material — a copper scroll which is believed to contain the secret locations of buried treasure, at least two hundred tons of gold and silver worth billions of dollars according to some calculations. Scholars have worked on the code, but no treasure has yet been unearthed.

Eventually archaeologists figured they had searched all possible caves and gave up the quest. But Bedouin continued the search. In the summer of 1952, after the official expedition had ended, Bedouin discovered the mother lode — later to be designated Cave 4Q — about three-quarters of a mile south of the cave which had yielded the original seven scrolls, and only a few hundred feet from where Roland de Vaux and a team of archaeologists were meticulously dusting off old ruins which they believed to have been the source of the scrolls. Bedouin began systematically looting the cave within view of the archaeologists. It was only after de Vaux had purchased an extraordinarily large lot of fragments from the Bedouin that the archaeologists became suspicious and discovered Bedouin working at Cave 4Q around the clock in shifts. The unauthorized digging was halted and archaeologists took over. It was several years and thousands of dollars later before the fragments the Bedouin had excavated from this cave were recovered.

In the ensuing years more caves yielding major finds of scrolls and scroll fragments were discovered in the vicinity — mostly by Bedouin — for a grand total of eleven caves. Had it not been for the work of the Bedouin most of the Dead Sea Scrolls would still be undiscovered.

And what of further discoveries? Are there fragments, or even whole scrolls which have been unearthed but are not yet made known? For some time Kando and the authorities worked together for mutual benefit. Some swear that he kept at least one well-preserved scroll — one individual claims he saw a manuscript which has since disappeared. On one occasion twenty scrolls were to be purchased, but Kando's multimillion-dollar price tag (goods unseen) was too steep and negotiation ceased. Did Kando have the scrolls, or was he bluffing?

When the new state of Israel was declared the caves fell within its territory. The Israeli authorities decided to pay Kando a visit. The evasive and wily Kando played innocent: Scrolls? What scrolls? What are you talking about? The authorities took Kando for a little drive. Two days later Kando's memory mysteriously returned. He led the officers to his bedroom. He pushed a heavy bureau aside and used a toilet plunger to remove some floor tiles. There, in a hidden compartment, was a scroll. When the scroll was lifted out of its hiding place much of it had the consistency of chocolate — this was not the dry desert environment which had preserved the scrolls for two thousand years. How had the authorities known? They hadn't. But they'd received a fragment from a "Mr. Z," an American who said he could get his hands on a whole scroll. They correctly guessed that Mr. Z was fronting for Kando.

Kando was likely not the only person marketing ancient manuscript material. At the time of the first Dead Sea Scrolls discovery a CIA agent was approached by an Egyptian merchant with a badly disintegrating scroll. As the agent tells it, he took the scroll onto a roof to photograph it. A wind came up and blew the scroll into fragments which were swept away, but not before some photographs had been taken. These were shown to an official in Beirut who knew ancient languages. He said the photographs were of the biblical book of Daniel. There was no follow-up and the photographs have disappeared.

Claims of ancient manuscripts are not unique to our times. Most notorious is "the Shapira affair." A hundred years ago the opportunity of a lifetime came to a shopkeeper named Moses Wilhelm Shapira. Born a Jew, Shapira had converted to Christianity and married a Lutheran. His modest little shop in Jerusalem displayed an assortment of trinkets calculated to appeal to tourists, for the railroad and steamship had made the Holy Land an achievable destination for wealthy Europeans eager to walk where Jesus had walked. Nurtured on fiction of the Romantic period, they sought adventure in the mysterious East.

Shapira did a good business inscribing Hebrew verses on olivewood Bible covers. For the very wealthy, and for ladies he found particularly attractive, Shapira had a back room full of rare treasures. Here he would unveil before wondering eyes manuscripts (both book and scroll) penned on parchment. Had these fine people noticed the sign over the entrance to his shop—"Correspondent to the British Museum"? He lovingly translated some Hebrew for these chosen clients and regaled them with fabulous tales of the origins of his precious documents—for Shapira was a romantic.

One day Shapira visited a friend who had just returned from Europe where he had been selling manuscripts and other rare and ancient artifacts from the Holy Land. When the topic of manuscripts came up, an Arab among the guests offered an interesting anecdote: Men hiding from the authorities in a cave east of the Dead Sea had discovered some old pieces of blackened leather inscribed with an ancient form of writing. Shapira asked if there was any way he might see this material.

Arrangements were made and Shapira was soon in possession of fifteen strips of parchment which did indeed contain strange writing, but not strange to Shapira. For he had read about the recent discovery of a stone with similar writing dating back to the ninth century B.C. He copied the writing on the parchment and sent this to a professor of Old Testament in Germany who specialized in paleography. His hopes were dashed when the professor wrote back to say that the text was similar to verses in the biblical book of Deuteronomy but not similar enough.

Shapira, ever the visionary, did not give up. He studied all he could about the Bible and ancient scripts. He read that German biblical scholars believed the present form of the first five books of the Old Testament resulted from a blend of three different sources. The text of the parchments which was similar to Deuteronomy but not similar enough ... could it be one of the original three sources for the biblical book?

Shapira spent hours every day poring over his manuscripts. He became convinced that the blackened parchments he had purchased for a paltry sum were the oldest biblical manuscripts in existence. He shared his dreams of fame and fortune with his darling daughter—a dreamer like her father. Even his doubting wife could smell money. Her stupid little man with his stupid little hobbies ... was it possible? Was he finally amounting to something? Would she become fabulously wealthy? Shapira bought his daughter a pony as an installment on the future, and headed off to Europe with his precious parchments.

First stop, Germany. After a one-and-a-half-hour cursory inspection an impressive committee of experts declared the parchments a forgery. A great disappointment, but Shapira had friends at the British Museum. On to London. A foremost British scholar studied the parchments for three weeks. While scholarly reticence prevented him from outrightly declaring the authenticity of the parchments, he could find no proof to the contrary. Soon newspapers were filled with accounts of Shapira's amazing discovery. He was interviewed by the British prime minister. It was rumored that the British Museum would pay hundreds of thousands of pounds for the parchments. Then the price rose to one million pounds.

But across the channel a jealous French scholar was determined to dash cold water on British enthusiasm. When he got to London his request to see the parchments was refused. So for two days he pushed and shoved with the crowds at the public display of two tiny fragments. Despite the bad lighting the Frenchman was able to pass judgment. Forgery. A definite forgery.

Soon British scholars jumped onto the bandwagon, including the one who had first given tacit validation. Scholar after scholar insisted that he didn't even need to view the parchments—it was surely obvious that parchment could not have lasted so many centuries. And the ink was as black as if penned a year ago ... which it probably was.

Scorn was poured on an embarrassed Shapira. Discredited, totally humiliated, he put a pistol to his head and shot himself. A London antiquarian purchased the manuscripts at a greatly reduced price, but they have since been lost.

Recently scholars have argued that the judgment of forgery was mistaken. The clarity of the writing, for example—the Dead Sea Scrolls show that writing can remain black for a very long time. Facsimilies of Shapira's manuscripts contain a script similar to that on the ninth-century-B.C. Moabite Stone. The same script has been found in some of the Dead Sea Scrolls, mixed with a later script. The older script was reintroduced much as we might use Old English typeface today—to give a feeling of religious tradition.

History records other discoveries of manuscripts in the area of the Dead Sea. Two were mentioned in Eusebius's fourth-century history of the early church: A Greek version of the Psalms had been discovered in a jar near Jericho, and on another occasion Greek and Hebrew manuscripts had been found in a jar in Jericho. A ninth-century letter from one churchman to another tells about Arabs who chased their dog into a cave and found "many books" written in Hebrew, some from the Old Testament. A century and a half later an historian wrote about "cave people" and books found in a cave.

In 1995, fearing that Israel might soon be forced to cede the West Bank to the Palestinians, the Israel Antiquities Authority launched Operation Scroll. Twenty teams of archaeologists searched four hundred caves in the cliffs along the western shore of the Dead Sea for buried artifacts that would be forever lost to Israel and her people should the land be transferred. But the Bedouin of earlier years had been thorough. No scrolls or fragments of scrolls were unearthed, despite the fact that new equipment and technology was available to facilitate the search.

Today the silence of the northwest corner of the Dead Sea is fractured by the whistling screech of military jet aircraft slicing through the murky sulphur-yellow haze. Their roar catches up and resonates off the rock, cascading into the distance. The highway which hugs the muddy black shore is busy with traffic, much of it military. Army patrols are on the alert night and day, guns obvious and ready. This desolate moonscape of the West Bank is an area of confrontation, of contention, of strife, of push and shove. An area where you grab what you can, and hold on possessively — like the tough thorns which suck life from the rocks.

The timeless figure of the Bedouin links present with past. Like his father and grandfather and great-grandfather, today's Bedouin feeds his goats on the sparse vegetation. The Bedouin is at home here; everything else seems out of place, artificial. Take away the convenient connecting road to Jerusalem; take away the seacoast highway and all its busyness. Accentuate the silence, the remoteness. Feel the eerie mystery of the place. No clouds, no trees. Just rock, and the relentless sun. A mile and a quarter away and one hundred feet below, a dead sea. This is where it all began half a century ago. Are there more ancient biblical manuscripts awaiting discovery? If so, what will they teach us about the text of the Bible?

# 24

# Scandal

Cave 4Q was the biggest Dead Sea Scrolls discovery. Out of a total of eight hundred manuscripts, five hundred were found in this one cave. But the material retrieved from Cave 4Q presented a major problem. The manuscripts were in fragments—over 15,000 pieces—many not bigger than a fingernail, containing no more than a few letters, sometimes just a single letter.

Assortments of decaying, soiled, warped, wrinkled, blackened, curled fragments continued to come from the Bedouin for several years after the initial discoveries. They came in containers of all shapes and sizes: shoe boxes, film boxes, cigarette boxes. The manuscript fragments were like pieces from five hundred jigsaw puzzles, all mixed together indiscriminately, with most pieces missing. There were no pictures of the finished puzzles to act as guides. Nor had the edges been cut to fit one another so they might be aligned by trial and error; instead, the edges had decayed or had been ravaged by insects and animals. This meant that the first task—before anyone could tackle putting the five hundred puzzles together (and at this stage no one even knew how many puzzles there were)—was to clean and flatten each piece.

Harding and de Vaux clearly needed help. They put out feelers to archaeological institutions and universities: Who could you spare for several months a year for a few years? Many established scholars could not make, or were not willing to make, such a sacrifice. The obvious solution was to use graduate students.

John Strugnell was one of these. One spring day the twenty-four-year-old was asked to remain behind after a seminar. To a student, that means bad news or good news. Fortunately for Strugnell it turned out to be the latter, an invitation to join de Vaux. Strugnell knew virtually nothing about the Dead Sea Scrolls. His professor at Oxford suggested some background reading — only a few documents had been published, he could read them on the plane en route. Heretofore Strugnell's only point of contact with the Middle East had been the portrait of Colonel T. E. Lawrence — Lawrence of Arabia — which hung in the dining hall of Jesus College. Forty years later he would remember only one thing about touching down in the Middle East on that warm day in 1954 — the beautiful girl sent to greet incoming tourists.

Strugnell was not prepared for the task which awaited him. Nor, it turned out, was anyone else. The international team of eight which would be responsible for publishing the manuscripts from Cave 4Q was assembled in an offhand and serendipitous way. Credentials? Training? How could you train someone for a task which was unique, a project the like of which had never been encountered before? The eight would simply have to wade into the mess and sort it out, developing their own techniques as they went along.

Many fragments were so friable and brittle they could scarcely be touched with a camel-hair brush. A process of humidification was developed to make them pliable, but too much humidity and you got a droplet of goo — one lost fragment. Sometimes several layers of manuscript came stuck together in a coagulated clump. When the pieces had passed through the initial stages of preparation they were cleaned, flattened between glass plates, and photographed.

Then came the problem of resolving the ultimate jigsaw puzzle. The Palestine Archaeological Museum had a long narrow room that was made-to-order. It was bathed in sunlight, and gentle breezes wafted through open windows. Trestle tables were laid out the length of the room. Spread out over these tables were some five hundred glass plates with their fragments. The eight members of the team learned as they went along, gradually developing a feel for different scribal hands. Hour after hour, day after day, week after week, month after month, the eye learned to recognize the idiosyncrasies of one scribe versus those of another. But the handwriting of one scribe was not always easily identified as such. A badly wrinkled fragment distorted the writing. A scribe's writing often varied depending on whether his quill was sharp or dull. To complicate matters, it wasn't always one scribe/one manuscript. Sometimes the team discovered that they had been trying to fit together fragments from two different documents transcribed by the same copyist. The reverse could occur: The same scribe did not always transcribe a whole manuscript.

Biblical manuscripts were checked with the standard text. Concordances helped match single words into phrases. But biblical manuscripts comprised only a fraction of the total. Half the manuscripts represented formerly unknown texts. Here there was no guide. In a normal jigsaw puzzle, color offers many clues. Not so with the Dead Sea Scrolls. While characteristics of the leather were helpful in matching fragments, the color of the leather — even for fragments of the same manuscript — often varied according to their degree of preservation. Fortunately at the time of sorting there existed new photographic techniques without which much of the recovered material would have been worthless. Some pieces had gone completely black, the writing indistinguishable from its background. Using infra-red technology a skilled technician could bring out the writing. In cases where the writing had virtually faded away ultra-violet techniques proved effective. (In the decades since, many of the fragments have badly decayed. But recent technology can provide enhanced images of the Scrolls. Each part of a Scroll fragment has a unique spectral signature. This information is fed into a computer and the result allows scholars to read texts which would otherwise have been virtually invisible.)

Gradually individual manuscripts began to come together. The manuscripts fell into literary genres: biblical texts, commentaries, other writings. A division of labor developed. Each individual on the team appropriated for himself specific texts. These would be his responsibility to assemble and to publish. It was all very casual at first. But as time passed responsibilities evolved into rights. The first letter of the serial number on a plate of fragments in the Rockefeller Museum came to indicate the exclusive intellectual property of a specific member of the team.

By 1960 the work of sorting the fragments from Cave 4Q was virtually complete. Yet extremely little of this material was published. Six years later John Allegro, a maverick member of the international team, and the only one who had quickly published the material assigned to him, urged the director of the Jordanian Department of Antiquities (which at that time owned the Scrolls) to oblige the international team to publish the documents they had worked on. Allegro also recommended a worldwide appeal for funds to construct a wing in the museum where scholars from all countries would have free and easy access to the Scrolls. He wanted funds to preserve the Scrolls — he feared they would decay in their present condition. He was right. During the decades of monopoly by the international team the Scrolls experienced considerable decay. None of Allegro's ideas came to fruition.

Thirty years after John Strugnell had arrived in the Middle East to begin work on the Scrolls he and Elisha Qimron were slated to present a paper titled "An Unpublished Halakhic Letter from Qumran" to twelve hundred scholars from around the world gathered in Jerusalem for the International Conference on Biblical Archaeology. Little had yet been published on the Cave 4Q scrolls.

By contrast, over 10,000 articles had appeared dealing with the original seven Dead Sea Scrolls manuscripts published shortly after their discovery by Trever and Sukenik. But since those early years scholars who studied anything that impinged on the time of the Scrolls—from two centuries before Jesus Christ to one century after—had lived in virtual suspended animation. Many were afraid to publish lest the unpublished Scrolls later make fools of them and contradict hypotheses they had labored so long to establish. They had been patient, contenting themselves with examining those documents already published. Now they were finally going to hear something about the manuscripts from Cave 4Q, some hint of what the fragments from the infamous cave revealed. The silence of several decades was about to be broken. Scholars waited spellbound.

An air of mystery and romance surrounded the possibilities which might unfold with the material from Cave 4Q. What light would be shed on the text of the Bible, on the foundation of Christianity and Judaism? Would there be major surprises? Certainly a wealth of newly available data, and a renewed avalanche of scholarly interpretation and debate. As Elisha Qimron ascended the podium — Strugnell was absent, rumor said "for political reasons"—the room was abuzz with excited anticipation. The press stood ready to sensationalize.

The paper dealt with a manuscript letter outlining legal rulings. But it was clear that this was no ordinary letter and that the rulings were neither minor nor secondary. The letter was nothing less than a foundation document concerning the ruins near Cave 4Q. It appeared to hold the key to many of the mysteries concerning the religious group which had at one time inhabited the ruins—who they were and why they were there. Theories about the scribes of the Scrolls might well have to be revised. Members of the audience took frantic notes.

Qimron finished reading. Those in attendance were galvanized, in shock. Here was a document of central significance which had been withheld from the academic community. How much more seminal material like this remained unpublished? Why had the international team been silent so long? The paper brought to the surface the displeasure academics felt regarding the tardiness of the international team's efforts. Displeasure had turned to outrage.

Enter Hershel Shanks, the crusading publisher of the popular and widely-circulated *Biblical Archaeology Review*. In an incisive report on the conference paper, he asked why Qimron had made public so few passages from the notorious letter. Why, when it had caused such a stir, was its text not made available in full to interested scholars? (It would be another ten years before the scholarly community would get a glimpse of the 121-line text, and then only as part of a published commentary running well over five hundred pages.) Shanks had opened to public view an academic can of worms.

Shanks's report was the first shot in a campaign to wrest the Scrolls from the small cartel — soon to be known as the Inner Circle — which held a virtual monopoly on their editing and publication, and make them available to all scholars. Shanks was not a professional archaeologist; he held no titled chair at a distinguished university. But he did recognize scandal when he saw it. A graduate of Harvard Law School and the author of several books, Shanks was no lightweight. He would prove to be a noisy and formidable opponent. Before this battle was over he would be hailed in the press and on television as a champion of intellectual freedom.

Shanks began in quite gentlemanly fashion: He didn't wish to question the credentials of the honorable scholars of the international team, but.... Shanks portrayed the international team as an exclusive club of "insiders," whose monopoly over the Scrolls gave them great status and power. His articles sounded a call to action. Prominent professors began to stand up and be counted. Morton Smith told a conference on the Scrolls at New York University that he found the "scandal" surrounding the Dead Sea Scrolls disgusting.

It was not the first time the word "scandal" had been used in connection with the Dead Sea Scrolls. Almost a decade earlier another scholar, Geza Vermes, had written that drastic measures must be taken immediately to avoid the greatest academic scandal of the twentieth century. Was there any valid reason the Scrolls could not be photographed and published? Vermes's suggestion failed to embarrass members of the international team.

One member of the team, J. T. Milik, had not returned to Jerusalem to examine "his" fragments since Israel took over the museum in 1967. But when John Allegro beat Milik to press with some of "Milik's" material, team members jumped to defend Milik. Strugnell, who had not published his own material, suddenly felt inspired to put pen to paper; he rushed off a 114-page line-by-line detailed criticism of Allegro's edition. To this day Allegro's name is a four-letter word among members of the international team, but he did indirectly force Milik to come out with his own edition.

Milik was not the only offender. Other members of the cartel had published virtually nothing. Moreover, the cartel perpetuated itself. When de Vaux died he bequeathed his "rights" to a colleague. When two more members died they did the same. Clearly, it would take more than isolated polite pleas in scholarly publications to break the monopoly on the Scrolls.

## 24. Scandal

When Professor Robert Eisenman arrived in Jerusalem as the National Endowment for the Humanities Fellow at the Albright Institute of Archaeological Research he naïvely expected to be welcomed into the Rockefeller Museum fraternity. He was treated politely but remained very definitely an outsider. When he sought access to Scroll material he was given the red tape runaround, and frankly told that he would never see the unpublished Scroll material in his lifetime. One day a museum employee brought him a computer printout listing the titles and inventory numbers of all the unpublished manuscripts. It was a gesture of sympathetic kindness which was to have far-reaching consequences. Frustrated, Eisenman decided to go public. He would make a formal request for specific Scroll material, now that he knew the names and numbers of the documents, and have this publicly documented. He submitted his request to John Strugnell, the chief editor at that time, offering to pay all expenses and promising not to publish the Scroll material itself. He merely wanted to see the documents to facilitate his research. He figured Strugnell would refuse. Strugnell obliged and went a step further; he didn't even respond. Much later, when outside forces prompted him to do so, Strugnell did respond: request denied.

Strugnell had unwittingly played into Eisenman's hands. First it was Shanks's *Biblical Archaeology Review*. Here Strugnell's reply to Eisenman's request was characterized as imperious and condescending. This slick magazine had a circulation of hundreds of thousands; it was here that the big American dailies and news magazines got their information regarding the field of archaeology. Freeing the scrolls became a cause célèbre. American, British, and Israeli presses hastened to record Eisenman's words. Moral issues took second place as journalists focused on personalities—stolid academic types bickering and sniping, academia displaying its dirty laundry. Normally boring academic conferences began to attract media attention. As polite colloquia turned into shouting matches, cameras rolled and tape machines recorded.

Eisenman had challenged the scholarly pecking order. Among the Inner Circle, the cartel, he became a target of scorn and wrath. Faxes which denigrated Eisenman's research and publications were sent to newspapers and universities around the world. Eisenman was ignored by the Inner Circle; he was not invited to their conferences, didn't get their handouts, and they refused to publish his submitted papers. The Inner Circle branded him a minor scholar. A minor scholar? Eisenman had a Ph.D. in Middle East languages and cultures from Columbia; he was chair of the Department of Religious Studies and Professor of Middle East Religions at California State University; he had held many academic honors including external fellow at Italy's University of Calabria, lecturer on the Dead Sea Scrolls at the Hebrew University in Jerusalem, visiting scholar at the Oxford Center for Postgraduate Hebrew Studies.

Then, in an infamous interview in an Israeli daily, Strugnell made derogatory comments about Jews (Eisenman was a Jew) and Judaism. Not mincing words, he asserted that "the solution to the Jewish problem" was mass conversion to Christianity. Judaism, he said, was a "horrible religion" that should not have survived. In his defense, friends pointed out that Strugnell was suffering from alcoholism and bouts of manic-depression and was not himself. Nevertheless, he was relieved of his official position as editor-in-chief of the Cave 4 material, and replaced by the Israeli Emanuel Tov.

The issue had now been sufficiently aired in public for events to move swiftly. Back in the days when the international team was busily engaged in piecing together the fragments from Cave 4Q four young scholars had been given the task of assembling a concordance which listed every word, the phrase and document in which it occurred, and the location in the document. Few people knew of the concordance's existence. One of few copies had been filed in the library of Hebrew Union College in Cincinnati. A professor at the college, Ben Wacholder, believed it was possible to work backwards from the words listed in the concordance to produce the text of the original manuscripts. One of his graduate students, Martin Abegg, a computer wiz, came up with a program to do the job, and Wacholder checked the results. Hershel Shanks published the reconstructed texts.

A few weeks later, in September 1991, a headline in the Sunday *New York Times* proclaimed the Dead Sea Scrolls monopoly ended. A picture showed a gentleman in white gloves examining a negative of the Scrolls. He was Dr. William A. Moffett, director of the Huntington Library, one of the most respected private research collections in the United States. He announced that the library's complete set of Scrolls photographs would immediately be made available to all qualified scholars.

How had the Huntington Library acquired the photographs? The philanthropist instrumental in establishing the Ancient Biblical Manuscript Center in California, Elizabeth Hays Bechtel, had financed a copy of photographs for the Center for security reasons. While the photographing was in progress she and an official of the Center had a falling out. So she had a duplicate copy made for herself, which she later donated to the Huntington Library. At the Center the Scrolls photographs could only be seen with the permission of the specific editors of the documents, the international team. Moffett's decision to release the Huntington's photographs was based on moral and intellectual principles and the right of free speech.

Now events began to trip over themselves. Other editions of photographs became available. There was some reorganization of the personnel responsible for publication of the Scrolls. Several new members were added to the international team. The Israel Antiquities Authority got involved. They authorized access to the photographs, but asked that no one usurp the right to publish of those who had labored so many years on the Scrolls. Now that the genie was out of the bottle and it was open season on the Scrolls, the enlarged international team began hastily cranking out long-awaited publications, eager to beat those outside the cartel to publication.

The international team surrendered slowly and grudgingly. They threatened legal action against the Huntington Library until strong reaction in the American press forced a withdrawal. Elisha Qimron sued Shanks and Eisenman for $200,000 for publishing the Scroll material contained in the controversial paper he had presented eight years previously. Qimron claimed loss of future income and academic reputation, and personal grief. He was awarded $50,000 by an Israeli judge. Lawyers for the defense claimed an ancient document could not be copyrighted; otherwise scholarship would be handcuffed.

To this day scholars complain about the continued power of the expanded Inner Circle, but as a result of the scandal over the Scrolls learned societies have issued policy statements regarding *new* discoveries. No longer will it be considered ethical to keep findings such as the Scrolls out of general circulation for more than a minimal period of time.

# 25

# The Original Text

When Trever's Dead Sea Scrolls manuscript of Isaiah was published over half a century ago there was great excitement concerning the text of the Bible. Observant students of Scripture had since earliest times noted that manuscripts presented differing texts. Jerome and Cassiodorus harped ceaselessly upon this fact. The Venerable Bede stressed the importance of obtaining a good text—which meant early manuscripts—for as a scribe he was fully aware of the types of errors to which copyists are prone. In his notes on the Greek and Latin texts of the book of Acts Bede anticipated many of the problems confronting modern textual scholars.

Late in the eighth century the Visigoth Theodulf, who had learned from Bede, produced a reference book for scholars—a collection and appraisal of variant texts. Despite his love of poetry and phrases from Ovid and Virgil, Theodulf curbed his creative tendencies and did not attempt to produce a revised and finished text. He realized that it was better simply to collect variant texts for future reference.

Centuries later those who produced the Wycliffite Bible knew that before translation began it was imperative to find the best possible text, the one closest to the original. Luther translated the earlier Greek text, not its later Latin translation, into the German tongue for his fellow countrymen. In the nineteenth century Tischendorf proclaimed in a direct and forceful manner that the goal of biblical scholars henceforth should be to determine the original text. And so, to this day, it has remained.

Tischendorf believed that the road to the original text was through the earliest available manuscripts. The most authentic text would be found in the oldest manuscripts. How the Dead Sea Scrolls would have excited Tischendorf! Paleographers have judged the handwriting in the Scrolls to range from 250 B.C. to A.D. 68. Archaeologists have dated pottery from the caves to the period within a few generations before and after the time of

Jesus's birth. Auspiciously, in the same year that the first scrolls were found in Cave 1Q, the carbon-14 method of dating was developed. Tests on the linen which wrapped the scrolls gave a date of A.D. 33 plus or minus two hundred years. But what if old linen had been used to wrap scrolls from a much later time? Or what if new linen had been used with older scrolls? Because carbon-14 tests require a fair amount of material the scrolls themselves had not been not used, but a recent process consumes such small quantities of material that the scrolls themselves could be tested. The results were consistent with the paleographic and carbon-14 methods. The Dead Sea Scrolls provide texts from the period around Jesus's lifetime.

Unfortunately, among the vast quantity of Dead Sea Scrolls material not a single fragment of New Testament Scripture has been confirmed. Nor, scholars tell us, is there anything in the Dead Sea Scrolls about Jesus, his teaching, his crucifixion, his resurrection, or his disciples. The Scrolls do, however, furnish material concerning the Judaism of Jesus's time, leading to considerable debate about the religious environment in which Jesus lived and taught.

That Trever's manuscript provided a virtually complete text of Isaiah caused biblical scholars at first to be overly optimistic. In fact, most of the Scrolls are non-biblical. Only one quarter of the eight hundred manuscripts represents literature from the Old Testament. Most of the Scrolls' material is in 25,000 fragments, many no larger than a fingernail. Only a dozen manuscripts were found in complete or nearly complete form. On average ninety percent of the material for all documents is missing. For many documents only a single fragment has been found.

On a positive note there is some manuscript material among the Dead Sea Scrolls for every Old Testament book except Esther. Although in many cases only the smallest of fragments remain of a particular manuscript, some Old Testament books are represented by several manuscripts. Thirty-six manuscripts of the book of Psalms have been identified. A few almost-complete manuscripts have been preserved in relatively good condition. Ironically the most complete and one of the best preserved manuscripts is the Isaiah manuscript examined by John Trever right at the beginning of the long Dead Sea Scrolls saga.

While precise dates are debated, it is clear that scholars now have Hebrew manuscripts of the Old Testament roughly one thousand years older than any possessed before. Formerly, the Greek Old Testament had been the primary tool of textual research because manuscripts of the Greek translation predated Hebrew manuscripts by several centuries. Scholars reconstructed the Hebrew exemplar by translating the Greek back into Hebrew. This process not only involved all the usual problems of translation, but the Greek text itself had not been determined with any precision. Even back in the fourth century Jerome knew of three major variant Greek texts.

In modern times the collection of divergent manuscripts has grown to mammoth proportions. A Greek text of the Old Testament is being compiled by scholars sifting through piles of variant texts. This composite edition of the Greek Old Testament contains detailed footnotes listing major textual variants and the manuscripts in which they are located. Often a few lines of text require a page of notes, and these by no means list all the variants in all known manuscripts. Textual scholars are quick to concede that the resultant text is only their best temporary opinion, one which is open to change with new discoveries.

It is little wonder scholars have regarded the Greek text as no royal road to the original Hebrew text of the Old Testament. While Greek and Hebrew texts usually differ only in numerous minor places, some Greek texts diverge widely from the Hebrew text. The Greek text of the book of Jeremiah is one eighth shorter than the Hebrew text. Large chunks of the Hebrew book of Samuel are missing from the Greek.

The discovery of the Dead Sea Scrolls opened a window of observation deep into the ancient past. No longer would scholars be restricted to indirect evidence and tortuous speculation. While the Scrolls have by no means answered all questions, and older methods continue to be pursued, scholars now possess some direct hard evidence. A fragment of the book of Daniel postdates the original writing of the book by a mere fifty years—the closest in time any biblical manuscript comes to its original text.

Only a fragment of Jeremiah was found among the Scrolls but its Hebrew text corresponds to that of the shorter Greek text. Were there originally two texts of Jeremiah, one shorter than the other? Or did the later medieval Hebrew text add material? These are just two of many possibilities facing textual scholars.

Hebrew manuscripts of the book of Samuel found among the Scrolls showed marked similarity to, and confirmed, the shorter Greek text. The extra psalm in the Greek text of Psalms had long posed a problem, until this extra psalm was discovered in a Hebrew manuscript among the Dead Sea Scrolls. Such discoveries have given scholars renewed confidence in the Greek text of these books. A divergent Greek text may not be the result of errors of translation or copying. Instead, the Greek translators appear to have used Hebrew exemplars which differed considerably from the later standardized medieval Hebrew text—exemplars similar to those manuscripts found among the Dead Sea Scrolls.

The larger Isaiah scroll photographed by John Trever contains virtually the whole sixty-six chapters of this long book. Although it is certainly not the original writing (the prophet Isaiah lived in the eighth century B.C.), this scroll goes back to approximately a century before Jesus's time. Yet its text varies in only minor ways from the much later medieval Hebrew text. The only other biblical scroll of the original seven was also from the book of Isaiah. Large parts of the text are missing but what remains is even closer to the medieval Hebrew text. Thirteen variations found in the Dead Sea Scrolls text of Isaiah have been incorporated in the Revised Standard Version of the Bible.

Some Scrolls agree to a great extent with the medieval Hebrew text, some do not. Every book of the Old Testament must be dealt with on its own. There are manuscripts for many Old Testament books in which some passages closely resemble a diverging Greek text, some passages mirror the medieval Hebrew text, and other passages correspond to no known text.

Most of the biblical manuscripts discovered near the Dead Sea are in Hebrew, but a few fragments of the Greek Old Testament were found. One of these from the book of Leviticus varies considerably from the Greek text as scholars had known it — fifteen variants in twenty-eight lines, lines that are far from complete.

One observation stands out: several different texts of the books of the Old Testament are found among the Dead Sea Scrolls. It appears that there was no single authoritative standardized text for most of these books. One looks in vain for one "Bible" among the Dead Sea Scrolls. Early sensationalist statements that the scrolls "proved the Bible" were mistaken. Even upon examining the relatively orthodox Isaiah scrolls, John Trever was compelled to observe that so optimistic a generalization was unwarranted.

The discovery of the Dead Sea Scrolls has helped refine the text of the Hebrew Bible, the Old Testament. Turn to the eleventh chapter of the first book of Samuel in an older translation. The chapter begins by telling about Nahash, king of the Ammonites, but important background details are lacking. Why did Nahash attack the Israelite city of Jabesh-Gilead? Why did he impose such cruel terms of surrender? One manuscript among the Scrolls provides answers to these questions, the missing background — the earlier history of an ongoing war. The omission of this history in later texts could have been the result of scribal error. The word "Nahash" appears at the beginning of the missing sentences and at the beginning of the verse following the omission. Glancing back to the manuscript he was copying, the scribe's eye may have gone to the second "Nahash" rather than the first, missing all that fell between. Scholars find support for the originality of the longer text in other parts of the Hebrew Bible. In the short version Nahash is introduced as "Nahash the Ammonite." This is unusual; the Hebrew Bible introduces kings as "so-and-so, king of such-and-such." The omitted text does introduce Hahash in this customary manner, which suggests the sentences in the Scroll were originally part of the Hebrew text. As a final piece of evidence, a passage from the ancient historian Josephus indicates that his book of Samuel included the omitted sentences. With such a preponderance of evidence scholars included the missing sentences in the New Revised Standard Version of the Bible.

Deuteronomy 32:8 in the standardized medieval Hebrew text tells how God established the borders of the nations according to "the sons of Israel." The Greek Old Testament read "the sons of God." A Scroll fragment for this portion of the Old Testament confirmed the Greek text. The Hebrew text which had been translated into Greek had clearly been altered in later Hebrew manuscripts. Why? In ancient times when Deuteronomy was written the Israelites believed that their god Yahweh was just one among many gods. In this passage Yahweh distributes the nations among his sons, the other gods. We know that the Canaanites worshiped Baal; the Moabites, Chemosh; the Edomites, Qos; and the Ammonites, Milkom. So the passage makes perfect sense in its historical context. But the Jews who were responsible for the later Hebrew text no longer believed in the existence of many gods; for them only one god existed, Yahweh. The embarrassing reference to the "sons" of *God* (other gods) was therefore altered.

The Dead Sea Scrolls have given scholars greater confidence in the Greek text of the Old Testament. Hence, even where no specific evidence is found in the Scrolls, the Greek text is often preferred over the later standardized Hebrew text. An example of this is found in Proverbs 14:32. The later Hebrew, "in their death the righteous have hope," might suggest life after death. Instead of "death" (Hebrew "bmtw") the Greek has "integrity" (from the Hebrew "btmw"). How profound a twist to text and interpretation and belief can result from the mere metathesis of two letters! The Revised Standard Version follows the Greek.

Because the Dead Sea Scrolls are of no help in the quest for the original text of the New Testament, the search for early manuscripts continues. Earlier manuscripts bypass generations of scribal errors and "corrections." Scribes did not always follow a single exemplar. Making textual decisions along the way, they took this phrase from one manuscript, that word from another, and here and there threw in some personal changes. Soon after the biblical books were written scribes were producing mongrel texts. Three hundred years ago a Greek New Testament listed 30,000 variant readings. The number has increased many times since. This does not count numerous unrecorded variants, for there are over five thousand New Testament manuscripts. With such a wealth of material, much has gone unexamined.

Manuscripts must be examined first-hand, not just a photograph. Tischendorf provided an example. His keen eyesight noticed ink of a slightly different color and letters of a different shape at the last verse of John's gospel (v 25) in Codex Sinaiticus. He concluded that the verse was a later addition to the original manuscript. Other scholars scoffed, but years later ultraviolet light revealed the words "the gospel according to John" at the end of the previous verse, signifying the end of the gospel. These had been scratched out by a later scribe and another verse added in their place.

Another example of the importance of direct examination of a manuscript is found at 1 Timothy 3:16 of the ancient Codex Alexandrinus. Here ink has bled through from the other side of the parchment. A later scribe, perhaps because of poor lighting, read the bleed-through as a standard abbreviation for the Greek word for "God." He added a stroke to clarify this reading, so that the sentence now read, "God was manifested in the flesh," instead of the original text, "He was manifested in the flesh." The altered wording suggests Jesus's divinity, while the original does not. Copies from this celebrated but altered manuscript gave new life to this error, spreading it outward like ripples on a pond.

The Dead Sea Scrolls have made it clear that earlier manuscripts differ to a great degree, in many instances, from later manuscripts for the same biblical passage. For this reason some scholars consider the quest for the original text of the Bible overly optimistic. Are they right? Is this quest for this textual Holy Grail futile? Textual study is as much art as science — it involves a great amount of guesswork. But the ideal of the original text nevertheless provides a worthwhile focal point for future endeavor. So biblical scholars continue to strive for a more authentic text, even if perfection is impossible.

There is always the possibility of major new manuscript discoveries. Who could have predicted the existence of the Dead Sea Scrolls? In recent years fragments of manuscripts from the second century have appeared. Some speculate that a fragment of one chapter of John's gospel may have been copied shortly after the original was written. But new problems arise. These early documents were preserved in the dry sands of Egypt, the place of origin for many ancient Christian heresies. Was the text of these early manuscripts corrupted by theologically motivated heretical scribes? Scripture has never existed in a pristine platonic realm, isolated from the motives of human beings.

# 26

# A Babel of Bibles

The continual discovery of more and more manuscripts has led to constant updating of the text of the Bible. In the quest for the original authentic text the latest discoveries are incorporated in new translations or revisions of Scripture for churches and personal study.

This process began in earnest in the late nineteenth century. Erasmus's New Testament was considered the "received text" until the weight of manuscripts, particularly the early Codex Sinaiticus and Codex Vaticanus, forced an updating of the biblical text. Because the King James Version was based upon the "received text" the time was ripe for a revision of this venerable English translation. A committee of scholars from several British denominations was assembled. The English text was altered only where the Hebrew and Greek texts demanded change, and its dignified Jacobean English was maintained.

Heavy reliance was placed on Codex Sinaiticus, a manuscript which goes back to within a few centuries of the writing of the New Testament books. It contains some unpleasant surprises. For centuries English-speaking Christians had reverently repeated the Lord's Prayer as found in the sixth chapter of Matthew in the King James Version, ending with words believed to have come from Jesus's lips: "For thine is the kingdom, and the power, and the glory, for ever." This passage is not found in Codex Sinaiticus, so the team responsible for the new revision left it out, relegating it to secondary importance in the marginal notes. Codex Sinaiticus lacks the story of Jesus and the woman accused of adultery, found in the eighth chapter of the gospel of John in the King James Version. An adulteress was about to be stoned, when Jesus suggested to the woman's accusers that whoever had not sinned should cast the first stone. One by one her accusers departed. The scholars who worked on the new revision omitted this beautiful story of toleration and forgiveness because it does not appear in the ancient codex. The final verses of Luke in the King James Version state that Jesus departed from his disciples and was "carried up into heaven." But this is not found in Codex Sinaiticus and was omitted from the new revision. Codex Sinaiticus lacks the last twelve verses of the gospel of Mark found in the King James Version, so these verses were relegated to the marginal notes. It is ironic that these changes resulted from Tischendorf's discovery, when his primary purpose had been to support Christian tradition.

The English Revised Version came out in 1881 but did not meet with great success. Few parish churches in England adopted the new text and it failed to replace the King James Version in the hearts of the people. New Bibles are never popular; the old phrases have too much tradition behind them. Previous to the new revision there had been an estimated 80,000 minor alterations in the text of the King James Version, but the populace was unaware of this and continued to regard it as a sacred monolith. Publishers, too, had held the line. For a long time they had known that the word "at" should be changed to "out" in the phrase "strain at a gnat" (the King James Version, Matthew 23:24), but new printings maintained the error.

Because so great an effort had been made to closely mirror the Greek and Hebrew, critics lamented that the new version read like a schoolboy's crib, that it was pedantic, harsh, unidiomatic, and in the final analysis just plain unreadable. While this word-for-word quality made it a poor choice for church use, to this day it remains the best text for anyone wishing to work back toward the Greek and Hebrew. Where the King James Version had rendered one Hebrew word ninety different ways, the revisers translated a Hebrew or Greek word consistently with the same English word.

Americans were not satisfied with the Revised Version. In the American Standard Version they modernized much of its archaic language and adapted it to American English. Many words in the King James Version had long since passed out of use, or had taken on different meanings, causing the text to be misunderstood. Who would realize that a "mean" man was a common man? Who would know that "peculiar people" were those who belonged to God? Who would understand that the "road" David made was really a raid, and that the "target" between Goliath's shoulders was a javelin?

For all its improvements, the American Standard Version of 1901 still retained archaic language and soon looked dated, but it proved more popular in the United States than had its British counterpart in Britain.

Soon after publication of the American Standard Version a series of discoveries vastly increased scholars' knowledge of biblical Greek and the cultural background of biblical times. Further revision of the text was deemed necessary. This time the committee did not rely almost exclusively upon Codex Sinaiticus and Codex Vaticanus for the New Testament, and aimed at a readable modern style which retained the dignified flavor of the King James Version: "says" replaced "saith"; "sendeth" became "sends." "Thou" and "thee" disappeared, except in passages addressing divinity: "you" was used for Jesus before his ascension; "thou" for Christ after. On the Damascus road Paul asks, "Who are you?," because he doesn't realize he is addressing the risen Christ. Critics charged that this dichotomy of wording denied the deity of Jesus while he was on this earth.

This Revised Standard Version of 1952 was not an immediate success. The King James Version continued to outsell it three to one. People thought of the older version with "thee" and "thou" as *the* Bible — a woman acknowledged that she liked the new version "almost as much as the Bible." A man wanted to know who this Tom Nelson was who had written a new Bible? (The name Thomas Nelson, the publisher, appeared on the title page.) He didn't want Tom Nelson's Bible; he wanted the real Bible — the King James Bible — the one written by the "apostle" James.

Nevertheless, the Revised Standard Version was read much more than previous revised editions, and it represented a milestone in the history of Christian Scripture. A Roman Catholic edition of the Revised Standard Version included notes congenial to Catholic doctrine. This was the first time in four hundred years that Catholics and non–Catholics had read, with official approval, from the same Bible. Soon Orthodox Christians had an edition of the Revised Standard Version. The Revised Standard Version is read by Christians from each of the three major divisions of Christianity, and therefore serves as an ecumenical bridge.

Soon new manuscript discoveries and cultural changes led to further extensive revision. A number of changes had been made to the text of Isaiah in the Revised Standard Version, based on initial findings in the Dead Sea Scrolls. As work on the Scrolls progressed it became clear that the text of other books needed altering as well.

While the committee for the Revised Standard Version had been almost exclusively Protestant, that for the New Revised Standard Version included scholars from the Roman Catholic church and the Greek Orthodox church. The language of the text was modernized further: the infelicitous "I will accept no bull from your house" became "I will not accept a bull from your house" (Psalm 50:9), and "once I was stoned" was changed to "once I received a stoning" (2 Corinthians 11:25). Respecting the fact that their efforts stood in a long line of descent from William Tyndale through the King James Version, the revision committee did not render a fresh translation but merely revised what had gone before.

## 26. A Babel of Bibles

The New Revised Standard Version of 1990 had its critics. But this was to be expected. No revised edition has met with universal approval. No biblical text appeals to all Christians. Christianity is not, and never has been, monolithic in doctrine and theology. It is for this reason that other biblical texts have been produced. The New International Version was designed to reflect an evangelical understanding of Scripture. It was a completely new translation, readable and based on sound scholarship.

Since the publication of the Revised Standard Version there have been over two dozen different translations of the complete Bible into English and another two dozen English translations of the New Testament. The large number of available translations reflects the fact that various constituencies of readers are being served. Among this babel of Bibles, which one is best?

There is no such thing as a best version. There are only better editions for a particular reader, for a particular purpose. For detailed study one of the new versions produced by committee is preferable, among which are the New International Version, the New Revised Standard Version, the Jerusalem Bible, the New English Bible. The New English Bible is not a revision of an existing English translation, but a new translation from the Greek. The Jerusalem Bible incorporates modern Roman Catholic biblical scholarship and the new Catholic approach to the Bible. Bibles which have excessive commentary along with the text should be read with caution. The editors may hold a particular theological viewpoint and interpretation, and their rendering of the text may reflect a gratuitous theological bias.

If a readable yet accurate account of the biblical story is wanted, with no need for precise detail or delicate shades of meaning, a good modern language paraphrase like *The Good News Bible* will suffice. A paraphrase is not a translation of the biblical text — and in that sense not really a Bible — but virtually a new literary creation.

One paraphrase favored by evangelicals, *The Living Bible*, has become a bestseller. Its hip street language appeals to many readers, but it has been widely criticized as inaccurate. Unlike the Revised Standard Version and the New International Version, it is not the work of large committees but of one man. In his preface the author candidly admits that he may in places be guilty of personal theological bias, that he may not always have perfectly understood what the original writers meant.

It is, of course, impossible to render the biblical text without some degree of theological nuance — the translators must understand the text before translating and this understanding is of necessity personal. Every translator brings to the translation some hint, no matter how subtle, of personal background, opinion, and belief. It is not surprising, therefore, that virtually every version has been criticized along theological lines. There does not exist, and never will exist, a perfect translation of the Bible.

Translation is an art. The translator can only hope to approach what is an ideal, a goal. The translator can strain at accuracy and precision and clarity, but it is possible to render only an approximation of its sense; overtones, allusions, nuances, feeling, and atmosphere are difficult to capture. The felicitous translation conveys the grace, beauty, and charm of the original, its rhythm, flow, emotion, figures of speech. Read from the pulpit, it should be euphonious, music to the ear, avoid harsh juxtaposition of word and phrase, maintain dignity of expression without stuffiness or catchy colloquialism.

Luther and Erasmus insisted that to appreciate fully the word-play and poetry of Scripture the Bible is best read in the original Greek and Hebrew. Rhyme, meter, and sound are sacrificed in translation. The elegance and beauty and richness of the original are lost. As a Jewish tradition expresses it: to read the Bible in translation is to kiss one's lover through a veil.

But to read the Bible in its original languages, to acquire a feel for Greek and Hebrew beyond mere acquaintance with these languages, is something to which few can aspire. An alternative is to read different vernacular versions. This frees the reader from dependency upon particular wording or phrasing. No version is cast in stone, but results from two levels of human decision: out of many possibilities, one text is chosen; then one translation of this text. Different versions yield passages which best speak to an individual's inner being. The reader of several versions benefits from the results of contemporary biblical scholarship, yet continues to enjoy the literary merit and splendor of phrase of the King James Version.

We can turn to words and phrases bound to our hearts when we first began to search for meaning in our lives. We can savor words of Scripture first heard in the quiet security of our parents' love, passages made sacred by repetition in times of joy and celebration. We can walk beside still waters and lie down in green pastures. But we do well to acquire a deep feeling and appreciation for the richness of the biblical text and its history, knowing that we shall never have before us the words of Scripture as they were originally penned. Instead, as the ancient Persian proverb says: we must be satisfied simply to see a man who saw a man who saw the sea.

# Bibliography

Abulafia, David, Michael Franklin, and Miri Rubin (eds.). *Church and City, 1000–1500.* Cambridge: Cambridge University Press, 1992.
Ackroyd, P. R., and C. F. Evans (eds.). *The Cambridge History of the Bible: From the Beginnings to Jerome.* Cambridge: Cambridge University Press, 1970.
Addison, James Thayer. *The Medieval Missionary: A Study of the Conversion of Northern Europe, A.D. 500–1300.* New York: International Missionary Council, 1936.
Aland, Kurt, and Barbara Aland. *The Text of the New Testament: An Introduction to the Critical Editions and to the Theory and Practice of Modern Textual Criticism.* 2nd ed. Grand Rapids: William B. Eerdmans, 1989.
Allegro, John M. *The Dead Sea Scrolls.* Harmondsworth: Penguin, 1956.
\_\_\_\_\_. *The Dead Sea Scrolls and the Christian Myth.* Buffalo: Prometheus, 1984.
\_\_\_\_\_. *The Shapira Affair.* Garden City: Doubleday, 1965.
Allen, P. S. *The Age of Erasmus.* New York: Russell & Russell, 1963.
\_\_\_\_\_. *Erasmus: Lectures and Wayfaring Sketches.* Oxford: Oxford University Press, 1934.
Almedingen, E. M. *St. Francis of Assisi: A Great Life in Brief.* New York: Alfred A. Knopf, 1967.
Anderson, Alan Orr, and Marjorie Ogilvie Anderson (eds.). *Adomnan's Life of Columba.* Oxford: Oxford University Press, 1991.
Anderson, G. W. "Canonical and Non-canonical," in *The Cambridge History of the Bible: From the Beginnings to Jerome*, edited by P. R. Ackroyd and C. F. Evans. Cambridge: Cambridge University Press, 1970. pp. 113–159.
Arce, Javier. "Otium et Negotium: The Great Estates, 4th–7th Century," in *The Transformation of the Roman World, AD 400–900*, edited by Leslie Webster and Michelle Brown. Berkeley: University of California Press, 1997. pp. 19–32.
Aston, Margaret. *The Fifteenth Century: The Prospect of Europe.* London: Thames and Hudson, 1968.
\_\_\_\_\_. *Lollards and Reformers: Images and Literacy in Late Medieval Religion.* London: Hambledon, 1984.
Augustijn, Cornelis. *Erasmus: His Life, Works, and Influence.* Toronto: University of Toronto Press, 1986.
Avrin, Leila. *Scribes, Script and Books: The Book Arts from Antiquity to the Renaissance.* Chicago: American Library Association, 1991.
Bachmann, E. Theodore (ed.). *Luther's Works, Vol. 35: Word and Sacrament I.* Philadelphia: Muhlenberg, 1960.
Backhouse, Janet. *The Lindisfarne Gospels.* Ithaca: Cornell University Press, 1981.
Baigent, Michael, and Richard Leigh. *The Dead Sea Scrolls Deception.* London: Jonathan Cape, 1991.
Bainton, Roland H. *Erasmus of Christendom.* London: Collins, 1970.

_____. *Here I Stand: A Life of Martin Luther*. New York: Abingdon-Cokesbury Press, 1950.
Baird, William. *History of New Testament Research, Vol. 1: From Deism to Tübingen.* Minneapolis: Fortress, 1992.
Bardy, Gustav. "St. Jerome and Greek Thought," in *A Monument to Saint Jerome: Essays on Some Aspects of His Life, Works and Influence*, edited by Francis X. Murphy. New York: Sheed & Ward, 1952. pp. 85–112.
Barnes, Timothy. "Pagan Perceptions of Christianity," in *Early Christianity: Origins and Evolution to AD 600*, edited by Ian Hazlett. Nashville: Abingdon, 1991. pp. 231–243.
Barr, James. "St. Jerome's Appreciation of Hebrew." *Bulletin of the John Rylands Library*, 49 (1966–67) 281–302.
Barrera, Julio Trebolle. *The Jewish Bible and the Christian Bible: An Introduction to the History of the Bible.* Leiden: Brill, 1998.
Basaglia, Enrico (ed.). *15th Century*. Seville: Centro Publicaciones, 1992.
Bedouelle, Guy. *Saint Dominic: The Grace of the Word.* San Francisco: Ignatius, 1987.
Bentley, James. *Secrets of Mount Sinai: The Story of Codex Sinaiticus.* London: Orbis, 1985.
Bentley, Jerry H. "Biblical Philology and Christian Humanism: Lorenzo Valla and Erasmus as Scholars of the Gospels." *The Sixteenth Century Journal*, 8.2 (1977) 9–28.
_____. "Erasmus' Annotationes in Novum Testamentum and the Textual Criticism of the Gospels." *Archiv für Reformationsgeschichte*, 67 (1976) 33–53.
_____. *Humanists and Holy Writ: New Testament Scholarship in the Renaissance.* Princeton: Princeton University Press, 1983.
Berger, Klaus. *The Truth Under Lock and Key? Jesus and the Dead Sea Scrolls.* Louisville: Westminster John Knox Press, 1995.
Betz, Otto, and Rainer Riesner. *Jesus, Qumran and the Vatican.* New York: Crossroad, 1994.
Bieler, Ludwig. *Ireland, Harbinger of the Middle Ages.* London: Oxford University Press, 1963.
_____. "Ireland's Contribution to the Culture of Northumbria," in *Famulus Christi: Essays in Commemoration of the Thirteenth Centenary of the Birth of the Venerable Bede*, edited by Gerald Bonner. London: SPCK, 1976. pp. 210–228.
Biller, Peter, and Anne Hudson (eds.). *Heresy and Literacy, 1000–1530.* Cambridge: Cambridge University Press, 1994.
Bitel, Lisa M. *Isle of the Saints: Monastic Settlement and Christian Community in Early Ireland.* Ithaca: Cornell University Press, 1990.
Blair, Peter Hunter. *The World of Bede.* Cambridge: Cambridge University Press, 1990.
Bloch, R. Howard, and Stephen G. Nichols (eds.). *Medievalism and the Modernist Temper.* Baltimore: The Johns Hopkins University Press, 1996.
Block, Edward A. *John Wyclif: Radical Dissenter.* San Diego: San Diego State College Press, 1962.
Bluhm, Heinz. *Martin Luther: Creative Translator.* St. Louis: Concordia, 1965.
Blumenfeld-Kosinski, Renate, Luise von Flotow, and Daniel Russell (eds.). *The Politics of Translation in the Middle Ages and the Renaissance.* Ottawa: University of Ottawa Press, 2001.
Boase, T. S. R. *St. Francis of Assisi.* London: Thames and Hudson, 1968.
Boccaccio, Giovanni. *The Decameron.* New York: W. W. Norton, 1977.
Bonner, Gerald (ed.). *Church and Faith in the Patristic Tradition: Augustine, Pelagianism, and Early Christian Northumbria.* Aldershot: Variorum, 1996.
_____ (ed.). *Famulus Christi: Essays in Commemoration of the Thirteenth Centenary of the Birth of the Venerable Bede.* London: SPCK, 1976.
Bowker, Margaret. *The Secular Clergy in the Diocese of Lincoln, 1495–1520.* Cambridge: Cambridge University Press, 1968.
Bowley, James E. (ed.). *Living Traditions of the Bible: Scripture in Jewish, Christian, and Muslim Practice.* St. Louis: Chalice, 1999.
Bradshaw, Paul F. "The Effects of the Coming of Christendom on Early Christian Worship," in *The Origins of Christendom in the West*, edited by Alan Kreider. Edinburgh: T. & T. Clark, 2001. pp. 269–286.

Brady, James F., and John C. Olin (eds.). *Collected Works of Erasmus: Patristic Scholarship, The Edition of St. Jerome*. Toronto: University of Toronto Press, 1992.
Brecht, Martin. *Martin Luther: His Road to Reformation, 1483–1521*. Philadelphia: Fortress, 1985.
\_\_\_\_\_. *Martin Luther: The Preservation of the Church, 1532–1546*. Minneapolis: Fortress, 1993.
\_\_\_\_\_. *Martin Luther: Shaping and Defining the Reformation, 1521–1532*. Minneapolis: Fortress, 1990.
Bredero, Adriaan H. *Christendom and Christianity in the Middle Ages: The Relations between Religion, Church, and Society*. Grand Rapids: William B. Eerdmans, 1994.
Brooke, George J. "The Scrolls and the Study of the New Testament," in *The Dead Sea Scrolls at Fifty*, edited by Robert A. Kugler and Eileen M. Schuller. Atlanta: Scholars Press, 1999. pp. 61–76.
\_\_\_\_\_, and Lawrence H. Schiffman. "The Past: On the History of Dead Sea Scrolls Research," in *The Dead Sea Scrolls at Fifty*, edited by Robert A. Kugler and Eileen M. Schuller. Atlanta: Scholars Press, 1999. pp. 9–20.
Brooke, Rosalind B. (ed.). *Scripta Leonis: The Writings of Leo, Rufino, and Angelo, Companions of St. Francis*. Oxford: Oxford University Press, 1970.
Brooks, Peter Newman (ed.). *Reformation Principle and Practice: Essays in Honour of Arthur Geoffrey Dickens*. London: Scholar Press, 1980.
Brown, Dennis. "Jerome," in *The Early Christian World*, edited by Philip F. Esler. London: Routledge, 2000. pp. 1151–1174.
Brown, George. "The Psalms as the Foundation of Anglo-Saxon Learning," in *The Place of the Psalms in the Intellectual Culture of the Middle Ages*, edited by Nancy van Deusen. Albany: State University of New York Press, 1999. pp. 1–24.
Brown, George Hardin. *Bede the Venerable*. Boston: Twayne, 1987.
Brown, Michelle P. *Anglo-Saxon Manuscripts*. Toronto: University of Toronto Press, 1991.
Brown, Peter. *The Book of Kells*. London: Thames and Hudson, 1980.
\_\_\_\_\_. *The Cult of the Saints: Its Rise and Function in Latin Christianity*. Chicago: University of Chicago Press, 1981.
\_\_\_\_\_. *The Making of Late Antiquity*. Cambridge. Harvard University Press, 1978.
\_\_\_\_\_. *The Rise of Western Christendom: Triumph and Diversity, AD 200–1000*. Cambridge: Blackwell, 1994.
\_\_\_\_\_. *Society and the Holy in Late Antiquity*. London: Faber and Faber, 1982.
\_\_\_\_\_. *The World of Late Antiquity, AD 150–750*. London: Thames and Hudson, 1971.
Brown, Raphael. *The Little Flowers of St. Francis*. Garden City: Image, 1958.
Bruce, F. F. *The English Bible: A History of Translations*. New York: Oxford University Press, 1961.
\_\_\_\_\_. *Second Thoughts on the Dead Sea Scrolls*. 2nd ed. London: Paternoster, 1961.
Buber, Martin, and Franz Rosenzweig. *Scripture and Translation*. Bloomington: Indiana University Press, 1994.
Buck, Lawrence P., and Jonathan W. Zophy (eds.). *The Social History of the Reformation*. Columbus: Ohio State University Press, 1972.
Bullough, D. A. "Columba, Adomnan and the Achievement of Iona." *Scottish Historical Review*, 43 (1964) 111–130.
Burckhardt, Jacob. *The Civilization of the Renaissance in Italy*. New York: Random House, 1954.
Burke, Eugene P. "St. Jerome as a Spiritual Director," in *A Monument to Saint Jerome: Essays on Some Aspects of His Life, Works and Influence*, edited by Francis X. Murphy. New York: Sheed & Ward, 1952. pp. 145–169.
Burke, Peter. *The Renaissance*. Atlantic Highlands: Humanities Press International, 1987.
Burnett, Charles. *Magic and Divination in the Middle Ages: Texts and Techniques in the Islamic and Christian Worlds*. Aldershot: Variorum, 1996.
Burns, Thomas S. *A History of the Ostrogoths*. Bloomington: Indiana University Press, 1984.

Burrows, Millar. *The Dead Sea Scrolls*. New York: Viking, 1955.
Bury, J. B. *The Life of St. Patrick and His Place in History*. London: Macmillan, 1905.
Calkins, Robert G. *Illuminated Books of the Middle Ages*. Ithaca: Cornell University Press, 1983.
Cameron, Averil. "Cult and Worship in East and West," in *The Transformation of the Roman World, AD 400–900*, edited by Leslie Webster and Michelle Brown. Berkeley: University of California Press, 1997. pp. 96–110.
Campbell, Gordon. "Popular Traditions of God in the Renaissance," in *Reconsidering the Renaissance*, edited by Mario A. Di Cesare. Binghamton: Medieval & Renaissance Texts and Studies, 1992. pp. 501–520.
Campbell, W. E. *Erasmus, Tyndale and More*. London: Eyre & Spottiswoode, 1949.
Campbell, William S. "Martin Luther and Paul's Epistle to the Romans," in *The Bible As Book: The Reformation*, edited by Orlaith O'Sullivan. London: The British Library, 2000. pp. 103–114.
Cantor, Norman F. *Inventing the Middle Ages: The Lives, Works, and Ideas of the Great Medievalists of the Twentieth Century*. New York: William Morrow, 1991.
_____. *Western Civilization: Its Genesis and Destiny*. Vol. 2. Glenview: Scott, Foresman, 1969.
_____, and Michael S. Werthman (eds.). *The History of Popular Culture*. New York: Macmillan, 1968.
Cardini, Franco. *Europe 1492: Portrait of a Continent Five Hundred Years Ago*. New York: Facts on File, 1989.
Carrick, J. C. *Wycliffe and the Lollards*. New York: Charles Scribner's Sons, 1908.
Carson, Donald A. "New Bible Translations: An Assessment and Prospect," in *The Bible in the Twenty-First Century*, edited by Howard Clark Kee. Philadelphia: Trinity Press International, 1993. pp. 37–67.
Cavallera, Ferdinand. "The Personality of St. Jerome," in *A Monument to Saint Jerome: Essays on Some Aspects of His Life, Works and Influence*, edited by Francis X. Murphy. New York: Sheed & Ward, 1952. pp. 15–34.
Chadwick, Henry. *The Early Church*. Grand Rapids: Eerdmans, 1968.
Chadwick, Nora. *The Age of the Saints in the Early Celtic Church*. London: Oxford University Press, 1961.
Chadwick, Owen. *The Reformation*. 2nd ed. Harmondsworth: Penguin, 1968.
Charles-Edwards, T. M. *Early Christian Ireland*. Cambridge: Cambridge University Press, 2000.
Charlesworth, James H. "Currents in Qumran Research," in *The Dead Sea Scrolls at Fifty*, edited by Robert A. Kugler and Eileen M. Schuller. Atlanta: Scholars Press, 1999. pp. 107–113.
_____. "The Dead Sea Scrolls and Christian Faith," in *The Dead Sea Scrolls and Christian Faith*, edited by James H. Charlesworth. Harrisburg: Trinity Press International, 1998. pp. 58–73.
_____. "John the Baptizer, Jesus, and the Essenes," in *Caves of Enlightenment*, edited by James H. Charlesworth. North Richland Hills: Bibal, 1998. pp. 75–103.
_____ (ed.). *Caves of Enlightenment*. North Richland Hills: Bibal, 1998.
_____, and Walter P. Weaver (eds.). *The Dead Sea Scrolls and Christian Faith*. Harrisburg: Trinity Press International, 1998.
Chaucer, Geoffrey. *The Canterbury Tales*. New York: Simon & Schuster, 1948.
Chavez, Fray Angelico. *The Song of Francis*. Flagstaff: Northland, 1973.
Cheyette, Fredric L. (ed.) *Lordship and Community in Medieval Europe: Selected Readings*. New York: Holt, Rinehart, and Winston, 1968.
Chrysos, Evangelos. "The Empire in East and West," in *The Transformation of the Roman World, AD 400–900*, edited by Leslie Webster and Michelle Brown. Berkeley: University of California Press, 1997. pp. 9–18.
Cobban, Alan B. "Reflections on the Role of Medieval Universities in Contemporary Soci-

ety," in *Intellectual Life in the Middle Ages*, edited by Lesley Smith and Benedicta Ward. London: Hambledon, 1992. pp. 227–241.

Colgrave, Bertram. "Bede's Miracle Stories," in *Bede: His Life, Times, and Writings*, edited by A. Hamilton Thompson. Oxford: Oxford University Press, 1935. pp. 201–229.

\_\_\_\_\_, and R. A. B. Mynors (eds.). *Bede's Ecclesiastical History of the English People*. London: Oxford University Press, 1969.

Comba, Emilio. *History of the Waldenses of Italy from Their Origin to the Reformation*. London: Truslove & Shirley, 1889.

Comfort, Philip Wesley (ed.). *The Origin of the Bible*. Wheaton: Tyndale House, 1992.

Cook, Edward M. *Solving the Mysteries of the Dead Sea Scrolls: New Light on the Bible*. Grand Rapids: Zondervan, 1994.

Craigie, William A. "The English Versions (to Wyclif)," in *The Bible in Its Ancient and English Versions*, edited by H. Wheeler Robinson. Oxford: Oxford University Press, 1954. pp. 128–145.

Crépin, André. "Bede and the Vernacular," in *Famulus Christi: Essays in Commemoration of the Thirteenth Centenary of the Birth of the Venerable Bede*, edited by Gerald Bonner. London: SPCK, 1976. pp. 170–192.

Crim, Keith R. "Bible Translation by Committees," in *The Bible and Bibles in America*, edited by Ernest S. Frerichs. Atlanta: Scholars Press, 1988. pp. 29–41.

Cross, Frank Moore, Jr. *The Ancient Library of Qumran and Modern Biblical Studies*. 2nd ed. Garden City: Doubleday, 1961.

\_\_\_\_\_. "Light on the Bible from the Dead Sea Caves," in *Understanding the Dead Sea Scrolls*, edited by Hershel Shanks. New York: Random House, 1992. pp. 156–166.

\_\_\_\_\_. "The Text behind the Text of the Hebrew Bible," in *Understanding the Dead Sea Scrolls*, edited by Hershel Shanks. New York: Random House, 1992. pp. 139–155.

\_\_\_\_\_, and Shemaryahu Talmon (eds.). *Qumran and the History of the Biblical Text*. Cambridge: Harvard University Press, 1975.

Cullmann, Oscar. "The Significance of the Qumran Texts for Research into the Beginnings of Christianity," in *The Scrolls and the New Testament*, edited by Krister Stendahl. Westport: Greenwood, 1975. pp. 18–32.

Cunningham, Lawrence. *Saint Francis of Assisi*. San Francisco: Harper & Row, 1981.

Curran, John. "Jerome and the Sham Christians of Rome," in *Recent Studies in Early Christianity*, edited by Everett Ferguson. New York: Garland, 1999. pp. 299–315.

Cuthbert, Fr. *The Life of St. Francis of Assisi*. London: Longmans, Green & Co., 1912.

Dahmus, Joseph H. *The Prosecution of John Wyclyf*. New Haven: Yale University Press, 1952.

Daiches, David. *The King James Version of the English Bible: An Account of the Development and Sources of the English Bible of 1611 with Special Reference to the Hebrew Tradition*. Chicago: University of Chicago Press, 1941.

Daniell, David. *William Tyndale: A Biography*. New Haven: Yale University Press, 1994.

\_\_\_\_\_. "William Tyndale, the English Bible, and the English Language," in *The Bible As Book: The Reformation*, edited by Orlaith O'Sullivan. London: The British Library, 2000. pp. 34–50.

Davies, Margaret. "The New Testament," in *The Oxford Illustrated History of the Bible*, edited by John Rogerson. Oxford: Oxford University Press, 2001. pp. 36–57.

Davies, Philip. "The Apocrypha," in *The Oxford Illustrated History of the Bible*, edited by John Rogerson. Oxford: Oxford University Press, 2001. pp. 26–35.

Davies, Wendy. "The Celtic Church." *Journal of Religious History*, 8 (1974–75) 406–411.

De Hamel, Christopher. *Medieval Craftsmen: Scribes and Illuminators*. Toronto: University of Toronto Press, 1992.

De la Bedoyere, Michael. *Francis: A Biography of the Saint of Assisi*. New York: Harper & Row, 1962.

De Paor, Liam. *Ireland and Early Europe: Essays and Occasional Writings on Art and Culture*. Dublin: Four Courts, 1997.

_____. *St. Patrick's World: The Christian Culture of Ireland's Apostolic Age.* Notre Dame: University of Notre Dame Press, 1993.
Deanesly, Margaret. *The Lollard Bible and Other Medieval Versions.* Cambridge: Cambridge University Press, 1920.
_____. *The Significance of the Lollard Bible.* London: University of London Press, 1951.
Décarreaux, Jean. *Monks and Civilization: From the Barbarian Invasions to the Reign of Charlemagne.* London: George Allen & Unwin, 1964.
Demaus, R. *William Tyndale: A Biography.* Rev. ed. Amsterdam: J. C. Gieben, 1971.
Desbonnets, Théophile. "The Franciscan Reading of the Scriptures," in *Francis of Assisi Today,* edited by Christian Duquoc and Casiano Floristan. New York: Seabury, 1981. pp. 37–45.
Di Cesare, Mario A. (ed.). *Reconsidering the Renaissance.* Binghamton: Medieval & Renaissance Texts and Studies, 1992.
Dickens, A. G. *The Counter Reformation.* London: Thames and Hudson, 1968.
_____. *Reformation and Society in Sixteenth-Century Europe.* London: Thames and Hudson, 1966.
_____, and Whitney R. D. Jones. *Erasmus the Reformer.* London: Methuen, 1994.
Dimant, Devorah. "The Scrolls and the Study of Early Judaism," in *The Dead Sea Scrolls at Fifty,* edited by Robert A. Kugler and Eileen M. Schuller. Atlanta: Scholars Press, 1999. pp. 43–59.
Diringer, David. *The Illuminated Book: Its History and Production.* London: Faber and Faber, 1958.
Dobson, James O. *The Little Poor Man of Assisi: A Consideration of the Life and Significance of St. Francis.* London: SCM, 1926.
Dorey, T. A. (ed.). *Erasmus.* London: Routledge & Kegan Paul, 1970.
Dost, Timothy P. *Renaissance Humanism in Support of the Gospel in Luther's Early Correspondence: Taking All Things Captive.* Aldershot: Ashgate, 2001.
Duckett, Eleanor Shipley. *Alcuin, Friend of Charlemagne: His World and His Work.* New York: Macmillan, 1951.
_____. *Anglo-Saxon Saints and Scholars.* Hamden: Archon Books, 1967.
Duerden, Richard. "Equivalence or Power?: Authority and Reformation Bible Translation," in *The Bible As Book: The Reformation,* edited by Orlaith O'Sullivan. London: The British Library, 2000. pp. 9–23.
Duerr, Hans Peter. *Dreamtime: Concerning the Boundary between Wilderness and Civilization.* Oxford: Basil Blackwell, 1985.
Dunn, J. D. G. "Paul and the Dead Sea Scrolls," in *Caves of Enlightenment,* edited by James H. Charlesworth. North Richland Hills: Bibal, 1998. pp. 105–127.
Dunn, Marilyn. *The Emergence of Monasticism: From the Desert Fathers to the Early Middle Ages.* Oxford: Blackwell, 2000.
Duparc, Pierre. "Cofraternities of the Holy Spirit and Village Communities in the Middle Ages," in *Lordship and Community in Medieval Europe: Selected Readings,* edited by Fredric L. Cheyette. New York: Holt, Rinehart, and Winston, 1968. pp. 341–356.
Duquoc, Christian, and Casiano Floristan (eds.). *Francis of Assisi Today.* New York: Seabury, 1981.
Dyer, Joseph. "The Psalms in Monastic Prayer," in *The Place of the Psalms in the Intellectual Culture of the Middle Ages,* edited by Nancy van Deusen. Albany: State University of New York Press, 1999. pp. 59–89.
Edwards, Brian H. *God's Outlaw.* Welwyn: Evangelical Press, 1976.
Edwards, Mark. "The Development of Office in the Early Church," in *The Early Christian World,* edited by Philip F. Esler. London: Routledge, 2000. pp. 316–329.
Edwards, Mark U., Jr. *Printing, Propaganda, and Martin Luther.* Berkeley: University of California Press, 1994.
Ehrman, Bart D. "Methodological Developments in the Analysis and Classification of New Testament Documentary Evidence." *Novum Testamentum,* 29 (1987) 22–45.

_____. *The Orthodox Corruption of Scripture: The Effect of Early Christological Controversies on the Text of the New Testament.* Oxford: Oxford University Press, 1993.
Eisenman, Robert H. *The Dead Sea Scrolls and the First Christians.* Shaftesbury: Element Books, 1996.
_____, and Michael Wise. *The Dead Sea Scrolls Uncovered.* Shaftesbury: Element Books, 1992.
Eisenstein, Elizabeth L. *The Printing Press as an Agent of Change: Communications and Cultural Transformations in Early-Modern Europe.* 2 vols. Cambridge: Cambridge University Press, 1979.
_____. *The Printing Revolution in Early Modern Europe.* Cambridge: Cambridge University Press, 1983.
Elliott, J. K. "Can We Recover The Original New Testament?" *Theology*, 77 (1974) 338–353.
Ellis, Roger, and Ren, Tixier (eds.). *The Medieval Translator.* Belgium: Brepols, 1996.
Englebert, Omer. *Saint Francis of Assisi: A Biography.* Chicago: Franciscan Herald Press, 1965.
Epp, Eldon Jay, and Gordon D. Fee (eds.). *New Testament Textual Criticism: Its Significance for Exegesis.* Oxford: Oxford University Press, 1981.
_____, and _____ (eds.). *Studies in the Theory and Method of New Testament Textual Criticism.* Grand Rapids: Eerdmans, 1993.
Erikson, Erik H. *Young Man Luther: A Study in Psychoanalysis and History.* New York: W. W. Norton, 1962.
Esler, Philip F. (ed.). *The Early Christian World.* 2 vols. London: Routledge, 2000.
Estep, William R. *Renaissance and Reformation.* Grand Rapids: William B. Eerdmans, 1986.
Evans, C. F. "The New Testament in the Making," in *The Cambridge History of the Bible: From the Beginnings to Jerome*, edited by P. R. Ackroyd and C. F. Evans. Cambridge: Cambridge University Press, 1970. pp. 232–284.
Evans, Craig A. "The Dead Sea Scrolls and the Canon of Scripture in the Time of Jesus," in *The Bible at Qumran: Text, Shape, and Interpretation*, edited by Peter W. Flint. Grand Rapids: William B. Eerdmans, 2001. pp. 67–79.
Ewert, David. *From Ancient Tablets to Modern Translations: A General Introduction to the Bible.* Grand Rapids: Zondervan, 1983.
Ferguson, Everett (ed.). *Missions and Regional Characteristics of the Early Church.* New York: Garland, 1993.
_____ (ed.). *Recent Studies in Early Christianity.* New York: Garland, 1999.
Ferguson, Wallace K. *The Renaissance.* New York: Holt, Rinehart and Winston, 1940.
Ferruolo, Stephen C. *The Origins of the University: The Schools of Paris and Their Critics, 1100–1215.* Stanford: Stanford University Press, 1985.
Finlay, Ian. *Columba.* London: Victor Gollancz, 1979.
Fitzmyer, Joseph A. "Scripture in the Catholic Tradition," in *Living Traditions of the Bible: Scripture in Jewish, Christian, and Muslim Practice*, edited by James E. Bowley. St. Louis: Chalice, 1999. pp. 145–161.
Fletcher, Richard. *The Barbarian Conversion: From Paganism to Christianity.* Berkeley: University of California Press, 1997.
Flint, Peter W. (ed.). *The Bible at Qumran: Text, Shape, and Interpretation.* Grand Rapids: William B. Eerdmans, 2001.
Flint, Valerie I. J. *The Rise of Magic in Early Medieval Europe.* Princeton: Princeton University Press, 1991.
Foley, W. Trent, and Arthur G. Holder. *Bede: A Biblical Miscellany.* Liverpool: Liverpool University Press, 1999.
Fortini, Arnaldo. *Francis of Assisi.* New York: Crossroad, 1981.
Fournier, Gabriel. "Rural Churches and Rural Communities in Early Medieval Auvergne," in *Lordship and Community in Medieval Europe: Selected Readings*, edited by Fredric L. Cheyette. New York: Holt, Rinehart, and Winston, 1968. pp. 315–340.

Frank, Harry Thomas. "Discovering the Scrolls," in *Understanding the Dead Sea Scrolls*, edited by Hershel Shanks. New York: Random House, 1992. pp. 3–19.
_____, Charles William Swain, and Courtlandt Canby. *The Bible through the Ages*. Cleveland: World, 1967.
Franklin, Michael. "The Cathedral as Parish Church: The Case of Southern England," in *Church and City, 1000–1500*, edited by David Abulafia, Michael Franklin, and Miri Rubin. Cambridge: Cambridge University Press, 1992. pp. 173–198.
Frantzen, Allen J. *King Alfred*. Boston: Twayne, 1986.
French, Katherine L. *The People of the Parish: Community Life in a Late Medieval English Diocese*. Philadelphia: University of Pennsylvania Press, 2001.
Frerichs, Ernest S. (ed.). *The Bible and Bibles in America*. Atlanta: Scholars Press, 1988.
Friedman, Jerome. *The Most Ancient Testimony: Sixteenth-Century Christian-Hebraica in the Age of Renaissance Nostalgia*. Athens: Ohio University Press, 1983.
Fuhrmann, Otto W. "The Invention of Printing," in *Reader in the History of Books and Printing*, edited by Paul A. Winckler. Englewood, Colorado: Information Handling Services, 1978. pp. 237–283.
Gameson, Richard. "The Royal 1.B vii Gospels and English Book Production in the Seventh and Eighth Centuries," in *The Early Medieval Bible: Its Production, Decoration and Use*, edited by Richard Gameson. Cambridge: Cambridge University Press, 1994. pp. 24–52.
_____. "Why Did Eadfrith Write the Lindisfarne Gospels?" in *Belief and Culture in the Middle Ages*, edited by Richard Gameson and Henrietta Leyser. Oxford: Oxford University Press, 2001. pp. 45–58.
_____ (ed.). *The Early Medieval Bible: Its Production, Decoration and Use*. Cambridge: Cambridge University Press, 1994.
_____, and Henrietta Leyser (eds.). *Belief and Culture in the Middle Ages*. Oxford: Oxford University Press, 2001.
Ganz, David. "Mass Production of Early Medieval Manuscripts: The Carolingian Bibles from Tours," in *The Early Medieval Bible: Its Production, Decoration and Use*, edited by Richard Gameson. Cambridge: Cambridge University Press, 1994. pp. 53–62.
Garin, Eugenio (ed.). *Renaissance Characters*. Chicago: Chicago University Press, 1991.
Gaskoin, C. J. B. *Alcuin: His Life and His Work*. New York: Russell & Russell, 1966.
Gasnick, Roy M. (ed.). *The Francis Book: 800 Years with the Saint from Assisi*. New York: Macmillan, 1980.
Geary, Patrick J. *Furta Sacra: Thefts of Relics in the Central Middle Ages*. Princeton: Princeton University Press, 1978.
Gentrup, William F. (ed.). *Reinventing the Middle Ages and the Renaissance: Constructions of the Medieval and Early Modern Periods*. Turnhout: Brepols, 1998.
Gibson, Margaret T. *The Bible in the Latin West*. Notre Dame: University of Notre Dame Press, 1993.
Gies, Joseph, and Frances. *Life in a Medieval City*. New York: Thomas Y. Crowell, 1969.
Gilkes, A. N. *The Impact of the Dead Sea Scrolls*. London: Macmillan, 1962.
Gillett, E. H. *The Life and Times of John Huss; Or the Bohemian Reformation of the Fifteenth Century*. 2 vols. Boston: Gould and Lincoln, 1863.
Golb, Norman. *Who Wrote the Dead Sea Scrolls? The Search for the Secret of Qumran*. New York: Scribner, 1995.
Goodich, Michael E. *From Birth to Old Age: The Human Life Cycle in Medieval Thought, 1250–1350*. Lanham: University Press of America, 1989.
Goodspeed, Edgar J. *As I Remember*. New York: Harper & Brothers, 1953.
Gottfried, Robert S. *The Black Death: Natural and Human Disaster in Medieval Europe*. London: Robert Hale, 1983.
Goudge, Elizabeth. *My God and My All: The Life of St. Francis of Assisi*. New York: Coward-McCann, 1959.
Graff, Harvey J. *The Legacies of Literacy: Continuities and Contradictions in Western Culture and Society*. Bloomington: Indiana University Press, 1987.

Grafton, Anthony (ed.). *Rome Reborn: The Vatican Library and Renaissance Culture.* New Haven: Yale University Press, 1993.
Grant, R. M. "The New Testament Canon," in *The Cambridge History of the Bible: From the Beginnings to Jerome,* edited by P. R. Ackroyd and C. F. Evans. Cambridge: Cambridge University Press, 1970. pp. 284–308.
Green, Dennis H. "Linguistic Evidence for the Early Migrations of the Goths," in *The Visigoths from the Migration Period to the Seventh Century: An Ethnographic Perspective,* edited by Peter Heather. Woodbridge: Boydell, 1999. pp. 11–32.
Greenslade, S. L. (ed.). *The Cambridge History of the Bible: The West from the Reformation to the Present Day.* Cambridge: Cambridge University Press, 1963.
Grossmann, Maria. *Humanism in Wittenberg, 1485–1517.* Nieuwkoop: B. DeGraaf, 1975.
Gurevich, Aaron. "Heresy and Literacy: Evidence of the Thirteenth-Century 'Exempla,'" in *Heresy and Literacy, 1000–1530,* edited by Peter Biller and Anne Hudson. Cambridge: Cambridge University Press, 1994. pp. 104–111.
_____. *Medieval Popular Culture: Problems of Belief and Perception.* Cambridge: Cambridge University Press, 1988.
Habig, Marion A. (ed.). *St. Francis of Assisi, Writings and Early Biographies: English Omnibus of the Sources for the Life of St. Francis.* 3rd rev. ed. London: The Society for Promoting Christian Knowledge, 1979.
Hague, Dyson. *The Life and Work of John Wycliffe.* London: The Church Book Room, 1935.
Hale, John. *The Civilization of Europe in the Renaissance.* London: Fontana, 1994.
Halkin, Léon-E. *Erasmus: A Critical Biography.* Oxford: Basil Blackwell, 1987.
Hall, B. "Erasmus: Biblical Scholar and Reformer," in *Erasmus,* edited by T. A. Dorey. London: Routledge & Kegan Paul, 1970. pp. 81–113.
Hall, Louis Brewer. *The Perilous Vision of John Wyclif.* Chicago: Nelson-Hall, 1983.
Hammond, Gerald. *The Making of the English Bible.* Manchester: Carcanet, 1982.
Hanawalt, Barbara A., and Kathryn L. Reyerson (eds.). *City and Spectacle in Medieval Europe.* Minneapolis: University of Minnesota Press, 1994.
Hankins, James. "The Popes and Humanism," in *Rome Reborn: The Vatican Library and Renaissance Culture,* edited by Anthony Grafton. New Haven: Yale University Press, 1993. pp. 47–85.
Hanson, Kenneth. *Dead Sea Scrolls: The Untold Story.* Tulsa: Council Oak Books, 1997.
Hanson, R. P. C. *The Life and Writings of the Historical Saint Patrick.* New York: Seabury, 1983.
Harbert, Maire. *Iona, Kells and Derry: The History and Hagiography of the Monastic Familia of Columba.* Oxford: Clarendon, 1988.
Harbison, E. Harris. *The Christian Scholar in the Age of the Reformation.* New York: Charles Scribner's Sons, 1956.
Harran, Marilyn J. (ed.). *Luther and Learning: The Wittenberg University Luther Symposium.* Mississauga: Associated University Presses, 1985.
Hart, A. Tindal. *The Country Priest in English History.* London: Phoenix House, 1959.
Harthan, John. *Books of Hours and Their Owners.* London: Thames and Hudson, 1977.
Hartmann, Louis N. "St. Jerome as an Exegete," in *A Monument to Saint Jerome: Essays on Some Aspects of His Life, Works and Influence,* edited by Francis X. Murphy. New York: Sheed & Ward, 1952. pp. 37–81.
Hay, Denys. "Fiat Lux," in *Reader in the History of Books and Printing,* edited by Paul A. Winckler. Englewood, Colorado: Information Handling Services, 1978. pp. 5–25.
_____ (ed.). *The Age of the Renaissance.* London: Thames and Hudson, 1986.
Hazlett, Ian (ed.). *Early Christianity: Origins and Evolution to AD 600.* Nashville: Abingdon, 1991.
Heather, Peter. "The Creation of the Visigoths," in *The Visigoths from the Migration Period to the Seventh Century: An Ethnographic Perspective,* edited by Peter Heather. Woodbridge: Boydell, 1999. pp. 43–73.

_____. *The Goths.* Oxford: Blackwell, 1996.
_____. *Goths and Romans, 332–489.* Oxford: Oxford University Press, 1991.
_____ (ed.). *The Visigoths from the Migration Period to the Seventh Century: An Ethnographic Perspective.* Woodbridge: Boydell, 1999.
_____, and John Matthews. *The Goths of the Fourth Century.* Liverpool: Liverpool University Press, 1991.
Henderson, Isabel. "Pictish Art and the Book of Kells," in *Ireland in Early Medieval Europe: Studies in Memory of Kathleen Hughes,* edited by Dorothy Whitelock, Rosamond McKitterick, and David Dumville. Cambridge: Cambridge University Press, 1982. pp. 79–105.
Herkless, John. *Francis and Dominic and the Mendicant Orders.* Edinburgh: T. & T. Clark, 1901.
Herklots, H. G. G. *How Our Bible Came to Us: Its Text and Versions.* New York: Oxford University Press, 1957.
Herlihy, David. *The Black Death and the Transformation of the West.* Cambridge: Harvard University Press, 1997.
Higman, Francis. "'Without great effort, and with pleasure': Sixteenth-Century Genevan Bibles and Reading Practices," in *The Bible As Book: The Reformation,* edited by Orlaith O'Sullivan. London: The British Library, 2000. pp. 115–122.
Hill, Rosalind. "Bede and the Boors," in *Famulus Christi: Essays in Commemoration of the Thirteenth Centenary of the Birth of the Venerable Bede,* edited by Gerald Bonner. London: SPCK, 1976. pp. 93–105.
Hillgarth, J. N. (ed.). *Christianity and Paganism, 350–750: The Conversion of Western Europe.* Philadelphia: University of Pennsylvania Press, 1986.
Hinson, E. Glenn. *The Church Triumphant: A History of Christianity up to 1300.* Macon: Mercer University Press, 1995.
_____. *The Evangelization of the Roman Empire: Identity and Adaptability.* Macon: Mercer University Press, 1981.
Hoffmann, Manfred. *Rhetoric and Theology: The Hermeneutic of Erasmus.* Toronto: University of Toronto Press, 1994.
Holl, Adolf. *The Last Christian.* Garden City: Doubleday, 1980.
Hollis, Christopher. *Erasmus.* Milwaukee: Bruce, 1933.
Holmes, Urban T., Jr. *Medieval Man: His Understanding of Himself, His Society and the World.* Chapel Hill: University of North Carolina Press, 1980.
Horrox, Rosemary. *The Black Death.* Manchester: Manchester University Press, 1994.
Hudson, Anne. *Lollards and Their Books.* London: Hambledon, 1985.
_____. *The Premature Reformation: Wycliffite Texts and Lollard History.* Oxford: Oxford University Press, 1988.
_____. "'Springing Cockel in Our Clene Corn': Lollard Preaching in England around 1400," in *Christendom and Its Discontents: Exclusion, Persecution, and Rebellion, 1000–1500,* edited by Scott L. Waugh and Peter D. Diehl. Cambridge: Cambridge University Press, 1996. pp. 132–147.
_____. "Wyclif and the English Language," in *Wyclif in His Times,* edited by Anthony Kenny. Oxford: Oxford University Press, 1986. pp. 85–103.
_____. "Wycliffism in Oxford 1381–1411," in *Wyclif in His Times,* edited by Anthony Kenny. Oxford: Oxford University Press, 1986. pp. 67–84.
Hughes, Kathleen. *The Church in Early Irish Society.* Ithaca: Cornell University Press, 1966.
Hughes, Philip Edgcumbe. *Lefèvre: Pioneer of Ecclesiastical Renewal in France.* Grand Rapids: William B. Eerdmans, 1984.
Huizinga, Johan. *The Autumn of the Middle Ages.* Chicago: University of Chicago Press, 1996.
_____. *Erasmus and the Age of Reformation.* New York: Harper & Row, 1957.
Hurtado, Larry W. *Text-Critical Methodology and the Pre-Caesarean Text: Codex W in the Gospel of Mark.* Grand Rapids: Eerdmans, 1981.

Hyma, Albert. *The Brethren of the Common Life*. Grand Rapids: Wm. B. Eerdmans, 1950.
_____. *The Christian Renaissance: A History of the "Devotio Moderna."* 2d ed. Hamden, Conn.: Archon, 1965.
_____. *The Life of Desiderius Erasmus*. Assen, The Netherlands: Van Gorcum, 1972.
Innes, Matthew. *State and Society in the Early Middle Ages: The Middle Rhine Valley, 400–1000*. Cambridge: Cambridge University Press, 2000.
Isaacs, J. "The Authorized Version and After," in *The Bible in Its Ancient and English Versions*, edited by H. Wheeler Robinson. Oxford: Oxford University Press, 1954. pp. 196–234.
_____. "The Sixteenth-Century English Versions," in *The Bible in Its Ancient and English Versions*, edited by H. Wheeler Robinson. Oxford: Oxford University Press, 1954. pp. 146–195.
Jørgensen, Johannes. *Saint Francis of Assisi: A Biography*. London: Longmans, Green, and Co., 1912.
Jardine, Lisa. *Worldly Goods: A New History of the Renaissance*. New York: Doubleday, 1996.
Jarrott, C. A. L. "Erasmus' Biblical Humanism." *Studies in the Renaissance*, 17 (1970) 119–152.
Jenkins, Claude. "Bede as Exegete and Theologian," in *Bede: His Life, Times, and Writings: Essays in Commemoration of the Twelfth Centenary of His Death*, edited by A. Hamilton Thompson. New York: Russell & Russell, 1966. pp. 152–200.
Jensen, De Lamar. *Renaissance Europe: Age of Recovery and Reconciliation*. Lexington: D. C. Heath, 1981.
Johnson, Paul. *The Renaissance: A Short History*. New York: Random House, 2000.
Jolly, Karen Louise. *Popular Religion in Late Saxon England*. Chapel Hill: University of North Carolina, 1996.
Jones, A. H. M. *The Later Roman Empire, 284–602: A Social, Economic and Administrative Survey*. 3 vols. Oxford: Basil Blackwell, 1964.
Jones, Charles W. *Bede, the Schools and the Computus*. Aldershot: Variorum, 1994.
_____. "Bede's Place in Medieval Schools," in *Famulus Christi: Essays in Commemoration of the Thirteenth Centenary of the Birth of the Venerable Bede*, edited by Gerald Bonner. London: SPCK, 1976. pp. 261–285.
Jones, G. Lloyd. *Robert Wakefield on the Three Languages*. Binghamton: SUNY at Binghamton, 1989.
Jones, Leslie Webber. *An Introduction to Divine and Human Readings, by Cassiodorus Senator*. New York: W.W. Norton, 1969.
Jones, Prudence, and Nigel Pennick. *A History of Pagan Europe*. London: Routledge, 1995.
Jones, R. Devonshire. *Erasmus and Luther*. London: Oxford University Press, 1968.
Jones, Tom B. *In the Twilight of Antiquity: The R. S. Hoyt Memorial Lectures (1973)*. Minneapolis: University of Minnesota Press, 1978.
Jordan, William Chester. *The Great Famine: Northern Europe in the Early Fourteenth Century*. Princeton: Princeton University Press, 1996.
Kaeuper, Richard W. *Chivalry and Violence in Medieval Europe*. Oxford: Oxford University Press, 1999.
_____. (ed.). *Violence in Medieval Society*. Woodbridge: Boydell Press, 2000.
Kamesar, Adam. "The Bible Comes to the West: The Text and Interpretation of the Bible in Its Greek and Latin Forms," in *Living Traditions of the Bible: Scripture in Jewish, Christian, and Muslim Practice*, edited by James E. Bowley. St. Louis: Chalice, 1999. pp. 35–61.
_____. *Jerome, Greek Scholarship, and the Hebrew Bible: A Study of Quaestiones Hebraicae in Genesim*. Oxford: Oxford University Press, 1993.
Karrer, Otto (ed.). *St. Francis of Assisi: The Legends and Lauds*. New York: Sheed & Ward, 1948.
Katz, Solomon. *The Decline of Rome and the Rise of Mediaeval Europe*. Ithaca: Cornell University Press, 1955.

Katzman, Avi. "Interview with Chief Scroll Editor John Strugnell," in *Understanding the Dead Sea Scrolls*, edited by Hershel Shanks. New York: Random House, 1992. pp. 259–263.
Kay, Richard (ed.). *The Broadview Book of Medieval Anecdotes*. Lewiston: Broadview, 1988.
Kee, Howard Clark (ed.). *The Bible in the Twenty-First Century*. Philadelphia: Trinity Press International, 1993.
Keen, Maurice. "The Influence of Wyclif," in *Wyclif in His Times*, edited by Anthony Kenny. Oxford: Oxford University Press, 1986. pp. 127–145.
_____. "Wyclif, the Bible, and Transubstantiation," in *Wyclif in His Times*, edited by Anthony Kenny. Oxford: Oxford University Press, 1986. pp. 1–16.
Kelly, J. N. D. *Jerome: His Life, Writings, and Controversies*. London: Gerald Duckworth, 1975.
Kelly, Joseph F. *The World of the Early Christians*. Collegeville: Liturgical Press, 1997.
Kelly, Susan. "Anglo-Saxon Lay Society and the Written Word," in *The Uses of Literacy in Early Medieval Europe*, edited by Rosamond McKitterick. Cambridge: Cambridge University Press, 1990. pp. 36–62.
Kenney, James F. "The Earliest Life of St. Columcille." *Catholic Historical Review*, (1926) 636–644.
Kenny, Anthony. "The Accursed Memory: The Counter-Reformation Reputation of John Wyclif," in *Wyclif in His Times*, edited by Anthony Kenny. Oxford: Oxford University Press, 1986. pp. 147–168.
_____. *Wyclif*. Oxford: Oxford University Press, 1985.
_____ (ed.). *Wyclif in His Times*. Oxford: Oxford University Press, 1986.
Kenyon, Sir Frederic. *Our Bible and the Ancient Manuscripts*. Rev. ed. London: Eyre & Spottiswoode, 1958.
_____. *The Story of the Bible: A Popular Account of How It Came to Us*. 2d ed. London: John Murray, 1964.
Kieckhefer, Richard. "The Holy and the Unholy: Sainthood, Witchcraft, and Magic in Late Medieval Europe," in *Christendom and Its Discontents: Exclusion, Persecution, and Rebellion, 1000–1500*, edited by Scott L. Waugh and Peter D. Diehl. Cambridge: Cambridge University Press, 1996. pp. 310–337.
Kirkpatrick, Robin. *The European Renaissance, 1400–1600*. Harlow: Longman, 2002.
Kitts, Eustace J. *Pope John the Twenty-third and Master John Hus of Bohemia*. London: Constable & Co., 1910.
Klein, Ralph W. *Textual Criticism of the Old Testament: The Septuagint after Qumran*. Philadelphia: Fortress, 1974.
Knowles, David. *Christian Monasticism*. New York: McGraw-Hill, 1969.
_____. *The Evolution of Medieval Thought*. London: Longmans, Green & Co., 1962.
_____. *Saints and Scholars: Twenty-five Medieval Portraits*. Cambridge: Cambridge University Press, 1962.
Kreider, Alan. "Changing Patterns of Conversion in the West," in *The Origins of Christendom in the West*, edited by Alan Kreider. Edinburgh: T. & T. Clark, 2001. pp. 3–46.
_____ (ed.). *The Origins of Christendom in the West*. Edinburgh: T. & T. Clark, 2001.
Kristeller, Paul Oskar. "Renaissance Humanism and Its Significance," in *Reconsidering the Renaissance*, edited by Mario A. Di Cesare. Binghamton: Medieval & Renaissance Texts and Studies, 1992. pp. 29–43.
Kubo, Sakae, and Walter F. Specht. *So Many Versions?: Twentieth-Century English Versions of the Bible*. Grand Rapids: Zondervan, 1983.
Kugler, Robert A., and Eileen M. Schuller (eds.). *The Dead Sea Scrolls at Fifty*. Atlanta: Scholars Press, 1999.
Kuhns, Oscar. *John Huss: The Witness*. New York: Abingdon, 1907.
Laistner, M. L. W. "The Library of the Venerable Bede," in *Bede: His Life, Times, and Writings*, edited by A. Hamilton Thompson. Oxford: Oxford University Press, 1935. pp. 237–266.

Lampe, G. W. H. (ed.). *The Cambridge History of the Bible: The West from the Fathers to the Reformation*. Cambridge: Cambridge University Press, 1969.
Latr, Guido. "The 1535 Coverdale Bible and its Antwerp Origins," in *The Bible As Book: The Reformation*, edited by Orlaith O'Sullivan. London: The British Library, 2000. pp. 89–102.
Lea, Henry Charles. *A History of the Inquisition of the Middle Ages*. 3 vols. New York: Harper & Brothers, 1887.
\_\_\_\_\_. *The Inquisition of the Middle Ages*. New York: Macmillan, 1961.
Leadbetter, Bill. "From Constantine to Theodosius (and Beyond)," in *The Early Christian World*, edited by Philip F. Esler. London: Routledge, 2000. pp. 258–292.
Leaney, A. R. C. *From Judaean Caves: The Story of the Dead Sea Scrolls*. Wallington: The Religious Education Press, 1961.
Leclerc, Eloi. *Francis of Assisi: Return to the Gospel*. Chicago: Franciscan Herald Press, 1983.
Leclercq, Jean. *The Love of Learning and the Desire for God: A Study of Monastic Culture*. 3rd ed. New York: Fordham University Press, 1982.
Leff, Gordon. *John Wyclif: The Path to Dissent*. London: Oxford University Press, 1966.
\_\_\_\_\_. *The Medieval Imagination*. Chicago: University of Chicago Press, 1988.
\_\_\_\_\_. *Time, Work, & Culture in the Middle Ages*. Chicago: University of Chicago Press, 1980.
\_\_\_\_\_. "Wyclif and Hus: A Doctrinal Comparison," in *Wyclif in His Times*, edited by Anthony Kenny. Oxford: Oxford University Press, 1986. pp. 105–125.
LeGoff, Jacques. *Intellectuals in the Middle Ages*. Oxford: Blackwell, 1993.
Lehane, Brendan. *The Quest of Three Abbots: Pioneers of Ireland's Golden Age*. London: John Murray, 1968.
Levenson, Jay A. (ed.). *Circa 1492*. New Haven: Yale University Press, 1991.
Lewis, Jack P. *The English Bible from KJV to NIV: A History and Evaluation*. 2nd ed. Grand Rapids: Baker Book House, 1991.
Lockwood, W. B. "Vernacular Scriptures in Germany and the Low Countries before 1500," in *The Cambridge History of the Bible: The West from the Fathers to the Reformation*, edited by G. W. H. Lampe. Cambridge. Cambridge University Press, 1969. pp 415–436.
Longford, Lord. *Francis of Assisi: A Life for All Seasons*. London: Weidenfeld and Nicolson, 1978.
Loserth, Johann. *Wiclif and Hus*. London: Hodder and Stoughton, 1884.
Lot, Ferdinand. *The End of the Ancient World and the Beginnings of the Middle Ages*. New York: Harper & Brothers, 1961.
Lützow, The Count. *The Life and Times of Master John Hus*. London: J. M. Dent, 1909.
Lynch, Joseph H. *The Medieval Church: A Brief History*. London: Longman, 1992.
MacGregor, Geddes. *The Bible in the Making*. Philadelphia: J. R. Lippincott, 1959.
\_\_\_\_\_. *A Literary History of the Bible: From the Middle Ages to the Present Day*. Nashville: Abingdon, 1968.
MacMullen, Ramsay. *Christianity and Paganism in the Fourth to Eighth Centuries*. New Haven: Yale University Press, 1997.
\_\_\_\_\_. "Christianity Shaped through Its Mission," in *The Origins of Christendom in the West*, edited by Alan Kreider. Edinburgh: T. & T. Clark, 2001. pp. 97–117.
\_\_\_\_\_. *Christianizing the Roman Empire (A.D. 100–400)*. New Haven: Yale University Press, 1984.
Macpherson, Robin. *Rome in Involution: Cassiodorus' Variae in Their Literary and Historical Setting*. Poznan, Poland: Adam Mickiewicz University Press, 1989.
Magill, Frank N. (ed.). *Great Lives from History: Ancient and Medieval Series*. Pasadena: Salem, 1988.
Manchester, William. *A World Lit Only By Fire: The Medieval Mind and the Renaissance, Portrait of an Age*. Boston: Little, Brown, 1992.

Mangan, John Joseph. *Life, Character & Influence of Desiderius Erasmus of Rotterdam.* 2 vols. New York: Macmillan, 1927.
Manns, Peter. *Martin Luther: An Illustrated Biography.* New York: Crossroad, 1982.
Mansoor, Menahem. *The Dead Sea Scrolls: A College Textbook and a Study Guide.* Grand Rapids: Eerdmans, 1964.
Marsden, John. *The Illustrated Bede.* London: Macmillan, 1989.
Martin, Luther H. "The Pagan Religious Background," in *Early Christianity: Origins and Evolution to AD 600*, edited by Ian Hazlett. Nashville: Abingdon, 1991. pp. 52–64.
Maynard, Theodore. *Richest of the Poor: The Life of St. Francis of Assisi.* Garden City: Echo Books, 1967.
McCarter, P. Kyle, Jr. *Textual Criticism: Recovering the Text of the Hebrew Bible.* Philadelphia: Fortress, 1986.
McConica, James. *Erasmus.* Oxford: Oxford University Press, 1991.
McCready, William D. *Miracles and the Venerable Bede.* Toronto: Pontifical Institute of Medieval Studies, 1994.
McFarlane, K. B. *The Origins of Religious Dissent in England.* New York: Collier, 1966.
McGoldrick, James Edward. *Luther's English Connection: The Reformation Thought of Robert Barnes and William Tyndale.* Milwaukee: Northwestern, 1979.
McGurk, Patrick. "The Oldest Manuscripts of the Latin Bible," in *The Early Medieval Bible: Its Production, Decoration and Use*, edited by Richard Gameson. Cambridge: Cambridge University Press, 1994. pp. 1–23.
McKane, William. *Selected Christian Hebraists.* Cambridge: Cambridge University Press, 1989.
McKinnon, James W. "The Book of Psalms, Monasticism, and the Western Liturgy," in *The Place of the Psalms in the Intellectual Culture of the Middle Ages*, edited by Nancy van Deusen. Albany: State University of New York Press, 1999. pp. 43–58.
McKitterick, Rosamond. "Carolingian Bible Production: The Tours Anomaly," in *The Early Medieval Bible: Its Production, Decoration and Use*, edited by Richard Gameson. Cambridge: Cambridge University Press, 1994. pp. 63–77.
_____ (ed.). *The Uses of Literacy in Early Medieval Europe.* Cambridge: Cambridge University Press, 1990.
McNeill, John T. *The Celtic Churches: A History A.D. 200 to 1200.* Chicago: Chicago University Press, 1974.
Meisel, Anthony C., and M. L. del Mastro. *The Rule of St. Benedict.* Garden City: Image, 1975.
Melia, Pius. *The Origin, Persecution and Doctrines of the Waldenses.* London: James Toovey, 1870.
Menzies, Lucy. *Saint Columba of Iona: A Study of His Life, His Times, & His Influence.* Felinfach: J.M.F. Books, 1992.
Metzger, Bruce M. *Chapters in the History of New Testament Textual Criticism.* Grand Rapids: Wm. B. Eerdmans, 1963.
_____. *The Making of the New Revised Standard Version of the Bible.* Grand Rapids: Eerdmans, 1991.
_____. *Manuscripts of the Greek Bible: An Introduction to Greek Palaeography.* Oxford: Oxford University Press, 1981.
_____. *The Text of the New Testament: Its Transmission, Corruption, and Restoration.* 3rd ed. Oxford: Oxford University Press, 1992.
Meyer, Carl S. (ed.). *Luther for an Ecumenical Age: Essays in Commemoration of the 450th Anniversary of the Reformation.* St. Louis: Concordia, 1967.
Meyvaert, Paul. "Bede the Scholar," in *Famulus Christi: Essays in Commemoration of the Thirteenth Centenary of the Birth of the Venerable Bede*, edited by Gerald Bonner. London: SPCK, 1976. pp. 40–69.
Milik, J. T. *Ten Years of Discovery in the Wilderness of Judaea.* London: SCM, 1959.
Miller, Edward. *The Abbey and Bishopric of Ely: The Social History of an Ecclesiastical*

*Estate from the Tenth Century to the Early Fourteenth Century.* Cambridge: Cambridge University Press, 1969.
Mitchell, Sabrina. *Medieval Manuscript Painting.* London: Weidenfeld & Nicolson, 1965.
Mockler, Anthony. *Francis of Assisi: The Wandering Years.* Oxford: Phaidon, 1976.
Mollat, Michel. *The Poor in the Middle Ages: An Essay in Social History.* New Haven: Yale University Press, 1986.
Moorman, John R. H. *Church Life in England in the Thirteenth Century.* Cambridge: Cambridge University Press, 1945.
Mozley, J. F. *Coverdale and His Bibles.* London: Lutterworth, 1953.
_____. *William Tyndale.* New York: Macmillan, 1937.
Mullett, Michael. *Popular Culture and Popular Protest in Late Medieval and Early Modern Europe.* London: Croom Helm, 1987.
Mundy, John Hine, and Kennerly M. Woody (eds.). *The Council of Constance: The Unification of the Church.* New York: Columbia University Press, 1961.
Murphy, Francis X. "St. Jerome: The Irascible Hermit," in *A Monument to Saint Jerome: Essays on Some Aspects of His Life, Works and Influence,* edited by Francis X. Murphy. New York: Sheed & Ward, 1952. pp. 3–12.
_____ (ed.). *A Monument to Saint Jerome: Essays on Some Aspects of His Life, Works and Influence.* New York: Sheed & Ward, 1952.
Nauert, Charles G., Jr. "The Clash of Humanists and Scholastics: An Approach to Pre-Reformation Controversies." *Sixteenth Century Journal,* 4 (1973) 1–18.
_____. *Humanism and the Culture of Renaissance Europe.* Cambridge: Cambridge University Press, 1995.
Needham, Paul. "The Changing Shape of the Vulgate Bible in Fifteenth-Century Printing Shops," in *The Bible As Book: The First Printed Editions,* edited by Paul Saenger and Kimberly Van Kampen. London: The British Library, 1999. pp. 53–70.
Neill, Stephen, and Tom Wright. *The Interpretation of the New Testament 1861–1986.* 2nd ed. Oxford: Oxford University Press, 1988.
New, David S. *Old Testament Quotations in the Synoptic Gospels, and the Two-Document Hypothesis.* Atlanta: Scholars Press, 1993.
Nickelsburg, George W. E. "Currents in Qumran Scholarship: The Interplay of Data, Agendas, and Methodology," in *The Dead Sea Scrolls at Fifty,* edited by Robert A. Kugler and Eileen M. Schuller. Atlanta: Scholars Press, 1999. pp. 79–99.
Nigg, Walter. *Francis of Assisi.* Chicago: Franciscan Herald, 1975.
Noble, Thomas F. X. "Literacy and the Papal Government in Late Antiquity and the Early Middle Ages," in *The Uses of Literacy in Early Medieval Europe,* edited by Rosamond McKitterick. Cambridge: Cambridge University Press, 1990. pp. 82–108.
Nordenfalk, Carl. *Celtic and Anglo-Saxon Painting: Book Illumination in the British Isles, 600–800.* New York: George Braziller, 1977.
Norton, David. *A History of the Bible As Literature.* 2 vols. Cambridge: Cambridge University Press, 1993.
_____. "Imagining Translation Committees at Work: The King James and the Revised Versions," in *The Bible As Book: The Reformation,* edited by Orlaith O'Sullivan. London: The British Library, 2000. pp. 157–168.
O'Croinin, Daibhi. *Early Medieval Ireland: 400–1200.* London: Longman, 1995.
O'Donnell, James J. *Cassiodorus.* Berkeley: University of California Press, 1979.
Olin, John C., James D. Smart and Robert E. McNally (eds.). *Luther, Erasmus and the Reformation: A Catholic-Protestant Reappraisal.* New York: Fordham University Press, 1969.
Orlinsky, Harry M., and Robert G. Bratcher. *A History of Bible Translation and the North American Contribution.* Atlanta: Scholars Press, 1991.
O'Sullivan, Orlaith (ed.). *The Bible As Book: The Reformation.* London: The British Library, 2000.
Owst, G. R. *Preaching in Medieval England: An Introduction to Sermon Manuscripts of the Period c.1350–1450.* Cambridge: Cambridge University Press, 1926.

Ozment, Steven E. (ed.). *The Reformation in Medieval Perspective*. Chicago: Quadrangle, 1971.
Paine, Gustavus S. *The Learned Men*. New York: Thomas Y. Crowell, 1959.
Palanque, Jean-Remy. "St. Jerome and the Barbarians," in *A Monument to Saint Jerome: Essays on Some Aspects of His Life, Works and Influence*, edited by Francis X. Murphy. New York: Sheed & Ward, 1952. pp. 173–199.
Palmer, Nigel F. "Biblical Block Books," in *The Bible As Book: The First Printed Editions*, edited by Paul Saenger and Kimberly Van Kampen. London: The British Library, 1999. pp. 23–30.
Pantin, W. A. *The English Church in the Fourteenth Century*. Cambridge: Cambridge University Press, 1955.
Parker, A. A. "An Age of Gold," in *The Age of the Renaissance*, edited by Denys Hay. London: Thames and Hudson, 1986. pp. 171–194.
Parry, Donald W., and Stephen D. Ricks (eds.). *Current Research and Technological Developments on the Dead Sea Scrolls*. Leiden: E. J. Brill, 1996.
Partridge, A. C. *English Biblical Translation*. London: Andr, Deutsch, 1973.
Patschovsky, Alexander. "The Literacy of Waldensianism from Valdes to c.1400," in *Heresy and Literacy, 1000–1530*, edited by Peter Biller and Anne Hudson. Cambridge: Cambridge University Press, 1994. pp. 112–136.
Pattie, T. S. "The Creation of the Great Codices," in *The Bible as Book: The Manuscript Tradition*, edited by John L. Sharpe III, and Kimberly van Kampen. London: The British Library, 1998. pp. 61–72.
Pernoud, Régine, and Madeleine. *Saint Jerome*. New York: Macmillan, 1962.
Petry, Ray C. *Francis of Assisi: Apostle of Poverty*. Durham: Duke University Press, 1941.
Phillips, Margaret Mann. *Erasmus and the Northern Renaissance*. London: Hodder & Stoughton, 1949.
Pohl, Walter. "The Barbarian Successor States," in *The Transformation of the Roman World, AD 400–900*, edited by Leslie Webster and Michelle Brown. Berkeley: University of California Press, 1997. pp. 33–47.
Porter, H. C. *Reformation and Reaction in Tudor Cambridge*. Hamden, Connecticut: Shoe String Press, 1972.
Porter, Stanley E. "The Contemporary English Version and the Ideology of Translation," in *Translating the Bible: Problems and Prospects*, edited by Stanley E. Porter and Richard S. Hess. Sheffield: Sheffield Academic Press, 1999. pp. 18–45.
_____. "Modern Translations," in *The Oxford Illustrated History of the Bible*, edited by John Rogerson. Oxford: Oxford University Press, 2001. pp. 134–161.
_____, and Craig A. Evans (eds.). *The Scrolls and the Scriptures: Qumran Fifty Years After*. Sheffield: Sheffield Academic Press, 1997.
_____, and Richard S. Hess (eds.). *Translating the Bible: Problems and Prospects*. Sheffield: Sheffield Academic Press, 1999.
Potter, G. R. "'The Egg That Luther Hatched,'" in *The Age of the Renaissance*, edited by Denys Hay. London: Thames and Hudson, 1986. pp. 123–144.
Pounds, N. J. G. *A History of the English Parish: The Culture of Religion from Augustine to Victoria*. Cambridge: Cambridge University Press, 2000.
Price, Ira Maurice, William A. Irwin, and Allen P. Wikgren. *The Ancestry of Our English Bible: An Account of Manuscripts, Texts, and Versions of the Bible*. New York: Harper & Brothers, 1956.
Proudfoot, Alice-Boyd (ed.). *Patrick: Sixteen Centuries with Ireland's Patron Saint*. New York: Macmillan, 1983.
Putnam, George Haven. *Books and Their Makers During the Middle Ages: A Study of the Conditions of the Production and Distribution of Literature from the Fall of the Roman Empire to the Close of the Seventeenth Century*. Vol. 1. New York: Hillary House, 1896.
Quain, Edwin A. "St. Jerome as a Humanist," in *A Monument to Saint Jerome: Essays on*

*Some Aspects of His Life, Works and Influence*, edited by Francis X. Murphy. New York: Sheed & Ward, 1952. pp. 203–232.
Rabb, Theodore K. *Renaissance Lives: Portraits of an Age*. New York: Pantheon, 1993.
Raymond, Ernest. *In the Steps of St. Francis*. London: Rich & Cowan, 1938.
Reumann, John H. P. *The Romance of Bible Scripts and Scholars: Chapters in the History of Bible Transmission and Translation*. Englewood Cliffs: Prentice-Hall, 1965.
Reynolds, L. D., and N. G. Wilson. *Scribes and Scholars: A Guide to the Transmission of Greek and Latin Literature*. 3rd ed. Oxford: Oxford University Press, 1991.
Rice, Eugene F., Jr. *Saint Jerome in the Renaissance*. Baltimore: Johns Hopkins University Press, 1985.
Richter, Michael. *Medieval Ireland: The Enduring Tradition*. New York: St. Martin's, 1988.
Rico, Francisco. "Humanism," in *15th Century*, edited by Enrico Basaglia. Seville: Centro Publicaciones, 1992. pp. 86–95.
Roberts, Colin H., and T. C. Skeat. *The Birth of the Codex*. London: Oxford University Press, 1983.
Robertson, Edwin. *Makers of the English Bible*. Cambridge: Lutterworth, 1990.
Robinson, H. Wheeler (ed.). *The Bible in Its Ancient and English Versions*. Oxford: Oxford University Press, 1954.
Rogerson, John (ed.). *The Oxford Illustrated History of the Bible*. Oxford: Oxford University Press, 2001.
_____, Christopher Rowland, and Barnabas Lindars. *The Study and Use of the Bible*. Grand Rapids: Eerdmans, 1988.
Rosenwein, Barbara H. *A Short History of the Middle Ages*. Peterborough: Broadview, 2002.
Rotzetter, Anton. "Mysticism and Literal Observance of the Gospel in Francis of Assisi," in *Francis of Assisi Today*, edited by Christian Duquoc and Casiano Floristan. New York: Seabury, 1981. pp. 56–64.
Rouse, Mary A., and Richard H. Rouse. "The Schools and the Waldensians: A New Work by Durand of Huesca," in *Christendom and Its Discontents: Exclusion, Persecution, and Rebellion, 1000–1500*, edited by Scott L. Waugh and Peter D. Diehl. Cambridge: Cambridge University Press, 1996. pp. 86–111.
Rousseau, Philip. "Christian Asceticism and the Early Monks," in *Early Christianity: Origins and Evolution to AD 600*, edited by Ian Hazlett. Nashville: Abingdon, 1991. pp. 112–122.
Rowling, Marjorie. *Everyday Life in Medieval Times*. London: B. T. Batsford, 1968.
Rubin, Miri. "Religious Culture in Town and Country: Reflections on a Great Divide," in *Church and City, 1000–1500*, edited by David Abulafia, Michael Franklin, and Miri Rubin. Cambridge: Cambridge University Press, 1992. pp. 3–22.
Rummel, Erika. *Erasmus As a Translator of the Classics*. Toronto: University of Toronto Press, 1985.
Rupp, Gordon. *Patterns of Reformation*. Philadelphia: Fortress, 1969.
Russell, James C. *The Germanization of Early Medieval Christianity: A Sociohistorical Approach to Religious Transformation*. New York: Oxford University Press, 1994.
Ryan, John. *Irish Monasticism: Origins and Early Development*. Ithaca: Cornell University Press, 1972.
Sabatier, Paul. *Life of St. Francis of Assisi*. New York: Charles Scribner's Sons, 1894.
Saenger, Paul. "The Impact of the Early Printed Page on the Reading of the Bible," in *The Bible As Book: The First Printed Editions*, edited by Paul Saenger and Kimberly Van Kampen. London: The British Library, 1999. pp. 31–51.
_____, and Kimberly Van Kampen (eds.). *The Bible As Book: The First Printed Editions*. London: The British Library, 1999.
Samuel, Athanasius Yeshue. *Treasure of Qumran: My Story of the Dead Sea Scrolls*. Philadelphia: The Westminster Press, 1966.
Sanders, James A. "Canon as Dialogue," in *The Bible at Qumran: Text, Shape, and Inter-

*pretation*, edited by Peter W. Flint. Grand Rapids: William B. Eerdmans, 2001. pp. 7-26.

\_\_\_\_\_. "The Judaean Desert Scrolls and the History of the Text of the Hebrew Bible," in *Caves of Enlightenment*, edited by James H. Charlesworth. North Richland Hills: Bibal, 1998. pp. 1-17.

Scanlin, Harold P. "Bible Translation by American Individuals," in *The Bible and Bibles in America*, edited by Ernest S. Frerichs. Atlanta: Scholars Press, 1988. pp. 43-82.

\_\_\_\_\_. *The Dead Sea Scrolls & Modern Translations of the Old Testament*. Wheaton: Tyndale House, 1993.

Schiffman, Lawrence H. *Reclaiming the Dead Sea Scrolls*. Philadelphia: The Jewish Publication Society, 1994.

Schoeck, R. J. *Erasmus of Europe: The Making of a Humanist, 1467-1500*. Edinburgh: Edinburgh University Press, 1990.

Schwarcz, Andreas. "Cult and Religion among the Tervingi and the Visigoths and Their Conversion to Christianity," in *The Visigoths from the Migration Period to the Seventh Century: An Ethnographic Perspective*, edited by Peter Heather. Woodbridge: Boydell, 1999. pp. 447-459.

Schwarz, W. *Principles and Problems of Biblical Translation: Some Reformation Controversies and Their Background*. Cambridge: Cambridge University Press, 1955.

Schwiebert, Ernest G. *Luther and His Times: The Reformation from a New Perspective*. St. Louis: Concordia, 1950.

\_\_\_\_\_. "New Groups and Ideas at the University of Wittenberg." *Archiv für Reformationsgeschichte*, 49 (1958) 60-79.

\_\_\_\_\_. "The Theses and Wittenberg," in *Luther for an Ecumenical Age: Essays in Commemoration of the 450th Anniversary of the Reformation*, edited by Carl S. Meyer. St. Louis: Concordia, 1967. pp. 120-143.

Semple, W. H. "St. Jerome As a Biblical Translator." *Bulletin of the John Rylands Library*, 48 (1965-66) 227-243.

Shanks, Hershel. *The Dead Sea Scrolls after Forty Years*. Washington: Biblical Archaeology Society, 1991.

\_\_\_\_\_. "Intrigue and the Scroll," in *Understanding the Dead Sea Scrolls*, edited by Hershel Shanks. New York: Random House, 1992. pp. 116-125.

\_\_\_\_\_. "Is the Vatican Suppressing the Dead Sea Scrolls?," in *Understanding the Dead Sea Scrolls*, edited by Hershel Shanks. New York: Random House, 1992. pp. 275-290.

\_\_\_\_\_. *The Mystery and Meaning of the Dead Sea Scrolls*. New York: Random House, 1998.

\_\_\_\_\_. "Of Caves and Scholars: An Overview," in *Understanding the Dead Sea Scrolls*, edited by Hershel Shanks. New York: Random House, 1992. pp. xv-xxxviii.

\_\_\_\_\_ (ed.). *Understanding the Dead Sea Scrolls*. New York: Random House, 1992.

Sharpe, John L., III, and Kimberly van Kampen (eds.). *The Bible as Book: The Manuscript Tradition*. London: The British Library, 1998.

Sharpe, Richard. *Medieval Irish Saints' Lives: An Introduction to Vitae Sanctorum Hiberniae*. Oxford: Clarendon, 1991.

Sheeley, Steven M., and Robert N. Nash, Jr. *The Bible in English Translation: An Essential Guide*. Nashville: Abingdon, 1997.

Sheler, Jeffery L. "Can Ideas Be Held Hostage?" *U.S. News & World Report*, June 25, 1990, 56-57.

Sherley-Price, Leo. *Bede: A History of the English Church and People*. Harmondsworth: Penguin, 1968.

Sherman, William H. "'The Book thus put in every vulgar hand': Impressions of Readers in Early English Printed Bibles," in *The Bible As Book: The First Printed Editions*, edited by Paul Saenger and Kimberly Van Kampen. London: The British Library, 1999. pp. 125-133.

Shinners, John (ed.). *Medieval Popular Religion, 1000-1500: A Reader*. Peterborough: Broadview, 1997.

Silberman, Neil Asher. *The Hidden Scrolls: Christianity, Judaism, & the War for the Dead Sea Scrolls.* New York: G. P. Putnam's Sons, 1994.
Simms, G. O. *The Book of Kells.* Dublin: Dolman, 1961.
Skehan, Patrick W. "St. Jerome and the Canon of the Holy Scriptures," in *A Monument to Saint Jerome: Essays on Some Aspects of His Life, Works and Influence,* edited by Francis X. Murphy. New York: Sheed & Ward, 1952. pp. 259–287.
Smalley, Beryl. "The Bible in the Medieval Schools," in *The Cambridge History of the Bible: The West from the Fathers to the Reformation,* edited by G. W. H. Lampe. Cambridge: Cambridge University Press, 1969. pp. 197–220.
\_\_\_\_\_. *The Study of the Bible in the Middle Ages.* Oxford: Basil Blackwell, 1984.
Smith, John Holland. *Francis of Assisi.* London: Sidgwick & Jackson, 1972.
Smith, Lesley. "Lending Books: The Growth of a Medieval Question from Langton to Bonaventure," in *Intellectual Life in the Middle Ages,* edited by Lesley Smith and Benedicta Ward. London: Hambledon, 1992. pp. 265–279.
\_\_\_\_\_, and Benedicta Ward (eds.). *Intellectual Life in the Middle Ages.* London: Hambledon, 1992.
Smith, Preserved. *Erasmus: A Study of His Life, Ideals, and Place in History.* New York: Frederick Unger, 1962.
Southern, R. W. *The Making of the Middle Ages.* New Haven: Yale University Press, 1959.
\_\_\_\_\_. *Western Society and the Church in the Middle Ages.* Harmondsworth: Penguin, 1970.
Sparks, H. F. D. "Jerome As Biblical Scholar," in *The Cambridge History of the Bible: From the Beginnings to Jerome,* edited by P. R. Ackroyd and C. F. Evans. Cambridge: Cambridge University Press, 1970. 510–541.
\_\_\_\_\_. "The Latin Bible," in *The Bible in Its Ancient and English Versions,* edited by H. Wheeler Robinson. Oxford: Oxford University Press, 1954. pp. 100–127.
\_\_\_\_\_. *On Translations of the Bible.* London: University of London Press, 1973.
Spinka, Matthew. *John Hus: A Biography.* Princeton: Princeton University Press, 1968.
\_\_\_\_\_. *John Hus at the Council of Constance.* New York: Columbia University Press, 1965.
\_\_\_\_\_. *John Hus and Czech Reform.* Chicago: University of Chicago Press, 1941.
Spitz, Lewis W. *Luther and German Humanism.* Aldershot: Variorum, 1996.
\_\_\_\_\_. *The Religious Renaissance of the German Humanists.* Cambridge: Harvard University Press, 1963.
Stacey, John. *John Wyclif and Reform.* London: Lutterworth, 1964.
Starck, Mary-Ann (ed.). *Medieval Saints: A Reader.* Peterborough: Broadview, 1999.
Stegemann, Hartmut. "How to Connect Dead Sea Scroll Fragments," in *Understanding the Dead Sea Scrolls,* edited by Hershel Shanks. New York: Random House, 1992. pp. 245–255.
Stegemann, Hartmut. *The Library of Qumran: On the Essenes, Qumran, John the Baptist, and Jesus.* Leiden: Brill Academic Publishers, 1998.
Steinmetz, David C. "Luther, the Reformers, and the Bible," in *Living Traditions of the Bible: Scripture in Jewish, Christian, and Muslim Practice,* edited by James E. Bowley. St. Louis: Chalice, 1999. pp. 163–176.
\_\_\_\_\_ (ed.). *The Bible in the Sixteenth Century.* Durham: Duke University Press, 1990.
Stendahl, Krister. "The Scrolls and the New Testament: An Introduction and a Perspective," in *The Scrolls and the New Testament,* edited by Krister Stendahl. Westport: Greenwood, 1975. pp. 1–17.
\_\_\_\_\_ (ed.). *The Scrolls and the New Testament.* Westport: Greenwood, 1975.
Stevenson, Jane. "Literacy in Ireland: The Evidence of the Patrick Dossier in the Book of Armagh," in *The Uses of Literacy in Early Medieval Europe,* edited by Rosamond McKitterick. Cambridge: Cambridge University Press, 1990. pp. 11–35.
Stevick, Robert D. *The Earliest Irish and English Bookarts: Visual and Poetic Forms before A.D. 1000.* Philadelphia: University of Pennsylvania Press, 1994.
Stewart, Columba. "Monasticism," in *The Early Christian World,* edited by Philip F. Esler. London: Routledge, 2000. pp. 344–366.

Strauss, Gerald. *Luther's House of Learning: Indoctrination of the Young in the German Reformation.* Baltimore: Johns Hopkins University Press, 1978.
Strayer, Joseph R. *Western Europe in the Middle Ages: A Short History.* 3rd ed. Glenview, Illinois: Scott, Foresman, 1982.
_____, and Dana C. Munro. *The Middle Ages: 395–1500.* New York: Appleton-Century-Crofts, 1959.
Stubbs, M. Wilma. *How Europe Was Won for Christianity: Being the Life-Stories of the Men Concerned in Its Conquest.* New York: Fleming H. Revell, 1913.
Sullivan, Edward. *The Book of Kells.* London: The Studio, 1914.
Sullivan, Richard E. *Christian Missionary Activity in the Early Middle Ages.* Aldershot: Variorum, 1994.
Sussmann, Ayala, and Ruth Peled. *Scrolls from the Dead Sea.* New York: George Braziller, 1993.
Swanson, R. N. *Church and Society in Late Medieval England.* Oxford: Basil Blackwell, 1989.
Taylor, David G. K. "Christian Regional Diversity," in *The Early Christian World,* edited by Philip F. Esler. London: Routledge, 2000. pp. 330–343.
Testa, Rita Lizzi. "Christianization and Conversion in Northern Italy," in *The Origins of Christendom in the West,* edited by Alan Kreider. Edinburgh: T. & T. Clark, 2001. pp. 47–95.
Thompson, A. Hamilton (ed.). *Bede: His Life, Times, and Writings: Essays in Commemoration of the Twelfth Centenary of His Death.* New York: Russell & Russell, 1966.
Thompson, E. A. *The Visigoths in the Time of Ulfila.* London: Oxford University Press, 1966.
_____. *Who Was Saint Patrick?* Woodbridge, Suffolk: Boydell, 1985.
*A Thousand Years of the Bible.* J. Paul Getty Museum and UCLA, 1991.
Timmermans, Felix. *The Perfect Joy of St. Francis.* Garden City: Image, 1955.
Tischendorf, Constantine. *Codex Sinaiticus: The Ancient Biblical Manuscript Now in the British Museum: Tischendorf's Story and Argument Related by Himself.* 8th ed. London: Lutterworth, 1934.
Todd, Malcolm. *Everyday Life of the Barbarians: Goths, Franks and Vandals.* London: B. T. Batsford, 1972.
Tov, Emanuel. "Hebrew Biblical Manuscripts from the Judaean Desert: Their Contribution to Textual Criticism." *Journal of Jewish Studies,* 39 (1988) 5–37.
_____. "The Publication of the Texts from the Judean Desert: Past, Present, and Future," in *The Dead Sea Scrolls at Fifty,* edited by Robert A. Kugler and Eileen M. Schuller. Atlanta: Scholars Press, 1999. pp. 21–27.
Tracy, James D. *Erasmus: The Growth of a Mind.* Geneva: Droz, 1972.
Trevelyan, George Macaulay. *England in the Age of Wycliffe.* 4th ed. London: Longmans, Green, 1909.
Trever, John C. *The Dead Sea Scrolls: A Personal Account.* Grand Rapids: William B. Eerdmans, 1977.
_____. *Scrolls from Qumran Cave I.* Jerusalem: The Albright Institute of Archaeological Research, 1972.
_____. *The Untold Story of Qumran.* Westwood, New Jersey: Fleming H. Revell, 1965.
Trevor-Roper, Hugh. *The Rise of Christian Europe.* London: Thames and Hudson, 1965.
Trexler, Richard C. *Naked Before the Father: The Renunciation of Francis of Assisi.* New York: Peter Lang, 1989.
Trinkaus, Charles. *The Scope of Renaissance Humanism.* Ann Arbor: University of Michigan Press, 1983.
Tuchman, Barbara W. *A Distant Mirror: The Calamitous 14th Century.* Alfred A. Knopf, 1978.
Twigg, Graham. *The Black Death: A Biological Reappraisal.* London: Batsford Academic and Educational, 1984.

Ulrich, Eugene. "The Bible in the Making: The Scriptures Found at Qumran," in *The Bible at Qumran: Text, Shape, and Interpretation*, edited by Peter W. Flint. Grand Rapids: William B. Eerdmans, 2001. pp. 51–66.

_____. *The Dead Sea Scrolls and the Origins of the Bible*. Leiden: Brill Academic Publishers, 1999.

_____. "Multiple Literary Editions: Reflections toward a Theory of the History of the Biblical Text," in *Current Research and Technological Developments on the Dead Sea Scrolls*, edited by Donald W. Parry and Stephen D. Ricks. Leiden: E. J. Brill, 1996. pp. 78–105.

_____. "The Scrolls and the Study of the Hebrew Bible," in *The Dead Sea Scrolls at Fifty*, edited by Robert A. Kugler and Eileen M. Schuller. Atlanta: Scholars Press, 1999. pp. 31–41.

Valantasis, Richard (ed.). *Religions of Late Antiquity in Practice*. Princeton: Princeton University Press, 2000.

Van Deusen, Nancy (ed.). *The Place of the Psalms in the Intellectual Culture of the Middle Ages*. Albany: State University of New York Press, 1999.

Van Doornik, N. G. *Francis of Assisi: A Prophet for Our Time*. Chicago: Franciscan Herald Press, 1979.

Van Engen, John. "'God is no Respecter of Persons': Sacred Texts and Social Realities," in *Intellectual Life in the Middle Ages*, edited by Lesley Smith and Benedicta Ward. London: Hambledon, 1992. pp. 243–264.

Van Zijl, Theodore P. *Gerard Groote, Ascetic and Reformer (1340–1384)*. Washington: Catholic University of America, 1963.

VanderKam, James C. "The Dead Sea Scrolls and Christianity," in *Understanding the Dead Sea Scrolls*, edited by Hershel Shanks. New York: Random House, 1992. pp. 181–202.

VanderKam, James C. *The Dead Sea Scrolls Today*. Grand Rapids: Eerdmans, 1994.

Vandriver, Elizabeth, Ralph Keen, and Thomas D. Frazel (eds.). *Luther's Lives: Two Contemporary Accounts of Martin Luther*. Manchester: Manchester University Press, 2002.

Vauchez, André. *The Laity in the Middle Ages: Religious Beliefs and Devotional Practices*. Notre Dame: University of Notre Dame Press, 1993.

Vermès, Géza. *Discovery in the Judean Desert*. New York: Desclee, 1956.

Von Campenhausen, H. *The Formation of the Christian Bible*. Philadelphia: Fortress, 1968.

Von Loewenich, Walther. *Martin Luther: The Man and His Work*. Minneapolis: Augsburg, 1986.

Von Nolcken, Christina. "Lay Literacy, the Democratization of God's Law and the Lollards," in *The Bible as Book: The Manuscript Tradition*, edited by John L. Sharpe III, and Kimberly van Kampen. London: The British Library, 1998. pp. 177–195.

Wagner, Klaus. "Printing in Europe in the 15th Century," in *15th Century*, edited by Enrico Basaglia. Seville: Centro Publicaciones, 1992. pp. 76–83.

Wakefield, Walter L. *Heresy, Crusade and Inquisition in Southern France, 1100–1250*. Berkeley: University of California Press, 1974.

Wallace-Hadrill, J. M. *The Barbarian West, 400–1000*. 4th ed. Oxford: Basil Blackwell, 1985.

_____. *The Frankish Church*. Oxford: Oxford University Press, 1983.

Walsh, Katherine, and Diana Wood (eds.). *The Bible in the Medieval World: Essays in Memory of Beryl Smalley*. Oxford: Basil Blackwell, 1985.

Waltke, Bruce K. "How We Got the Hebrew Bible: The Text and Canon of the Old Testament," in *The Bible at Qumran: Text, Shape, and Interpretation*, edited by Peter W. Flint. Grand Rapids: William B. Eerdmans, 2001. pp. 27–50.

Ward, Benedicta. "Miracles and History: A Reconsideration of the Miracle Stories Used by Bede," in *Famulus Christi: Essays in Commemoration of the Thirteenth Centenary of the Birth of the Venerable Bede*, edited by Gerald Bonner. London: SPCK, 1976. pp. 70–76.

Waterman, John T. *A History of the German Language*. Rev. ed. Seattle: University of Washington Press, 1976.
Waugh, Scott L., and Peter D. Diehl (eds.). *Christendom and Its Discontents: Exclusion, Persecution, and Rebellion, 1000–1500*. Cambridge: Cambridge University Press, 1996.
Webster, Leslie, and Michelle Brown (eds.). *The Transformation of the Roman World, AD 400–900*. Berkeley: University of California Press, 1997.
Weiland, J. Sperna, and W. Th. M. Frijhoff (eds.). *Erasmus of Rotterdam: The Man and the Scholar*. Leiden: E.J. Brill, 1988.
Weiss, Roberto. "The New Learning," in *The Age of the Renaissance*, edited by Denys Hay. London: Thames and Hudson, 1986. pp. 101–122.
Weitzmann, Kurt. *Late Antique and Early Christian Book Illumination*. New York: George Braziller, 1977.
West, Andrew Fleming. *Alcuin and the Rise of the Christian Schools*. London: William Heinemann, 1893.
Westcott, Brooke Foss. *A General View of the History of the English Bible*. 3rd ed. London: Macmillan, 1905.
Whitelock, Dorothy, Rosamond McKitterick, and David Dumville (eds.). *Ireland in Early Medieval Europe: Studies in Memory of Kathleen Hughes*. Cambridge: Cambridge University Press, 1982.
Whitelock, Dorothy. "Bede and His Teachers and Friends," in *Famulus Christi: Essays in Commemoration of the Thirteenth Centenary of the Birth of the Venerable Bede*, edited by Gerald Bonner. London: SPCK, 1976. pp. 19–39.
Whiting, C. E. "The Life of the Venerable Bede," in *Bede: His Life, Times, and Writings*, edited by A. Hamilton Thompson. Oxford: Oxford University Press, 1935. pp. 1–38.
Wieruszowski, Helene. *The Medieval University: Masters, Students, Learning*. Princeton: D. Van Nostrand, 1966.
Wilson, Edmund. *The Dead Sea Scrolls 1947–1969*. New York: Oxford University Press, 1969.
Winckler, Paul A. (ed.). *Reader in the History of Books and Printing*. Englewood, Colorado: Information Handling Services, 1978.
Winship, George Parker. *Gutenberg to Plantin: An Outline of the Early History of Printing*. New York: Burt Franklin, 1968.
Wise, Michael, Martin Abegg, Jr., and Edward Cook. *The Dead Sea Scrolls: A New Translation*. San Francisco: HarperSanFrancisco, 1996.
Wolfram, Herwig. *History of the Goths*. Berkeley: University of California Press, 1988.
Wood, Ian. "The Transmission of Ideas," in *The Transformation of the Roman World, AD 400–900*, edited by Leslie Webster and Michelle Brown. Berkeley: University of California Press, 1997. pp. 111–126.
Woodward, Scott R., Gila Kahila, Patricia Smith, Charles Greenblatt, Joe Zias, and Magen Broshi. "Analysis of Parchment Fragments from the Judean Desert Using DNA Techniques," in *Current Research and Technological Developments on the Dead Sea Scrolls*, edited by Donald W. Parry and Stephen D. Ricks. Leiden: E. J. Brill, 1996. pp. 215–238.
Worth, Roland H., Jr. *Bible Translations: A History through Source Documents*. Jefferson: McFarland, 1992.
_____. *Church, Monarch and Bible in Sixteenth-Century England: The Political Context of Biblical Translation*. Jefferson: McFarland, 2000.
Yadin, Yigael. "The Temple Scroll—the Longest Dead Sea Scroll," in *Understanding the Dead Sea Scrolls*, edited by Hershel Shanks. New York: Random House, 1992. pp. 87–112.
Yarom, Nitza. *Body, Blood and Sexuality: A Psychoanalytic Study of St. Francis' Stigmata and their Historical Context*. New York: Peter Lang, 1992.
Yates, Frances A. *Ideas and Ideals in the North European Renaissance: Collected Essays*. Vol. 3. London: Routledge & Kegan Paul, 1984.
Ziegler, Philip. *The Black Death*. Stroud: Alan Sutton, 1991.

# Index

abbot 44
Abegg, Martin 180
*Acta Sanctorum* 33
Acts (biblical book) 8, 10, 182
Acts of Andrew 15
Acts of John 15
Acts of Paul 14
Acts of Paul and Thecla 11
Acts of Pilate 52
*Address to the Christian Nobility of the German Nation* 134
Adelbert 40
Afghanistan 54
Alaric 22, 33
Albright, William Foxwell 159
Albright Institute of Archaeological Research 179
Alexander VI (pope) 113–114
Alexandria 13, 15, 18
Alexis (saint) 65
Alfonso VI (of Spain) 23
Allegro, John 176, 178
*Altus Prosator* 51
Amazons 20, 116
Ambrose (bishop of Milan) 41
American School of Oriental Research, Jerusalem 158–159, 161, 166
American Standard Version (1901) 189
Amiens 69
anchorites 27
Ancient Biblical Manuscript Center, California 180
Angles 57, 89
Anglo-Norman (language) 89
Anglo-Saxon 54, 59, 62
*Antibarbari* 107
Antioch 13–14, 26–27
Antwerp 135, 142
Apocalypse of Peter 14–15
Apocrypha 12–13
Apostles' Creed 18, 137
Apulia 73, 75

Aquileia 26
Aquinas, Thomas 101
Aquitaine 56
Aramaic 9
Arian Christianity 21–24, 34
Arian controversy 18, 24
Aristotle 102
Arius 18
Asia Minor (now Turkey) 14
Asperius 36
Athanasius 15
Attila the Hun 23
Augustine 32, 60, 109
Augustinian order 98–99
Aurogallus, Matthew 124
Aventine 29
Azores 116

Babylon 12
Bacon, Roger 109
Ball, John 88
"barbarian" 23
bard 45, 47, 51
Basel 109–110
"Be Thou My Vision" (hymn) 51
Bechtel, Elizabeth Hays 180
Bede, the Venerable 56–58, 60–63, 84, 89, 103, 182
Benedict (saint) 35
Bernardone, Pietro 72
Bethlehem 30–31, 42
Bible: significance and dissemination 3–4, 8, 42–43, 64, 66–67, 87, 89, 94–96, 101–104, 107, 115, 124–126, 131, 134, 137, 149, 192
Bible in English 13, 62, 91–92, 94, 150, 191; see also American Standard Version (1901); Bishops' Bible; Coverdale Bible (1535); English Revised Version (1881); Geneva Bible (1560); Great Bible; Jerusalem Bible; King James Bible; Matthew's Bible (1537); New English

Bible; New International Version; New Revised Standard Version (1990); Revised Standard Version (1952); Rheims-Douai Bible; Tyndale's Bible; Wycliffite Bible
*Biblical Archaeology Review* 177, 179
Bibliothèque Nationale, Paris 67, 151
Biscop, Benedict 58–60
bishop 44
Bishops' Bible 148
Bisticci, Vespasiano da 132
Black Death 82–83
black-letter 147
Black Sea 82, 88
Boccaccio, Giovanni 42
Bohemia (now the Czech Republic) 94
Boleyn, Anne 145–146
Book of Durrow 53, 151
Book of Hours 124
Book of Kells 53–54, 151
Borgia, Lucrezia 114
Bourges 69
Breviary, Roman 31, 91
Britain *see* England
British Museum 151–152, 157, 172
Brussels 143
Bulgaria 21
*Bulletin of the American Schools of Oriental Research* 165
Byblos 8
Byzantine empire 117
Byzantium *see* Constantinople

Caedmon 61
Caedmonian poems 61
Caesarea 31, 157
calligraphy 131, 151, 157
Calvary 42, 69, 79
Cambridge University 137
Cannae 22
canon of Scripture 11–16
*Canterbury Tales* 89
Cape Nothing 116
Cape Verde Islands 116
carbon-14 dating 183
Cassiodorus 20, 33–38, 59–60, 182
Cathach 48, 52, 151
Cathars 77
cathedral schools 83–84
Catholic Christianity 22–24, 39, 57, 149, 190–191; *see also* Roman Catholic Church
Celtic tradition *see* paganism
Ceolfrid 58–60
Challoner, Richard 149
Charlemagne 40, 42, 108
Charles the Bald 52
Charles I (English monarch) 151
Charles I (king of Spain) 117
Chartres 69
Chaucer, Geoffrey 89

China 82, 117; Han Dynasty 132
Christina (queen of Sweden) 17
Christmas 8, 39, 51, 78–79, 125
church, medieval 66–70, 77–78, 81, 84–85, 88, 94–95; abuses 84–87, 90, 94, 105, 113–114
Church of England 13
Cicero 25, 27, 107
city, medieval 64, 68–69, 82
Cochlaeus, John 139–140
codex 15
Codex Alexandrinus 151, 187
Codex Amiatinus 59, 108
Codex Argenteus (Silver Codex) 17, 23–24
Codex Claromontanus 151
Codex Ephraemi 151
Codex Grandior 59
Codex Sinaiticus 15, 157, 187–189
Codex Vaticanus 152, 188
Cologne 17, 40, 69, 140
Cologne Chronicle of 1499 129
Colossians 4:16 11
Columba (saint) 45–51, 53
Columbus, Christopher 12, 116
computer technology 176
*Concerning Christian Liberty* 134
Constantine 15, 18, 21, 26, 56, 157
Constantinople (formerly named Byzantium) 15, 19, 27, 36, 117
copper scroll 169
Coptic church 18
Corinthians I 11
Corinthians II 190
corruption of biblical text 3, 28, 37–38, 108–109, 131–134, 149–151, 182, 185–187
Council of Constance 94–96
Council of Hippo 15
Council of Nicea 26
Council of Trent 13, 149
Count of Brienne 73, 75
Coverdale, Miles 142, 145
Coverdale Bible (1535) 144–146, 148
Crete 9
Crusades 73
Cuthbert (saint) 55

Dacia 20–22
Daniel (biblical book) 170, 184
Dante 57
Dark Ages 23, 39, 56
Dead Sea 1–2, 171–173
Dead Sea Scrolls 2–3, 158–170, 172, 174–187, 190; assessment and significance 182–186; Cave 4Q 169, 174–181
Decapolis 6
*The Decline and Fall of the Roman Empire* 150
demons 6, 40, 97
Denmark 57
Desert Fathers of Egypt 152

# Index 217

Deuteronomy (biblical book) 171, 186
diocese 44
division of text: into chapters 147; into paragraphs 141, 147; by punctuation 54; into verses 147; into words 54
divorce 9
Donatus, Aelius 25
Douai 149
druid 45
drunkenness 81
Duns Scotus, John 101

Eadfrith 54, 60
Easter 78
Ecclesiastes 12:12 11
*Ecclesiastical History* 14, 172
École Biblique et Archéologique, Jerusalem 166
Edward VI (English monarch) 146
Eisenman, Robert 179–181
Elizabeth I (English monarch) 147–149
Emersen, Margaret von 139, 142
Emersen, Matthias von 139
Emser, Jerome 127
England 44, 52, 54–57, 59, 62–63, 82, 88, 94, 130, 135, 138–140, 144, 146, 149
English Bible *see* Bible in English
*English Psalter* 89–90
English Revised Version (1881) 188–189
Ephraem (saint) 151
Epictetus 19
Epistle of Barnabas 15
Erasmus, Desiderius 103–110, 115, 127, 137, 150, 152, 188, 192; Greek New Testament 108–112, 137, 141, 150; and Jerome 107–108
Erigena, John Scotus 52, 103
eschaton 8
Estienne, Robert 110, 147
Eusebius (bishop of Nicomedia) 18–19
Eusebius of Caesarea 14–15
excommunication 78, 86–87, 90
Ezra (the scribe) 12, 59

famine 81, 97, 140
Fêng Tao 132
Finnian 47–48
Florence 82
Folger Shakespeare Library, Washington 133
Fontevrault (abbey) 66
food laws 9
Francis of Assisi 72–80, 87, 125
Francis I (king of France) 117
Frederick Barbarossa (emperor) 71
Frederick the Wise 42, 100–103, 114, 117, 119, 121
Froben, Johann 103, 109, 112
Fronto 27

Gallican Psalter 31
Gama, Vasco da 116

Garden of Eden 116
Gaul 22
Genesis (biblical book) 1, 79, 142
Geneva Bible (1560) 147–149
George, duke of Albertine Saxony 127
German language 125–126, 128–129
Gerritszoon, Gerrit 104
Gervasius (saint) 41
Ghibellines 106
Gibbon, Edward 150
*The Good News Bible* 191
Gospel of Nicodemus 52
Gospel of Philip 10
Gospel of the Hebrews 15
Gospel of Thomas 10, 15
Gospel of Truth 10
gospels ascribed to Peter, Thomas, Matthias 15
Gothia 20–21
Gothic Bible 17, 21, 23–24
Gothic language 17, 21
Goths 17, 19, 20–21, 34
Great Bible 146, 148
Great Famine 81
Greccio 78, 125
Greek Bible 31
Greek language 9, 13, 103, 137, 189
Greek New Testament 103, 109, 112, 157
Gregory I (pope) 35, 56
Gregory the Great (pope) *see* Gregory I
Guelfs 106
Gutenberg, Johannes 129–130
Gutenberg Bible 129–131

Hadrian's Wall 56
Hamburg 139, 142
Hannibal 22
Harding, Gerald Lankester 165–168, 174
Harvard University 147
Hebrew language 12, 31–32
Hebrew Union College, Cincinnati 180
Hebrew University, Jerusalem 162, 180
Hebrews (biblical book) 15
Helena (saint) 42
Henry VIII (English king) 117, 135, 137, 140–141, 143–146
Henry the Navigator, Prince 116
Hereford, Nicholas 90–91
"heresy" 24
Herod 5–6
Herodias 6
Hexapla 31–32
Hisperica Famina 51
*Historia Ecclesiastica Gentis Anglorum* 60
Hobbes, Thomas 97
Holland 17
Holy Land 30, 79, 93, 102, 159, 171
Holy Roman Empire 99, 113, 117
Holy Spirit 14, 42, 50
Hugh of Lincoln 41

Hundred Years' War 88
Huns 21–22
Huntington Library 180
Hupei 82
Hus, John 93–96, 115

Ignatius 8
illiteracy 8, 19, 38–39, 43, 69, 86, 101, 108, 125, 134
illumination of manuscripts 52–55
India 18, 116
indulgences 114
Infancy Story of Thomas 11
infra-red technology 176
Inner Circle 178–181
*Institutiones* 36
International Conference on Biblical Archaeology 176
interpretation of Scripture 68, 102, 141, 187, 191
Iona 49–50, 53–54, 57
Irish monastic culture 44, 48, 50–54, 103
Isaiah (biblical book) 7, 105, 158, 183–185, 190
Israel Antiquities Authority 173, 181
Italy 23, 74

James I (English monarch) 148–149
Jamnia 11–12
Jarrow 57
Jeremiah (biblical book) 184
Jerome (saint) 12, 25–32, 54, 109, 182, 184; appreciated during Renaissance 107–109; revises Latin gospels 28; revises Latin Old Testament 31; translates Hebrew Old Testament into Latin 31–32
Jerusalem Bible 191
Jesus 6–11, 35, 38–39, 42, 46, 58, 66, 68–69, 77–79, 94–95, 183, 187
Jewish Scripture 7–9, 11
Job (biblical book) 71
John (biblical gospel) 9–10, 62, 187–188
John the Baptist 5–6, 42, 72
John I 150
John XXIII (the "antipope") 95
Jordanes 20
Jordanian Department of Antiquities 165, 176
Josephus 36, 60, 186
Judaea 6
Julius Caesar 5
Julius II (pope) 113
Justinian (emperor) 153

Kando 162, 165–168, 170
Kells 53
kill-the-cat 74
King James Bible 3, 11–13, 89, 110–111, 134, 141, 148–149, 188–190, 192
Kingdom of Heaven 5

Kings (biblical books) 21
Koberger, House of (Nuremberg) 132

Langton, Stephen 147
lapis lazuli 54
Latin Bible 28, 31–32, 59, 70, 89–91, 101, 108–110, 112, 129, 131, 145
Latin language 12, 36, 43, 51, 62, 67, 70, 76, 86, 101, 103, 105
lector 19
Leo X (pope) 113, 115, 117–118
Leviticus (biblical book) 126, 185
*Life of Ceolfrid* 59
Lindisfarne 54–55, 57
Lindisfarne Gospels 54–55, 59
literacy *see* illiteracy
Little Sodbury Manor 137, 139
*The Living Bible* 191
Loch Ness monster 46
Lollards 88–89, 91–92, 137
Lombard, Peter: *Sentences* 99
Lombard Kingdom 23
Lombards 23, 38
London 137, 139, 140, 146
Lord's Prayer 62, 109–110, 137, 188
Luke (biblical book) 10, 189
Luther, Martin 12, 97–99, 101–105, 112–115, 117–125, 127–128, 134, 137–140, 192; German Bible 124, 126–128, 145; German translation of the New Testament 123–124, 126–127, 134, 138, 141; German translation of the Old Testament 124, 126, 142
Lutterworth, England 89
Lyons 64

magic 8, 39, 42–48, 55
Magna Carta 147
Malacca 116
Manetti, Giannozzo 110
manuscripts 35–37, 47–48, 109–112, 131–132, 150–159, 172, 174–176, 182–187; *see also* corruption of biblical text
Manutius, Aldus 103
Marcellinus, Ammianus 22
Marcion 13
Mark (biblical book) 10, 68, 189
Maro Grammaticus, Virgilius 52
Mary Magdalene 41
Mary I (English monarch) 146
Matthew (biblical book) 9–10, 35, 66, 76–77, 79, 112, 140, 189
Matthew's Bible (1537) 146, 148
*Mayflower* 147
messiah 5–6, 9
Messina 82
Middle English (language) 89
Milik, J.T. 178
miracles 6, 8, 46, 55, 60–61, 79, 105
missionaries 8, 44, 54, 57, 108

Index 219

Moabite Stone 172
Moffett, William A. 180
Mohammed 153
Moluccas 116
monasticism 35, 44–45, 51, 62, 79, 83–85, 98–99, 101, 108, 130–131, 153; *see also* Irish monastic culture
Montanus 14
Monte Amiata, abbey of 59
More, Thomas 141, 143
Morrigan 52,
Moses (patriarch) 31
Mount La Verna 79
Mount Sinai 152–153
mystery plays 125

Nag Hammadi 10
Napoleon 152
Nathan, Rabbi 147
Netherlands 135
New English Bible 191
New International Version 191
New Latin Psalter 31
New Revised Standard Version (1990) 186, 190–191
New Testament 7, 9, 15, 183, 186–188, 191
*The New York Times* 180
New York University 178
Nicene Creed 18
Nicomedia 18
Northumbria 57, 62
Noseley, England 82
Notre Dame (cathedral) 69
Nuremberg 110

O'Donnell clan 48
Odovacar 34
Oecolampadius 140
*Of the Freedom of a Christian Man* 118
ogham, Celtic 55
Old English language 61–62, 89
Old Testament 7–8, 11–12, 14–15, 31, 173, 183–185
ollamh 51
Onesimus 19
*An Open Letter to the Christian Nobility of the German Nation Concerning the Reform of the Christian Estate* 118
Operation Scroll 173
orgies at the Vatican 113–114
Origen 14
Orthodox Christianity 13, 103, 190
orthography 36, 108
Ostrogoths 20–21, 23, 34
Ottoman Turks 117
Oxford 83
Oxford University 83, 90, 94, 136, 174–175

paganism 39–40, 44–45, 47–48, 52–53, 55, 97

paleography 151, 158–160, 163, 171, 182–183
Palestine 5, 12, 31, 159
Palestine Archaeological Museum (Rockefeller Museum) 165, 175–176
papacy 27–28, 35, 41, 113–114, 117
papyrus 8, 14
Paris 82, 110
parish 68–69
Parker, Matthew 148
*Pasturella pestis* 82
Patrick (saint) 44, 46
Paul (the apostle) 8–10, 13, 15, 19
Paul's letter to the Laodiceans 11
Peasants' Revolt (1381) 88–89
Persia 72
Perugia 74, 80
Peter (saint) 41
Peter of Lombardy 59
Peter the Venerable 37
Pharisees 6, 11
Philemon (biblical book) 19
Philip (Jesus's disciple) 18
Phillips, Henry 142–143
Pilgrim Fathers 147
Pliny 27, 60
Polo, Marco 129
Poyntz, Thomas 139, 142–143
Prague 17, 95
preaching 68, 70–71, 77–78, 88, 90, 94, 120, 125
printing 128–134, 138
Protasius (saint) 41
Protevangelium of James 11
Provençal (language) 68, 73
Provence 72–73
Proverbs 14:32 186
Psalms (biblical book) 36–37, 47–48, 60, 102, 145, 172, 183–184, 190
psalter 48, 58, 71, 80, 91, 101, 108, 131
purgatory 13, 114
Puritans 147–148
Purvey, John 91

Qimron, Elisha 176–177, 181
Quentel publishing house, Cologne 139–140
Quintilian 27

*The Reason and Cause of Why Luther's Translation of the New Testament Has Been Justly Forbidden to the Common Man...* 127
"received text" 110–111, 188
Reformation, Protestant 12, 42, 97, 103, 113, 134, 139, 144
*regula fidei* 16
relics 40–43, 52, 55, 60–61, 67, 74, 80, 94, 105, 114, 153; *see also* magic; miracles
Rembrandt 80
Renaissance 12, 17, 25, 32, 100–104, 106–

107, 113, 128, 137; *see also* scholasticism, medieval
resurrection 7–8, 10
Revelation (biblical book) 15
Revised Standard Version (1952) 185–186, 189–190
Rheims 69
Rheims-Douai Bible 149
Richard II (king of England) 89
Rockefeller Museum *see* Palestine Archaeological Museum
Rogers, John 142, 146–147
Rolle, Richard 89
Roman Catholic Bibles 25, 149, 190–191
Roman Catholic Church 13, 23, 32, 52, 93, 103, 190; *see also* Catholic Christianity; church, medieval
Roman empire 15, 19–21, 34, 44, 51
Roman Index of prohibited books 127
Romania 20
Romanum (language) 68
Rome 22, 25, 44
Romuald (saint) 40
*The Rule of Saint Benedict* 35
runes, Germanic 55
Russian Orthodox Church 13

Saad, Yusif 166–168
Sabbath law 6
St. Alexis *see* Alexis (saint)
St. Ambrose *see* Ambrose (bishop of Milan)
St. Augustine *see* Augustine
St. Benedict *see* Benedict (saint)
Saint Catherine's monastery 152–157
St. Columba *see* Columba (saint)
St. Ephraem *see* Ephraem (saint)
St. Francis *see* Francis of Assisi
Saint Gall, monastery of 38
St. Ignatius *see* Ignatius
St. Jerome *see* Jerome (saint)
Saint Mark's Syrian Orthodox Monastery 158, 166
St. Patrick *see* Patrick (saint)
St. Peter *see* Peter (saint)
saints 40–43
Salvian 24
Samuel (biblical book) 184–186
Samuel, Athanasius Yeshue 159–161, 163–164, 167
Saturnalia 39
Saxons 89
Saxony 97, 99–100
Scandza 20
Schoeffer, Peter 140
scholasticism, medieval 102, 106–107, 136–137
Scotland 49, 54, 147
Scots 49, 52
scriptorium 2, 36–38

scroll 14
Scythian desert 21
Scythians 20
Septuagint 12–13, 31
Seven Deadly Sins 62
Seven Sacraments 62
Shahin, Khalil Iskander *see* Kando
shamrock 46
Shanks, Hershel 177–178, 180–181
Shapira, Moses Wilhelm 170–172
Shapira affair 170–172
Shaya 162, 166
Shepherd of Hermas 14–15
Shrine of the Book 164
Sickingen, Franz von 119–120
Siena 82
Sixtus IV (pope) 114
Smith, Morton 178
Sodom and Gomorrah 1
Soncino Hebrew text 124
sorcery 8, 97
Spain 23
Spalatin, Georg 102–103, 121, 123, 140
Spice Islands *see* Moluccas
Sponheim, Abbot of: *Praise of Scribes* 132
Squillace 35
Steelyard, London 139–140
Stephen of Bourbon 67
Strassburg 110
Strugnell, John 174, 176–180
Sukenik, Eleazar 162–164, 177
supernatural forces and powers 8, 40–41
synagogue 11
Synod of Carthage 15
Syriac language 27

Tacitus 20
Tartars 82
Temple in Jerusalem 11
Ten Commandments 62, 137, 152
Theodoric the Great 20, 34
Theodulf 182
Thomas (Jesus's disciple) 18
Timothy I 187
Tischendorf, Lobegott Friedrich Constantin 150–152, 154–157, 182, 187, 189
Tonstall, Cuthbert 137–138, 141
Toulouse 91
Tov, Emanuel 180
translation and interpretation 127, 191–192
translation, the art of 123–124, 192
translations *see* Erasmus, Desiderius; Jerome (saint); vernacular translations
Transylvania 20
Trever, John 158–161, 177, 183–185
trinity 46, 51, 150
troubadours 73
Tyndale, William 135–143, 145, 147; English translation of New Testament 136–

142, 146; English translation of Old Testament 142, 146
Tyndale's Bible 148–149

Ulm 69
ultra-violet technology 59, 176, 187
Umbria 72, 74
United Nations Truce Supervision Organization 166
universities 83–84, 130
University of Bologna 84
University of Erfurt 99, 101
University of Leipzig 100–101, 115, 150, 155
University of Paris 84, 131, 147
University of Prague 94
University of Wittenberg 99–103, 113, 138–139
"An Unpublished Halakhic Letter from Qumran" 176–177
Uppsala University 17

Valdes *see* Waldo
Valla, Lorenzo: *Annotationes* 108
vampires 97
Vandals 20
Vatican library 152–153
Vaughan, Stephen 135–136
Vaux, Roland de 166, 168–169, 174, 178
Venice 82, 110, 132
Vermes, Geza 178
vernacular translations 68, 71, 91, 96, 123, 126–127, 150, 192; *see also* Bible in English; Luther, Martin

Vespucci, Amerigo 117
Vikings 53, 55, 62–63
Virgil 60, 107
Virgin Mary 78, 80, 114
Visigoths 20–24
Vulgate 25, 145, 147, 149

Wacholder, Ben 180
Waldensians 71, 77–78, 87
Waldo 64–68, 70–71, 78, 87
Wales 54
*The Wall Street Journal* 164
Wartburg Castle 121
Wearmouth 57
Werden, monastery at 17
Westminster Confession of 1648 13
witches 21, 97
Wittenberg 100, 134, 138
Worms 140
Wulfila 19–22, 24
Wyclif, John 83–85, 87–89, 91–92, 94–95, 137
Wycliffite Bible 89–92, 137, 141, 182

Yahweh (god of ancient Israel) 1
Ydros, Bernard 67
Yellow Plague 58
York 36

Zealots 6, 11
Zeus 9

www.ingramcontent.com/pod-product-compliance
Ingram Content Group UK Ltd.
Pitfield, Milton Keynes, MK11 3LW, UK
UKHW041954140426
5217IPUK00015B/797